Economic Rights in Canada and the United States

Pennsylvania Studies in Human Rights

Bert B. Lockwood, Jr., Series Editor

A complete list of books in the series is available from the publisher.

Economic Rights in Canada and the United States

Edited by Rhoda E. Howard-Hassmann
and Claude E. Welch, Jr.

PENN

University of Pennsylvania Press

Philadelphia

Copyright © 2006 University of Pennsylvania Press

Printed in the United States of America on acid-free paper

10 9 8 7 6 5 4 3 2 1

Published by
University of Pennsylvania Press
Philadelphia, Pennsylvania 19104-4112

Library of Congress Cataloging-in-Publication Data

Economic rights in Canada and the United States / edited by Rhoda E. Howard-Hassmann
and Claude E. Welch, Jr.
  p. cm. — (Pennsylvania studies in human rights)
  Includes bibliographical references and index.
  ISBN-13: 978-0-8122-3925-6
  ISBN-10: 0-8122-3925-3 (alk. paper)
  1. Human rights—Canada. 2. Human rights—United States. 3. Canada—
Economic policy. 4. United States—Economic policy. 5. Canada—Social policy.
6. United States—Social policy. 7. Capitalism. 8. Equality. I. Howard-Hassmann,
Rhoda E., 1948– II. Welch, Claude Emerson. III. Series.
JC599.C2E36   2006
330—dc22   2005054669

Contents

Introduction
Looking at Ourselves

Rhoda E. Howard-Hassmann and
Claude E. Welch, Jr.

In 1910, the novelist Anatole France wrote of his country, "We in France are . . . citizens. Our citizenship is [an] . . . occasion for pride! For the poor it consists in supporting and maintaining the rich in their power and their idleness. At this task they must labor in the face of the majestic equality of the laws, which forbid rich and poor alike to sleep under the bridges, to beg in the streets, and to steal their bread."[1] Only the poor were inconvenienced by the prohibition on sleeping under bridges.

Anatole France's aphorism shows the danger of assuming that equality before the law can result in an outcome that satisfies common-sense ideas of substantive material security. Indeed, his comment reflects an earlier observation by Karl Marx. In unequal economic situations, said Marx, an "equal" right was a right of inequality. "Right by its very nature can consist only in the application of an equal standard: but unequal individuals . . . are measurable only by an equal standard in so far as they are brought under an equal point of view . . . and nothing more is seen in them, everything else being ignored. . . . To avoid all these defects, right instead of being equal would have to be unequal."[2] The only right that made sense to the proletariat (the working class) according to Marx's collaborator, Friedrich Engels, was the "spontaneous reaction against the crying social inequalities" that characterized life in their times.[3] The debate about the relationship between equality of opportunity and substantive material equality has continued since Marx and Engels's time. In human rights terms, we are now interested in minimal economic security, recognizing that economic equality is impossible.

The international human rights regime includes a set of laws regarding economic rights, most especially those that are enumerated in the 1976 International Covenant on Economic, Social and Cultural Rights (hereafter ICESCR), included in this book as Appendix 1. These include inter alia the right to work and to just and favorable conditions of work (Articles 6 and 7); the right to join and form trade unions (Article 8); the right to social security, including social insurance (Article 9); specific rights for the family, special protection to mothers before and after childbirth and to children and young persons (Article 10); the right to "an adequate standard of living," including food, clothing, housing, and "the continuous improvement of living conditions" (Article 11); and the right to the "highest attainable standard of physical and mental health" (Article 12). This volume contains chapters on how Canada and the United States realize—or violate—these rights.

In law, there is generally an expectation that once a rule is made, it should be respected. International human rights lawyers try to establish economic rights as justiciable rights, as firmly protected as civil and political rights. Standards can be changed and made law. For example, David Weissbrodt, the author of Chapter 2, was elected chairperson in 2001 of the UN Sub-Commission on the Promotion and Protection of Human Rights, which deals especially with economic rights. The philosophical justification for economic rights is still not as robust and widely accepted as is the justification for civil and political rights, but progress is also being made in that direction. Brian Orend, in Chapter 1, offers a strong defense of economic rights, rooted in his conception of the vital needs and fundamental interests of all human beings.

For many countries, it is difficult to provide economic rights because of shortages of three kinds of resources—(1) material; (2) institutional; and (3) organizational. Therefore, as Weissbrodt explains, the ICESCR stresses "progressive implementation" of economic rights, rather than immediate. States are required to implement economic rights as their resources permit. It would seem, however, that Canada and the United States should be able to implement the full range of economic rights immediately. Both are extremely wealthy countries. In 2002, the per capita gross domestic product of the United States was US$36,300, while the comparable figure for Canada was US$29,300.[4]

Capitalist Societies and Class Inequalities

That Canada and the United States, like other wealthy developed countries, do not protect the basic economic rights of all their citizens is in part a function of their economic structure. The economies of both countries are capitalist. One can use this word without implying that one is an old-fashioned Marxist, dedicated to the overthrow of the capitalist system and its replacement by communism. Communism has been discredited by its application over several decades in the former Soviet

Union and other states in Eastern and Central Europe, and its substantial modification in China. Capitalism is the most efficient and productive economic system known to humankind, and it is because capitalism developed so early in Western Europe and North America that those two regions of the world are so prosperous.

But capitalism also breeds its own set of inequalities. In particular, capitalism divides the population into owning and nonowning classes. In general, it stratifies the population into rich, middle class, and poor. Those too incapacitated or lacking in opportunity to have any type of job at all are the worst off. They are the ones who are often homeless, especially if they also suffer the debilitating effects of mental illness, as Barbara Carroll points out in Chapter 4. But even the working poor in Canada and the United States frequently live insecure lives on the margins of society. Income distribution figures show a picture far different from average income in both Canada and the United States. In 2000, the top 10 percent of American households had an income 15.7 times the bottom 10 percent, while in Canada, in 1998, the figure was 10 times.[5] These inequalities are not inevitable consequences of the way capitalist societies are organized. They are the consequence in large part of conscious political decision making, often by individuals with their own material self-interest in mind.

To be a member of the working class, or to be unemployed, in Canada or the United States is often to live on the margins of society. The margins became even more remote from the center in the late twentieth and early twenty-first centuries. Poverty was exacerbated by declining social supports and the proliferation of low-wage, dead-end jobs, at the same time that the number of secure, unionized industrial jobs declined. The rate of unionization dropped in the United States from 35.5 percent at the end of World War II to 13.2 percent in 2004. More than half of the full-time employed workers in the United States in 2001 made less than $35,000 per year.[6] Lacking incomes that could support a family, many Americans did not bother trying to form families at all.

The enormous retail chain Wal-Mart employed 1.2 million people in the United States in 2004 whose average income was less than $18,000. One-third of Wal-Mart's employees could not afford company-sponsored health care.[7] This is a tragedy in a country that does not have any provision for universal medical insurance, as Virginia Leary explains in Chapter 7. The investigative journalist Barbara Ehrenreich worked for a time at Wal-Mart. She discovered there a class of people so poor that they could never afford permanent accommodation with decent kitchens, and so relied on fast food lacking in nutritive value: one of her colleagues, a fellow "associate" at Wal-Mart, ate hot dog buns for lunch.[8] It is difficult for comfortable middle-class people (including academics) to imagine the situation of Caroline Payne, an otherwise responsible individual rendered unemployable because she lacked health insurance and therefore lacked teeth.[9]

These class inequalities are grafted onto older sets of inequalities, so that particular sections of the population suffer the worst. In both Canada and the United States, Native Americans suffer from endemic poverty.[10] Native Americans were forced off their lands by colonizers, sometimes subjected to genocide,[11] granted highly exploitative "treaties" with their conquerors, and in Canada denied the civil and political rights that could enable them to seek economic betterment.[12] Race is also a marker of inequalities; to be black in both countries, and to be Hispanic in the United States, is to experience greater poverty than whites. Indeed, Kenneth Neubeck argues in Chapter 5 that racism is a factor in shaping American welfare policies. Women are less well paid than men, and female-headed families are the poorest of the poor. In Canada in 1995 56.8 percent of single-parent female-headed families were considered poor.[13] Migrants, both legal and illegal, often lack even the minimal protections that labor and other laws provide to citizens, and their incomes are accordingly low for both Canada and the United States, as Vic Satzewich documents in Chapter 10. People with disabilities—at least those among them who cannot compete in the labor market—often also live on the margins of society, as Chapter 9, by Sarah Armstrong, Mindy Noble, and Pauline Rosenbaum, shows for Canada.

Great strides have been made since the 1960s in both North American countries to ameliorate the disadvantages consequent upon gender and race or ethnicity, and latterly also sexual orientation. But there has been no significant social movement dedicated to ameliorating the condition of the poor as such. Indeed, in the fiscally conservative 1990s, the poor in many North American jurisdictions suffered cuts to their entitlements. In the Canadian province of Ontario, those subsisting on welfare were subject to the shock of 21.6 percent cuts in their incomes in the 1990s.[14] Between 1975 and 1995, Canadians endured a 15 percent decline in sickness benefits and a 13 percent decline in unemployment benefits; Americans also endured a 13 percent decline in unemployment benefits.[15] There are antipoverty movements in both countries, but they have not attracted significant backing. Many people in both countries believe that the poor are partly, or even mostly, to blame for their own fate: the poor should be able to avail themselves of formal equality of opportunity to find jobs and thereby support themselves at an adequate level.

Mary Bricker-Jenkins and Willie Baptist describe in Chapter 6 the movement to end poverty in the United States. They particularly note that poverty is not a race-specific phenomenon, as the figures cited earlier confirm. To organize the poor is decidedly an uphill struggle, although the movement can draw upon the international law of economic rights both for educational purposes and to legitimize itself. Bricker-Jenkins and Baptist express confidence that efforts to organize the poor as a national group can succeed. But without the "threat power" and capacity to disrupt everyday social relations that characterized the civil rights and black power movements of the 1960s, a poor people's social movement may well be something that the ruling elite can ignore.[16]

The Imperative of Self-Criticism

From within Canada and the United States, there is comparatively little criticism of the economic structure of capitalism, compared to the debates that take place in those Western European countries that possess strong socialist—and some even communist—political parties. In the United States, there have historically been reformers such as Jacob Riis, the late nineteenth century New York photographer and crusader against poverty; the Chicago welfare reformer Jane Addams; and the left-wing political thinker of the 1960s and 1970s, Michael Harrington.[17] Academic critics such as William Julius Wilson have noted the importance of social class, as opposed to skin color, in determining the life chances of African Americans.[18]

But from the late eighteenth century until well into the twentieth, governments in the United States persecuted left-wing political parties and trade unions, thus preventing any critical, anti-capitalist party from taking strong enough root to effectively regulate the workings of capitalism. At least 700 people were killed in American labor struggles between 1870 and 1940, 500 labor activists were deported during the post-World War I Palmer raids, and the political left was effectively intimidated during the McCarthy period of the 1950s.[19] In Canada, in 1961, the New Democratic Party (NDP), a fairly strong national social democratic political party, was formed. It united a predecessor called the Cooperative Commonwealth Confederation with some trade unions. From the 1960s to the 1980s, the NDP sometimes held the balance of power in Canada's then-tripartite parliamentary system and was sometimes able to influence the ruling party to introduce reforms that protected citizens' economic rights. Provincial governments controlled by the NDP also introduced economic rights, such as health care in Saskatchewan, as Leary describes.

The failures of both Canada and the United States to protect the economic rights of all their citizens demand reflection on the part of Canadian and American human rights jurists and scholars. Yet, remarkably little attention is paid to this category of rights, as Louis Henkin observed about the United States in 1981: "Few judges . . . have been prepared to declare basic human needs—subsistence, education—to be fundamental rights. . . . Even when some societal responsibility for individual welfare was finally accepted, it was seen as secondary and supplemental. Especially in austere, conservative times, that responsibility is seen only as residual, only to help those who cannot help themselves, and only with respect to minimum necessities at poverty levels. The primary responsibility for individual welfare . . . was on the individual."[20]

Yet, as the eminent Sudanese American scholar Abdullahi An-Na'im has pointed out, if Americans (and Canadians) do not heed their own violations of human rights, they will undermine their credibility in international discussions: "[A]ll cultures must be held to the same standards . . . of all . . . human rights. . . . [I]n the United States . . . racism and economic and social rights are large problems for the majority culture. So American human rights advocates should be equally concerned with all human rights issues that are problematic in their own situation. . . . Only by engaging in such an 'internal discourse' can American human rights advocates gain the moral credibility required to encourage such discourse elsewhere."[21]

As editors, we agree with An-Na'im, and we recall the Socratic principle "Know yourself." *Economic Rights in Canada and the United States* attempts to make a start in analyzing the weak protection of economic rights in Canada and the United States. We recognize the serious criticisms made of the concept of human rights, particularly its historical and philosophical beginnings in the Western liberal tradition that originally privileged civil and political rights over economic and social rights. These criticisms are by no means limited to persons from Africa, the Asia-Pacific area, or other "developing" or "southern" parts of the world. Indeed, philosophical and practical debate is in many respects as vigorous in the "developed" or "northern" parts of the globe. At the heart of contention is the issue of what claims on resources come first. Are there priorities among human rights, regardless of the 1993 assertion that they are "universal, indivisible and interdependent and interrelated"?[22]

We agree with Henry Shue that there are certain basic rights whose fulfillment is requisite to the enjoyment of all others, namely subsistence and security.[23] Orend's view that human rights respond to basic needs and fundamental interests strengthens Shue's point of view. To insist on economic rights is not to engage in "rights inflation," as Michael Ignatieff suggests.[24] Civil and political rights are indeed strategically crucial to the attainment of economic rights, as Ignatieff argues, but economic rights are also intrinsically valuable. One of the purposes of *Economic and Social Rights in Canada and the United States* is to show how fundamental these rights are to any reasonable conception of human dignity. Ignatieff argues that human rights rely on the "basic intuition that what is pain and humiliation for you is bound to be pain and humiliation for me."[25] Poverty, ill health, homelessness, and general lack of minimum economic security are both painful and humiliating. Minimum economic rights should be attainable for all in wealthy societies.

To "know oneself," countries like Canada and the United States must be willing to turn their critical scrutiny inward. It is telling that the United States' Department of State annually publishes a massive report on human rights conditions in close to 200 countries, but is barred from examining its own, as the impetus for these reports is foreign policy. Examination of internal human rights policy is a task of civil society in America, performed by a myriad of public interest and not-for-profit groups such as the American Civil Liberties Union and Human Rights Watch. But to resolve violations, the public sector—the government—plays the central role. We must thus concentrate less on the law of economic and social rights and more on their implementation.

Particularly heavy burdens of justification with respect to human rights performance fall upon the United States. The United States has set itself up as a paragon of achievement to which other states should—perhaps must—aspire. Such preaching about morality has rarely been absent from American history. Witness the bold assertion of the Declaration of Independence with respect to truths that were "self-evident." Witness also Woodrow Wilson's Fourteen Points intended to provide an appropriate framework within which the combatants could heal the rancor of World War I. During World War II, Franklin Delano Roosevelt proclaimed the Four Freedoms, discussed further in the following section. In the 1970s, Jimmy Carter's electoral promises brought human rights front and center after the moral sleaze and realpolitik of the Nixon-Kissinger years.[26] Republican presidents added their own voices to these prior Democratic assertions. Ronald Reagan stressed the need for democracy in the Soviet Union before it collapsed, and George W. Bush emphasized the evils of authoritarianism in Iraq. All these examples can be brushed aside by non-Americans, however, as manifestations of America's desire to preach to the world, to set itself up as a human rights paragon while turning a blind eye to continuing inequalities and abuses within its own borders. While hypocrisy is not unknown among other governments and their leaders, it is particularly resented when coupled with American economic and military power and a rarely restrained propensity to hold up the United States as the ideal.

Assessing Conformity to International Law

Are there ways in which states can be successfully pressured to improve their performance? This question is central to *Economic Rights in Canada and the United States*. As editors and authors, we begin with the organizing framework provided by the ICESCR.

International human rights law combines several elements. Most important are treaties negotiated and ratified by governments. States pledge faithfully to carry out the obligations specified in the agreements. There are no enforcement mechanisms, however, unlike in domestic settings. International society is usually described as "anarchic," depending on its members to police themselves. When countries are unwilling or unable to meet their human rights obligations, little can be done internationally. Yet this does not stop the use—and abuse—of human rights as a tool of global politics.

For many decades, the principle of economic rights was used by the Soviet Union as an ideological weapon of the Cold War. The Soviet Union claimed that the economic rights of its citizens were constitutionally protected. In practice, although housing was very cheap and health care free, the quality of each was abysmal.[27] Without any civil and political rights, Soviet citizens could not call their government to account and demand that its actions in the economic realm conform to its ideology. The Soviet Union's hypocrisy regarding economic rights rendered it easy for the United States to ignore criticism of its own serious shortcomings. The United States, in turn, touted the supremacy of civil and political rights. The rights promulgated in the 1948 Universal Declaration of Human Rights were separated into two Covenants, dividing civil and political from economic, social, and cultural rights. This separation was a clear reflection of the Cold War, in which the United States saw itself as the leader of the democratic, capitalist West. For several decades, the human rights debate was mired in this false either/or dichotomy of which category of rights—economic, social and cultural or civil and political—ought to take precedence.

The end of the Cold War ushered in a major transition in the global balance of power. It appeared that democracy and capitalism had triumphed. The United States emerged at the top of the heap, its power unquestionably great, suggesting that its was the only correct path to the protection of human rights. Yet democracy and capitalism do not necessarily protect economic rights. The devastating condition of the poor in the United States—most especially the African American poor, as Neubeck shows—is obvious to all informed observers and puts the lie to American claims to moral superiority in the arena of human rights.

This, then, is the political background to the formal international discussion of economic rights, focused around the ICESCR. The ICESCR was drafted and came into force two centuries after the American Declaration of Independence was penned, but only six years before the Canadian Charter of Rights and Freedoms (henceforth Charter) was adopted. The different historical contexts are meaningful. Thus, while the 1787 American Constitution spoke broadly of goals, such as to "promote the general Welfare," it did so only in the Preamble. The role of the national government, limited to a small number of essential functions (e.g., diplomacy, coinage, tariffs, and interstate commerce), was one of coordination of former colonies with divergent backgrounds and interests. Its role grew gradually, largely as a result of emergencies such as the Civil War, the Great Depression, and international conflict. By contrast, the Canadian Charter is a modern document. It was written at a time when women's rights, native peoples' rights, and new ideals such as multiculturalism dominated many Canadian and international discussions of the meaning of social justice. Yet despite its modernity, despite the fact that it was drafted in a country with a highly developed social welfare system, and despite Canada's ratification of the ICESCR, the Charter does not protect economic rights. This is surprising, given the obligations of the ICESCR.

Each country that ratifies the ICESCR pledges to implement its provisions, yet the Covenant's capacity to monitor states' achievements is extremely weak in comparison to its companion International Covenant on Civil and Political Rights. The latter provides for an eighteen-member committee of independent experts, which meets three times annually to review reports from the ratifying countries and forwards its observations both to the countries themselves and to the UN General Assembly.[28] No similar provision originally existed for the ICESCR, for which an optional protocol had to be drafted to create an oversight group.[29]

The resulting agenda for action by the Committee on Economic, Social and Cultural Rights, and for the governments that implement policies, is extensive but not exhaustive. The committee has myriad areas on which it can work and on which it is pressured by civil society. Developments subsequent to the drafting and ratification of the ICESCR have been incorporated into new international declarations and/or treaties, usually as a result of pressures from below. Likewise, as editors, we had to choose from myriad issues in putting together *Economic Rights in Canada and the United States*. The result is a volume that is extensive but not exhaustive; our coverage is necessarily selective and reflects the context of the early twenty-first century. For example, the chapters by Bricker-Jenkins and Baptist, on the antipoverty movement in the United States, and by Armstrong, Noble, and Rosenbaum, on the rights of persons with disabilities, reflect the rise of relatively new human rights issues in North America, as well as recent developments at the United Nations.

Given the loose definitions of human rights found in the ICESCR, how is effectuation of its provisions to be measured? The most significant efforts to define standards have come from the Committee on Economic, Social and Cultural Rights and from Western European academic lawyers.[30] The most important steps in monitoring and advocacy have come through national and international nongovernmental organizations (NGOs) and through intergovernmental organizations, although few report or act on economic, social, and cultural rights as well as civil and political rights. Amnesty International, which was established in 1961 in Britain with a focus on prisoners of conscience, the death penalty, and torture, has broadened its mandate to include economic rights, along with all the other rights contained in the Universal Declaration. Amnesty's annual report covers all countries.[31] Freedom House, a private, nonpartisan American organization, concentrates on civil and political rights, ranking states and summarizing them as "free," "partly free," and "not free," but does not report on economic rights. Human Rights Watch, an American organization, does not aim to be global in its coverage, concentrating instead on those countries in which it focuses its efforts, sixty-nine in 2002. Human Rights Watch does include both Canada and the United States among the countries on which it focuses but concentrates mainly on violations of civil and political rights.[32]

There are also numerous publications under intergovernmental auspices. Through the European Convention on Human Rights and the European Social Charter, the Council of Europe produces regular reports. The UN Development Report appears annually through the UN Development Program and is notable for its Human Development Index, based on three indicators. These are life expectancy at birth; the adult literacy rate and the combined gross enrollment rates in the primary, secondary, and tertiary educational levels; and the standard of living by gross domestic product (GDP) per capita.[33] The yearly report of the United Nations Educational, Scientific and Cultural Organization (UNESCO) is a valuable source for data on education. The World Bank's annual development report includes data relevant to economic and social rights. Its 2000 report (its cover completely black save for the title) concentrated on human rights. The World Health Organization publishes its annual World Health Report, again a survey relevant to *Economic Rights in Canada and the United States*.

With one exception, consistent and universal monitoring by individual governments has been nonexistent. Acting under congressional mandate, the U.S. Department of State has published country-by-country reports on human rights since the mid-1970s. These reports are organized idiosyncratically, however, categorizing rights by respect for the integrity of the person; respect for civil liberties; discrimination based on race, sex, disability, language, or social status; and worker rights.[34] Of these categories, only worker rights are directly relevant to this volume, and it is telling that the United States provides very little protection for workers and trade unions, as James Atleson shows in Chapter 8. China has offered several critiques of human rights practices in the United States since 1997, a year China faced a U.S.-backed possible censure in the UN Commission on Human Rights.[35] A European Yearbook of Human Rights has been published by a consortium of academic research institutes annually since 1985, but tends to focus on issue areas rather than country assessments. Finally, several academics have focused on quantitative analysis of economic and social rights.[36]

Reports on the economic human rights performances of states are also available through the UN Committee on Economic, Social and Cultural Rights, described earlier, to which States Party to the ICESCR must report periodically. As a State Party, Canada reports to this body and, as of mid-2003, had made three full reports, with a fourth in preparation. Having signed but not ratified the Covenant, the United States has no such obligation. Thus, the United States illustrates its exceptionalist position on international relations, about which David Forsythe and Eric Heinze write in Chapter 3. Although both countries are derelict in their domestic protection of economic rights, only Canada is subject to United Nations' monitoring and criticism. Without giving Canada credit it does not deserve, it seems overall to be a better protector of economic rights than the United States, although there may be some exceptions, such as policies for the homeless, as Carroll argues.

The authors in this book analyze a number of key economic rights, discussing domestic protection and violation in the United States and Canada. Human rights discourse in the West has been carried out largely by those trained in law. This is a result in part of the relative primacy of the emphasis on civil and political rights, in which the rule of law is central. Many law schools publish human rights journals. This contrasts with the relative rarity of scholarly attention to human rights in political science (except in international relations) or sociology. The single major book we have located dealing with human rights in Canada and the United States was written largely by and for legal scholars.[37] We adopt a different approach to human rights. While several distinguished lawyers have contributed chapters to *Economic Rights in Canada and the United States*, so too have well-known political scientists, sociologists, and persons from other social science disciplines.

Human rights discourse also tends to focus on individuals and individual cases, rather than on underlying conditions. Nongovernmental organizations chronicle abuses of specific persons or groups, calling for change, while international human rights treaty bodies respond to "communications" in which harms done to individuals or groups can be documented. But human rights can be violated unintentionally as a result of social structure, as well as intentionally by individuals or governments. We believe that human rights abuses arising from widespread structural, social, and political conditions should be analyzed by social scientists as well as by legal scholars, so that the resulting dialogue can contribute more fully to understanding the particular human rights problems of wealthy capitalist societies.

Canadian/American Comparison

Canada and the United States provide an ideal basis on which to show how nations similar in most respects—"probably as alike as any other two peoples on earth"[38]—differ with respect to implementing social and economic rights. Considering both countries' affluence, neither is very close to implementing the aspirations of the ICESCR. As discussed earlier, the United States has long depicted itself as unique, claiming a distinctive position globally. Indeed, it is distinctive among wealthy industrialized countries in paying far less attention to economic rights than most others. Canada, by contrast, occupies an intermediate position between the United States and highly industrialized Western European states, such as the Nordic states, France, or the Benelux countries. The political systems of these countries include social democratic political parties, which sometimes form governments, and they demonstrate a more corporatist attitude to social relations than is found in either North American country.

The purpose of *Economic Rights in Canada and the United States* is not explicitly to compare Canada and the United States. Rather, it is to show that both countries are derelict in their protection of economic rights. Nevertheless, there are some noticeable differences in their attitudes to this category of rights, especially the right to health care, as Leary explains. Canada has had a national health insurance program since 1966. The United States still does not have such a program, and the attempt in 1993 by then-president Bill Clinton and his wife, Hillary Clinton, to introduce one failed miserably. In 2002, about 43.6 million Americans, or 15.2 percent of the population, were uninsured.[39] This is not an insignificant difference, and Canadians, aware of this, balk at any suggestion that their universal program of health insurance should be modified in directions that might bring it closer to the U.S. system. In this section, we explore some ideas about why there is a difference between the two countries in regard to economic rights such as health care.

Both Canada and the United States are highly developed, Western, capitalist countries. They have a common historical background in British colonial rule and a resulting constitutional heritage of the British legal and parliamentary systems. Their economies are also highly interdependent. Both have supported international law and institutions, albeit with significantly greater enthusiasm north of the border. In short, Canada and the United States are countries that invite comparison across numerous dimensions.

The United States, however, broke away from the British model in 1776. While Canada remained a colony, subject to the common-law British tradition, with its incremental and decidedly incomplete approach to human rights, the United States drafted its own Constitution, including a Bill of Rights. This Constitution, with its various amendments, is one of the world's most inspiring guarantors of civil and political rights, but there is no mention in it of economic rights. Nor do American courts interpret the reference in the Constitution's Preamble to the promotion of general welfare as an enforceable provision.

Nevertheless, the United States has contributed to the international debate on economic rights. During World War II, then-president Franklin Delano Roosevelt proclaimed his Four Freedoms, included in this book as Appendix 2. These were freedom of speech and expression, the freedom of each person to worship God in his own way, freedom from want, and freedom from fear. In his 1944 State of the Union Address, a selection from which is in this volume as Appendix 3, President Roosevelt advocated more widespread old-age pensions and unemployment insurance for American citizens and a broadening of opportunities for adequate medical care. His wife, Eleanor Roosevelt, presided over the formulation of the United Nations' first human rights document, the Universal Declaration of Human Rights, which contained many of the economic rights that later became international law in the 1976 ICESCR. Yet sixty-two years after Roosevelt proclaimed the Four Freedoms, his visionary approach to economic rights had little influence on American political culture.

Canada entered the international debate on economic rights at about the same time as the United States. One of the drafters of the first version of the Universal Declaration of Human Rights was John Humphrey, a Canadian legal scholar working with Eleanor Roosevelt at the United Nations. Humphrey inserted economic rights into the Declaration, over the objections of Canadian politicians, the country's legal community, and its business elite.[40] At that time, human rights were not protected in Canada itself. The political culture in English Canada was one of an easy belief in the rectitude of the English-speaking, Anglo-Scottish ruling class, while in French Canada, the Church still ruled both institutional and ideational life. Human rights only gradually became a Canadian value, the first Bill of Rights not being introduced into Parliament until 1960.

Nevertheless, from this less than inspiring early history, Canada emerged in the last quarter of the twentieth century as a strong supporter of the international law of human rights, ratifying the ICESCR in 1976. Canada tends to accept judgments against it by the United Nations' Human Rights Committee, which oversees civil and political rights. For example, Canada accepted the committee's instructions in the 1981 Sandra Lovelace case to restore Native women's rights. The rights in question were to live on reserves and retain Native status, even after marriage to non-Natives.[41] In 1982, Canada rewrote its constitution and introduced its Charter of Rights and Freedoms. As already discussed earlier, the Charter did not protect economic rights.

Canada does have a reputation for being more peaceful, law-abiding, and rights-protective than the United States. Many readers of this book will have seen Michael Moore's 2002 movie *Bowling for Columbine.* Moore made this film after two students massacred thirteen people at Columbine High School in Littleton, Colorado, in April 1999. In one scene in this film, Moore visits Canada. He portrays a much friendlier, more trusting society than the United States, at one point showing a Canadian happily greeting Moore as he walks unannounced through the Canadian's unlocked door. While attractive to many Americans, this picture was probably quite surprising to Canadians, among whom are many with alarm systems on their doors. In fact, the rate of theft in Canada in 2001 was almost 90 percent of the rate in the United States in 2000. The homicide rate, however, was significantly lower, at 1.8 homicides per one hundred thousand people in 2001, as compared to 5.5 homicides per one hundred thousand people in the United States in 2000, or about one-third the American rate.[42] In 1996, 21.9 percent of Canadian households owned at least one gun, as compared to 48.5 percent of American households.[43]

Much of the alleged contrast between Canada and the United States, then, is a myth. Poverty rates in Canada approach those in the United States. In 1991, 21.0 percent of Americans and 21.6 percent of Canadians were considered poor before taxes and transfer payments. On the other hand, there may be some differences in Canadian attitudes to the poor. When transfer payments are taken into account, the poor in Canada are better off than the poor in the United States, although they are worse off than the poor in many countries in Western Europe. Only 5.6 percent of Canadians were considered poor in 1991 after taxes and transfers, as opposed to 11.7 percent of Americans who remained poor.[44] These differences between Canada and the United States in post-transfer rates of poverty may have lessened after the financial retrenchments in Canada during the 1990s.

Canadians pay much higher rates of income tax than do Americans, in part to support their more expansive system of health care and social safety nets. Exact comparisons are difficult, but some illustrative figures exist. In 1997, taxes constituted 36.8 percent of Canada's GDP, as compared to 29.7 percent of the United States'. In 1999, the combined federal and provincial income tax rate in Canada for income over CAN\$63,050 was 46.1 percent, while at a comparable level the figure for the United States was 34.5 percent.[45] Federal tax cuts enacted in the United States in 2001 (often necessitating increased state and local taxes) accentuate the contrast with Canada.

If a more sincere commitment to economic rights exists in Canada than in the United States, it may be a result of a difference in political culture. In the United States, there is no viable political party to the left of the Democrats. The two-party system effectively means that all new political tendencies must either be folded into the Democrats or the Republicans or disappear. Individuals in the Democratic Party who hold social democratic views find them watered down in bargaining with other members of the party. Trade unionism—the single biggest protection of the economic rights of workers, as Atleson explains—hardly exists in the United States. In 1999, 13.9 percent of American workers belonged to trade unions, while in Canada the figure was 30.1 percent.[46]

This does not mean that Canada has been free of the kind of politics that have permeated American conflict over what is now known as economic rights. For example, Canada deported labor leaders immediately after World War I. As did political leaders in the United States, Canadian politicians feared the left-wing politics sweeping over Europe in the aftermath of the War and the Bolshevik Revolution in Russia.[47] Again like the United States, after World War II, Canada engaged in a period of persecution and harassment of left-wing thinkers and activists.[48]

The persecution of leftist activists was somewhat offset by a tendency in Canada toward communitarian and corporatist thinking that was absent in the United States and that promoted a sense of civic obligation toward all. In one older reading of this tendency, Canada was characterized by a "feudal remnant." In feudal societies, the nobility were obliged to help provide for peasants' minimal economic needs in return for loyalty and military support. So in Canada, a country that never experienced a bourgeois revolution as did the United States, remnants of this ethic remained in both the quasi-feudal *seigneuries* of pre-Conquest Quebec, and among the Anglo elite of English Canada.[49] Added to this were the strong Catholic Church in Quebec and the Protestant beliefs of the Christian socialists who started the Co-operative Commonwealth Federation. Socialist and Communist immigrants could also be found among the farmers of the Canadian West, as well as among the urban workers of Montreal and Toronto.[50]

The idea that Canadians are ideologically different from Americans has some currency. A common contrast is the reputed Canadian stress on "peace, order and good government" as opposed to the American stress on "life, liberty, and the pursuit of happiness." Canadians are thought to trust the state more than do Americans and to be less individualistic. Seymour Martin Lipset, an American sociologist who studied Canada in depth, attributed this contrast to the differential effects of the American Revolution on both countries. While the United States, he argued, celebrates "the overthrow of an oppressive state," Canada "commemorates a defeat."[51] Thus, Lipset continued, "Canada . . . was formed as a counterrevolutionary monarchical society that valued hierarchy in class relations and religion and authority and deference in politics. . . . In contrast, the United States was founded as a nation seeking to explicate a set of political and religious ideals that emphasized liberty, saw danger in concentrated government power, and increasingly stressed populism and equality of opportunity and of social relations."[52] As proof of his thesis, Lipset noted that "crossnational polls . . . continue to reveal Americans as less favoring large welfare programs and an active role for government in the economy than the citizens of Canada."[53]

Lipset's thesis was, however, challenged by Canadian scholars. Carefully constructed national surveys show that Canadians are less deferential to government than are Americans and are more individualistic.[54] Moreover, to argue that national "characters" in the late twentieth century could be traced to events that occurred two hundred years earlier is to ignore significant social change of various kinds. These include the processes of urbanization and industrialization and huge immigration movements into both countries from parts of the world other than Britain.

In any case, even if Canadians do have a more corporatist or communitarian value system than Americans, its beneficial effects should not be exaggerated. Large numbers of people lived in dire poverty in Canada until well after World War II. Blacks and members of other racial minorities were denied the equal opportunity and legal standing that might have helped them better their economic status. People of Chinese and Japanese ancestry were long denied the right to vote, a political right crucial to the attainment of economic benefits. Women and children were almost entirely dependent for their economic well-being on men. Corporatist thinking often took the form of a patronizing charity, its recipients dependent on the givers' interpretation of their worthiness.

Nor has poverty disappeared in Canada. In the late twentieth century there were still low-income mothers who compromised their own nutrition at the end of the month, when their welfare checks fed their children but not themselves.[55] In 1996, 21.1 percent of Canadian children lived in poverty,[56] although by 2001, the rate of child poverty was 15.7 percent, as compared to more than 20 percent in the United States.[57] A 1994 study estimated that 1.2 percent of Canadian children were malnourished.[58] By comparison, in 2002, 11.1 percent of American households were found to be "food insecure," with 3.5 percent of households experiencing "food insecurity with hunger."[59]

If indeed it exists, the greater Canadian commitment to the common good may also be a consequence of the more homogeneous (until very recently) racial structure of Canada, compared to that of the United States. Canada does not have a good historical record of welcoming strangers into its midst. The great migrations of Eastern Europeans, especially Poles and Ukrainians, into Canada in the early twentieth century coincided with a social eugenics movement to reduce the number of "feeble-minded" in the country. Immigrants who often could not speak English were counted among these "feeble-minded."[60] (This was also the policy in the United States, the elites of both countries being influenced by the eugenics movement of the late nineteenth and early twentieth centuries.)[61] In an effort to maintain the country as a white colony, Canada enacted legislation excluding Chinese immigrants in 1923, one year before the U.S. Chinese Exclusion Act. Since the late 1960s, Canada has had a much more open immigration policy, so that by 2000 three-fourths of its immigrants were from regions other than Europe, and in the 2001 census 13.5 percent of the population identified itself as members of "visible minorities" (with another 3.3 percent identifying itself as Aboriginal).[62] In an attempt to adjust to this, the federal government instituted an official policy of multiculturalism in 1971. Nevertheless, nonwhite immigrants experience much difficulty in economically catching up with native born Canadians. And black males are particularly disadvantaged, even if they are native-born. A 1999 study showed that native-born black males earned 24 percent less than native-born male Canadians as a whole, even after controlling for educational level and work experience.[63]

If Canada is not able to maintain its collective commitment to the common welfare in the future, it may end up, like the United States, as a country in which black males, as a group, suffer severe violations of human rights, both civil/political and economic.[64] If the poor are not seen as part of "us"—if they are not seen as related to those who make decisions and distribute resources—then they may be deemed less worthy of assistance.

Regulating Capitalism

That Canada and the United States are more similar than different is not surprising: both are capitalist countries. They rely on free market economies in which the intention of private producers is to make a profit. As we noted at the beginning of this introduction, such economies are the most efficient known to mankind. Yet they produce class inequalities—inequalities in access to basic economic rights—that must be ameliorated by public policy if all citizens are to be protected under international human rights law. In their public policies, neither Canada nor the United States has ever addressed the problem of class inequality as a human rights issue. Nor has either one instituted constitutionally protected economic rights. Yet there is little by way of social movements in Canada and the United States to pressure the respective governments to institute economic rights as legally enforceable human rights. The Kensington Welfare Rights Movement, described by Bricker-Jenkins and Baptist, is unfortunately a rare instance of organization of the poor by the poor.

Margaret Keck and Kathryn Sikkink suggest that human rights social movements succeed when there is evidence of direct harm from human rights abuses, as in torture; when core values such as equality are undermined; and when the causal chain between the action or inaction and the harm is short and obvious.[65] These conditions do not apply to violations of economic rights in Canada and the United States. Direct harm such as starvation—as opposed to the slow harm of malnutrition—rarely occurs in North America. The core value with regard to economic well-being is equality of opportunity, not the idea of a solid floor below which no Canadian or American should sink. The link between public policy measures such as cuts in welfare allowances and poverty "on the ground" involves other factors such as family dynamics, individual initiative, and racial or ethnic status. Without compelling evidence of direct harm, attacks on core values, and a short causal chain, it is difficult to generate a large social movement in favor of economic rights.

There are also many people in North America whose interests would be harmed were economic human rights better protected. The business and property-owning classes might well rebel if minimum wages, unemployment insurance benefits, and social welfare payments were raised to a level at which recipients might live a life of dignity instead of a life spent scraping by. The ordinary taxpayer might be concerned about increased taxes and how such increases would affect her or his standard of living. Among both groups, some might also worry that too great a stress on economic rights would create a society of irresponsible people, unwilling to earn their own way in society.[66] Yet ordinary taxpayers often do not realize how their own economic security has been ensured by earlier rights-seeking activities. Had trade unions not demanded limited hours of work, minimum wages, and other social benefits in the late nineteenth and early twentieth centuries, there would be no stable, working middle class in the early twenty-first. Atleson documents how the recognition that labor rights are human rights impelled early legislation protecting trade unions in the United States, yet the American government and legal profession frequently do not remember that connection now.

Unfortunately, then, there is so far no indication that "ordinary" Canadians and Americans view economic rights as of the same importance as civil and political rights. Human rights are wrested from below. But in this case, "below" comprises those people whose economic betterment might impose a real monetary cost on their fellow citizens. Even in rich societies, wealth is not infinite. The rich prefer to stay rich. Middle-income citizens enjoy their standard of living but worry about economic insecurity in times of unemployment, illness, or old age. Human rights that directly attack the pocketbook meet much more resistance than human rights that only indirectly affect citizens' financial interests.

And there is even greater hostility to the idea that citizens of rich democracies should share their wealth with people who live in other countries. This inability to overcome the constraints of direct financial interest is what often strikes commentators from the "rest" of the world as hypocritical about Western human rights policies. Economic human rights are indeed the "stepchild" of the international human rights movement, Forsythe and Heinze argue. As they point out, even those Western democracies, such as Canada, that are more oriented to the global "South" than is the United States have not formed an alliance to promote economic rights on the international scene. Canada's moralistic foreign policy preaching about its democratic and multicultural values conceals a policy based on national interest, especially trade promotion.[67] As for Americans, it seems to outsiders that they are steeped in hypocrisy. The Information Office of the State Council of the People's Republic of China concluded its study of the United States' human rights record for 2000 with these words: "China would like to offer this advice to the U.S. government: abandon your old ways and make a new start, take effective measures to improve the human rights record in your own country, take steps to promote international cooperation in human rights, and stop ordering other countries on the pretext of safeguarding human rights."[68]

We believe that both our countries should pay more attention to economic rights, both to defuse international accusations of hypocrisy and to protect our fellow citizens. We admire social democratic states that protect economic rights more carefully than does either of our own two societies, even though the protections in such states are far from perfect. Social democracy combines concern for economic rights with a firm commitment to civil and political rights, a commitment that is lacking in communist states such as the former Soviet Union or present-day China. We also acknowledge that capitalist economic systems are here to stay. Capitalism should be regulated, however, and states should protect the human rights of their citizens over the interests of private corporations or the extremely wealthy property-owning class.

The advantages of the capitalist economic system must be acknowledged. Capitalism creates wealth. As Orend notes, in wealthy societies, most adult citizens are able to take care of their own economic needs without resort to state support. In democratic capitalist societies, moreover, citizens are able to win substantial economic benefits from their governments, even if those benefits are not recognized as rights. Canada and the United States both offer social programs that promote economic security, even if economic rights are not recognized. In both countries, minimal levels of benefits are provided for the poor and unemployed, for the disabled, and for (some) low-income parents with children. In both countries there are old-age pensions. In both countries there is universal, free education at the primary and secondary levels. In the United States, many citizens benefit from state health benefits. Indeed, if one takes into account the different manner in which the United States promotes its citizens' economic security, for example, via tax deductions on mortgage interest (but not on rent), it may be that the difference between the United States and Canada, or the Netherlands, our European comparison state, is not as great as is often thought. Christopher Howard suggests that if all such measures are taken into account, the United States in 1997 spent $4,809 per capita on its citizens' welfare, compared to $4,443 spent by Canada and $4,495 by the Netherlands.[69]

Capitalism, moreover, is not necessarily a recipe for a dog-eat-dog society. Canadians and Americans both have vibrant civil societies and large volunteer sectors. These volunteers not only help the weak but also act as their advocates. But even when volunteer action is combined with social programs, that is not enough to protect the economic rights of the most disadvantaged citizens. Per capita figures hide race, ethnic, gender, and other inequalities, as well as masking programs such as Social Security for the aged that benefit the wealthy as well as the poor. A particularly shocking example of racially biased outcomes of public policy is seen in rates of AIDS in the United States. In 2002, the AIDS diagnosis rate was almost eleven times higher among African Americans than among whites.[70] Excluding assaults, homicides and accidents, in 2001 AIDS was the biggest killer of African Americans aged twenty-five to thirty-nine.[71]

Conscientious fulfillment of the ICESCR's provisions requires much more—and more dedicated—social action than presently exists in either Canada or the United States. Public policies to protect human rights must be directed in particular to the poor and other marginalized groups. Being destitute or even a member of the working poor often entails not merely economic disadvantage compared to the upper and middle classes but actual denial of economic rights. Many men, women, and children are locked into poverty. In both countries, being disabled can also mean not enjoying fundamental economic rights, as Armstrong, Noble, and Rosenbaum show for Canada.

Structural economic inequalities produce human rights abuses that pass largely unnoticed, especially when combined with racial minority, immigrant, or other such disadvantaged statuses. We believe that more than lip service must be offered to those needing affirmative action or employment equity, whether they be women, native peoples, the disabled, or members of racial minorities. Such individuals must benefit from policies that (at least for varying periods of transition) allow for positive discrimination. We also advocate more progressive income taxes, together with their mirror, "negative" income taxes. In the United States, universal health insurance is also a key necessity. In both countries, a social safety net that embraces the working poor as well as the truly destitute is needed, as are more universal, affordable systems of child care. The United States also needs a national system of paid parental leave similar to that which already exists in Canada. Both state-financed and private pensions should be universal and portable, with periodic adjustments for the cost of living. Wages must be fair, adequate to maintain at least a basic standard of living. Within the workplace, labor conditions must be healthful, and workers must enjoy freedom of association. Taken together, these obligations dictate a considerable policy agenda: social democracy.

Nevertheless, there is no guarantee that even in the best case, exemplified by Western European countries with strong social democratic traditions, states will or can protect all human rights. In Chapter 11, Peter Baehr warns us that all may not be what it seems in one such country, the Netherlands. We agree that Western Europe is not perfect. Indeed, like citizens of Canada and the United States, citizens of the Netherlands endured severe cuts to their social benefits between 1975 and 1995, with declines of 15 percent in sickness benefits and 13 percent in unemployment benefits.[72] This reflects a pattern of retrenchment in almost all Western countries in the late twentieth century, as governments found themselves no longer able to sustain the social welfare commitments of the post-World War II period. But European social democracies do provide a contrast to the United States and, to a lesser extent, to Canada. They suggest a model to strive for, other than the stridently capitalist social structure of the United States. They answer to some extent the criticism from the "rest" that Western countries disregard economic rights.

Part I
Philosophy, Law, and
Politics of Economic Rights

Chapter 1
Justifying Socioeconomic Rights

Brian Orend

Justifying socioeconomic rights—rights to things like subsistence income, education, and health care—is difficult, but doable. It is difficult, especially in North America, because there is substantial suspicion to deal with. The suspicion is mainly twofold: of the concept itself; and of the cost of its implementation.

Those suspicious of the concept itself tend to have no problems whatsoever with civil and political rights. Such rights, also called "first-generation rights," involve claims to security of the person, property, due process, and standard political and social liberties, such as freedom of speech and religion. Critics of the concept of socioeconomic rights, also called "second-generation rights," view them as abuses of the very concept of natural or human rights, which in their view involves only first-generation claims. Such critics, when feeling strident, even allege that defending socioeconomic rights is tantamount to supporting socialism, when that boat has so clearly sailed, historically. There is a clear constituency in North America, especially on the American right, for the notion that to defend socioeconomic rights is to inject malignant old world socialism into the healthy heart of modern free-market democracy. Other critics, who might be more sympathetic to the idea of socioeconomic rights, nevertheless finally reject them on grounds that implementing them would be ruinously costly. One often hears such assertions as "it would be wonderful if everyone in North America had livable housing, but we simply can't afford it!"

This chapter must adequately respond to these two suspicions, and before that it must show positive grounds for believing that socioeconomic rights are fully justified human rights in the first place.

Quick Stipulations

We must first define our terms. A human right is a general moral right that every human being has. Sometimes it finds legal expression and protection, sometimes not. This legal variability does not undermine the existence and firmness of the moral right, and it actually provides focus for contemporary human rights activism, where the goal is often to translate the pre-existing moral claim into an effective legal entitlement.

A human right is a high-priority claim to a set of objects that are owed to each human person as a matter of minimally decent treatment. Internationally, the United Nations' 1948 Universal Declaration of Human Rights (UDHR)—which includes both first- and second-generation human rights—is seen as providing a fairly authoritative list of human rights objects. Two separate International Covenants came out of the UDHR, the first on Civil and Political Rights (ICCPR), the second on Economic, Social and Cultural Rights (ICESCR). They were both ratified as pieces of international law in 1966 and came into force in 1976. America has ratified only the ICCPR, whereas Canada has ratified both.[1] Ratification means the country in question is legally committed to providing all listed objects, as a matter of human right, to each of its citizens. In general terms, the objects of human rights are those fundamental benefits that every human being can reasonably claim from other people, and from social institutions, as a matter of justice. As I have elsewhere argued,[2] in my view there are a group of "foundational five" human rights objects: personal security, material subsistence, personal freedom, elemental equality, and social recognition. All other human rights are derived from one, or a combination, of these foundational five. Failing to provide such objects, or acting to take away such objects, counts as rights violation. The violation of human rights is a vicious and ugly phenomenon indeed and is something we have overriding reasons to resist and, ultimately, to remedy.

Elements of a Good Justification

Before we can justify socioeconomic rights, we need to develop a justification for human rights in general, and then show how socioeconomic claims flow from the core concepts. Now, to justify something is literally to show that thing's justice, rightness, or correctness. In general, to justify some claim is to show adequate grounds for people to believe in that claim and to guide their conduct accordingly. So to justify human rights is to show adequate grounds, or sufficient reasons, why people should believe that human rights exist and are important—why people should adjust their conduct in light of the claims that human rights make on all of us.

A good justification has to rest on some basic set of premises and principles that are themselves *not* argued for. This is the case because we cannot keep arguing forever: philosophers have referred to such a never-ending chain of reasoning as an "infinite regress," and thus as something that we finite creatures—with lives to live and choices to make—should avoid. *Every argument has to rest somewhere*: it is thus part of the art of argument to decide where one is going to stand satisfied. Usually in moral and political debate, these premises will involve some conception of human nature and some understanding of a foremost requirement of morality and justice. The justification for human rights that we will be looking at in this chapter will rest on a conception of human nature that assumes a set of vital needs we all share and a core principle that it is deeply, and manifestly, wrong to inflict harm on people in connection with their vital needs. Such harm is grievous and unjust, falling below the threshold of minimally decent treatment we have the right as human beings to expect and demand. The only justification for intentionally inflicting such grievous harm is to protect others from suffering such grievous harm themselves.[3]

A good justification not only starts out from plausible initial premises and principles, which it ultimately rests on, but also arrives at attractive conclusions. It is often said "you shall know them by the fruits of their actions." We should ask not merely, "Are the initial assumptions plausible?" but also, "Would I like to live in a society where that idea is finally implemented?" John Rawls refers to this process as "reflective equilibrium," searching for a satisfying balance between plausible starting points and desirable ending points. Such a strategy of justification combines the strengths of appealing to abstract first principles and of stressing the predictable outcomes of implementing such principles.[4]

Starting Points

All human beings have vital needs and fundamental interests in living a life of at least minimal value to themselves and the world. To make such an assertion is not at all to downplay the wondrous diversity of human experience. It is merely an accurate observation regarding the necessary conditions of our survival—not only as biological human beings but also as creatures with desires and aspirations, both personal and social. For all our achievements and potential, we remain finite and needy creatures desirous of living a life we see as at least minimally worthwhile. As the ancient Greeks first observed, *it is not just about life, it is also about the good life.* But the good life must here be understood as composed of elements that we might call, after Michael Walzer, thick and thin.[5]

A thick vision of the good life is highly personal, diverse, relative, and subjective. A thin vision, by contrast, is of those objects genuinely needed to survive *and* to be able to pursue one's thick vision at all. No one has the human right to succeed in securing their thick vision of the good life. Someone may very much want to be a movie star or a head of state, but that person has no human right to claim that the rest of us are duty-bound to do our part in realizing his aspirations. The first reason why is that such a claim is inconsistent with the universality and equality residing at the heart of human rights. If there are human rights, they exist equally for every person. Because we cannot all become movie stars, or heads of state, such lifestyles cannot be claimed as a matter of human right. The second reason has to do with the burden that would fall on the rest of us if we were duty-bound to aid someone's political or film career. The burden, clearly, would be unreasonable: we have our own lives to lead and have better things to do than play a role as props in another person's thick projects. Human rights claims, therefore, must be confined to the *essential* ingredients of a *thin* vision of the good life: the objects of vital need, which James Nickel has referred to as those needed to both *have* and *lead* a life.[6] If we want to survive and be able to pursue our personal goals at all, we must have the objects of our vital needs.

To need something, of course, is to require it—to be dependent on it in some important sense. Importantly, to need something is to be harmed if one is deprived of it or is lacking it to begin with. To vitally need something is for it to be required to sustain one's functioning as the very kind of creature one is. For one to fail to have an object of one's vital needs is for one to suffer grievous harm—for one to face a grave threat to one's ability to lead a minimally good life, or perhaps even any life at all. David Wiggins has made important contributions to this line of thought. He suggests that, for someone to vitally need an object, call it *x*, three things need to hold: (1) the deprivation, or lack, of *x* would harm that person's very functioning in life as a human being; (2) there are no acceptable substitutes for *x* available to that person; and (3) *x* is integral to that person's living a life of minimal value.[7]

As noted earlier, I contend that there are five abstractly defined items that meet each of Wiggins's three criteria for the vital needs of the human person living in our time: (1) personal security, (2) material subsistence, (3) elemental equality, (4) personal freedom, and (5) recognition as a member of the human community. I submit that these five vital needs are also the ultimate objects of our human rights claims. I thus refer to them, as I've mentioned earlier, as the "foundational five" objects of human rights.

Personal security means reliable protection from, or freedom from, a context of violence that threatens either one's very life or at least the core aspects of one's physical and mental well-being. Material subsistence means having secure access to those resources one requires to meet one's biological needs—notably a minimal level of nutritious food, drinkable water, breathable air, some clothing and shelter, and basic preventative health care. Elemental equality means our need to be regarded as equal in initial status with other moral agents and not to suffer from vicious and groundless social discrimination. In particular, it means that whatever is acknowledged as a human right must be extended to every individual human person. Personal freedom means the need to follow one's own path in life, not subject to coercive interference with one's critical life choices. Liberty also implies the need to have some space to enjoy some privacy, and earlier all to develop a degree of personal identity, integrity, and autonomy. Finally, recognition means our deep need as social beings for acknowledgment from others of our own humanity, of our own independent worth, and of our own belonging to, and full membership within, the human community.

Not having any one of these five core elements does real damage—verifiable harm—to one's functioning as a human being in the contemporary world. This is perhaps clearest with physical security and material subsistence, but it does not take much imagination to realize that lacking the other elements also harms human functioning: why else, for example, would we make the deprivation of liberty the core ingredient in criminal punishment? It is indeed interesting that socioeconomic rights are the ones so often under the cloud of suspicion, when their justification is here so palpably evident, whereas additional comment has to be added for the other kinds of human rights objects.

Similarly, it is clear that there are no acceptable substitutes for any one of the five core elements of vital human need. What, for instance, would one trade one's physical security for, or a subsistence level of income, or one's need for social recognition as a human being? Such are goods beyond price and measure, so instrumental are they to one's present and future.

All five elements together appear necessary for living a minimally good life in the modern world. We know this by reflection on the alternatives: without enough food and water, without basic medical care, without freedom from serious violence, we clearly cannot live minimally well, or even for long at all, in this world. To suffer from vicious social discrimination, or to be forced to live a life not of one's choice, is to suffer grievous harm as a human being. It is to endure a life that none of us would find worth living, considering the kinds of creatures we are and with reference to the kind of decent and respectful treatment we deserve. However we each, individually, understand the full or thick picture of the good life; we need these five core elements to pursue it.

These five elements are what we truly and vitally *need*, no matter what else we might *want* out of life. Of course, we should want what we vitally need, and most of us as rational agents do so. But wanting what one vitally needs is not necessary to ground one's entitlement to the objects of those needs. The grounding of the entitlement comes not from one's subjective wanting but rather from one's objective needing—and, moreover, from the core moral principle that *one should not be inflicted with grievous harm in connection with one's vital needs.*

Much has been made thus far of the connection between human rights and vital human needs. But it must be stressed that this connection is not one of straightforward equivalence. In particular, one does *not* have the human right to claim *absolutely everything* in which one might come to have vital need. Judith Thomson illustrates this point vividly with her thought experiment regarding the dying violinist.[8] Suppose a world-famous violinist is dying, and for whatever reason, he can survive only by being hooked up to you by machine, for twenty-four hours a day, nine months in a row. During this time, your kidneys and liver will cleanse his blood of the poison that is killing him. There is no denying that, in this hypothetical case, the dying violinist vitally needs to be hooked up to you: without such action, he will die. But it seems wrong to suggest that he has the human right to be so hooked up, since the burdens imposed on you would be very heavy and unreasonable. The hooking up would directly interfere with your ability to lead your life in a manner of your choosing, at least for nine months; and this is supposing that the procedure would pose no physical danger to your own life, which is not on the face of it obvious. Here, then, we have at least a hypothetical case where there is genuine vital need for something, but no corresponding human right to that something.

What the case of the dying violinist illustrates is that what we have human rights to is *not* simply the objects of all our vital needs but rather that others and social institutions *do their fair share* in enabling us to have the objects of our vital needs. Doing one's fair share means that, on the one hand, if someone already has an object of their vital needs, one ought not take it away from them. If the person, on the other hand, does not yet have the object, a fair share means doing one's part in providing that object to the person *provided that one's part in the provision comes with a readily absorbable cost to oneself.* In particular, one's part in the provision cannot come at the price of one's own vital needs and fundamental interests in both *having* and *leading* a life. It would, after all, be unfair and unreasonable to require one person to sacrifice his/her own vital needs so that the needs of another can be met.

To fail to do one's fair share in enabling others to have the objects of their vital needs is to do them grievous harm. Such failure amounts either to positively thwarting and hindering their possession of their vital needs or else to negatively, and negligently, ignoring their serious suffering when one could do something about it at readily absorbable cost. Such failure denies to others their capacity to live minimally good lives and may actually attack their very ability to survive at all. The core principle, on which this reasoning rests, is that *it is fundamentally wrong to do grievous harm to people without just cause.* The only just cause for doing such harm would be that the harm is being done to a human rights violator, in the name of protecting the human rights of another person.

The duty not to do grievous harm is one of the most widely shared, and deeply moving, conceptions of universal moral duty. The only thing capable of dislodging this duty is if the person in question has forfeited his/her right not to be grievously harmed by performing an act of human rights violation. Otherwise, we ought not do him/her grievous harm, and that means doing our fair share in enabling everyone to have the objects—including socioeconomic objects—of his/her vital needs. Thus, the reason each of us has to respect the human rights of others—in addition to demanding respect for our own—is that failure to show such respect is to cause them grievous harm. And causing grievous harm to a human being, without just cause, violates a primary and powerful moral duty whose vital importance we all acknowledge.

To put it at its most elemental, this strain of justification runs thus: we each have every self-interested reason to demand the objects of our human rights, since we vitally need them to survive and live a life of minimal value. But what reason do we have to respect the human rights of others? Several: we want them to respect ours; the value of fairness lets us see they have vital needs of their own to fulfill; and there's a fundamental duty not to harm people in connection with their vital needs. We then saw that, strictly speaking, what we all have the right to claim is that everyone—every person and social institution—does his/her fair share in connection with human rights realization. We will return to the notion of a fair share when we talk about the costs of realizing human rights, especially those of the socioeconomic variety.

Ending Points

The key notion here is that respecting human rights, as here conceived, would result in a better and more enjoyable society than not. We have to be persuaded not just of the sense and moral power of the first principles but also of the live possibility to effectively realize human rights in society and to see society thereby improved. What do we mean by "improved"? The general response is an increase in subjective happiness, and objective well-being, across individuals in society. John Stuart Mill defended the desirability of human rights in this way:[9]

1. We should, through our actions and institutions, advance and not detract from human happiness and general well-being.
2. Human rights promote human happiness and well-being because they protect people's vital needs, allowing them to pursue those things they find enjoyable and worthwhile.
3. Disrespecting, or violating, human rights, causes serious pain, both to those victimized and to those close to the victims. It also more generally undermines everyone else's confidence that they can count on having their human rights respected. Human rights violations cause particular pain and general insecurity.
4. *Therefore*, we should, through our actions and institutions, respect people's human rights.

In support of this line of reasoning, we could refer to the historical record and argue compellingly that those societies which respect human rights are societies where human happiness and flourishing are more in evidence than in societies disrespectful of them. People who live in rights-respecting societies are certainly better off, and generally happier, than those suffering under conditions of rights violation. Compare, for example, the quality and enjoyment of life of the average citizen in America, Australia, Canada, or Western Europe with, say, that of the average citizen in China, Cuba, the Congo, or North Korea. The facts speak for themselves: if people in a society care about their own overall happiness and well-being, they ought to ensure that their own behavior, and the social institutions they share, respects human rights.

There is much to be said for this view: it makes a frank and compelling case, indeed. Some might dispute the quality-of-life comparison, noting in particular the far-from-perfect record of rights respect in the first set of countries.[10] That is fine, but the general point that respect for rights *on the whole* generates a happier, more enjoyable society than the alternative is, in my judgment, decisively supported by the facts of history.

I suggest that any reasonable person would answer strongly in the affirmative to the question "Would I like to live in a human rights respecting society?" Moreover, I argue that such a person would still answer "yes," knowing that vital socioeconomic claims are included in this vision of human rights. Why? Such a person certainly wants basic socioeconomic objects as a matter of her own vital need in having and living a life. Such a person also recognizes that it's only fair that, if she can have hers, other people should get theirs. Would she be willing to help foot the bill? She should be, because we are (only) talking about a *thin* set of *genuinely vital* objects for all, and failure to do her part means that other people are severely harmed as a result of her choice, which is a severe violation of a basic moral duty.

Responding to the First Objection

Now that we've witnessed a strong justification for human rights in general, and socioeconomic rights in particular, let's return to the two big objections: that socioeconomic rights aren't really human rights and that socioeconomic rights aren't really affordable. In response to the first issue, we properly ask, "Why should we limit ourselves to first-generation civil and political rights when we list objects of human rights? The raw fact that they were the first set of claims?" But this is to honor the past too much and, moreover, to commit to a rigid, frozen conception of human rights. It honors the past too much, because it assumes they got it all right the first time out—and how often has that happened in human affairs? The Enlightenment-era defenders of first-generation human rights—such as the American Founding Fathers—were geniuses, but we can wonder whether this conception remains complete in the face of all that has happened since then. It is, I admit, simpler to stick to a static conception of human rights; indeed, I suspect that it is an active psychological factor here. But more compelling, I suggest, is a model that allows for the gradual—but responsible—growth of human rights over time. After all, our society is much more complex, capable, and wealthy than those during the Enlightenment. So more things are possible and affordable, and our sense of what is needed for a minimally good life in our world is probably larger than that needed in Enlightenment societies.[11]

It does not violate the very concept of a human right to contend that it includes socioeconomic claims. For a human right, as we have seen, is a universal moral entitlement to those objects vitally needed to live a life of minimal value. In fact, the more plausible allegation goes the other way: that critics of socioeconomic human rights have an obviously incomplete understanding of vital human need and a minimally good life. Freedom and security are integral parts of these things, yes, but they are not sufficient. What good is freedom of conscience to one who is starving? Or the right to a fair trial to one dying of easily preventable disease? It seems plain that we need our vital material needs satisfied if we are to survive at all, much less enjoy a worthwhile life.

Furthermore, it's not as though first-generation thinkers were oblivious to anything save aspects of freedom, due process, and security. They also staunchly defended the right to own private property. This is clearly a socioeconomic claim, a material benefit. Moreover, it is not inconsistent with the view suggested here. I believe that most adults—at least in North America—can provide, for themselves and their dependents, the level of material subsistence genuinely denoted by human rights.[12] Again, we are only talking about a thin set of objectively vital needs. In the case of these adults, realizing their socioeconomic rights simply means *not depriving them* of this level of personal property. That hardly seems burdensome, much less ruinous.

But there are some, a small minority, who genuinely cannot—perhaps due to war, abandonment, abuse, illness, addiction—provide material subsistence for themselves. These people—both children and adults— do exist, even though some choose to ignore them, preferring that they "sleep under bridges," where they are out of sight, out of mind.[13] These are the people mainly in mind when we speak of socioeconomic rights, because they need provision, not merely respect for what they've already earned. Note that this provision need not entail massive, invasive government programs, much less old world socialism. All it should entail, in my view—and, interestingly enough, in that of arch-capitalist thinker Milton Friedman—is a program providing a guaranteed minimal income to those who genuinely cannot provide material subsistence for themselves.[14]

There are compelling historical reasons to wonder about the cost and universal effectiveness of things like government housing, government food stamps, government make-work projects, and even, in places, aspects of government Medicare. But it's wrong to confuse the assertion that people have rights to food, clothing, shelter, education, clean water, and medical care with the view that the government must set up a huge, separate program for each to actually provide these things for everyone. Why not simply have government, through the taxation and transfer system, provide those—and only those—who genuinely cannot provide for themselves, as determined by a means test, with an amount sufficient to purchase a subsistence amount of these goods? The subsistence amount will clearly vary from place to place, pending cost of living, but that would be for talented economists to determine. Measures against abuse would have to be taken, earlier and beyond a means test. Fraud would have to be prosecuted, and any claim for a second payment in one year would have to be investigated. If a person frittered away his payment, for instance on a drug addiction, then that would probably justify some state intervention, for example, mandatory treatment and counseling, on threat of being cut off.[15]

States have their own vested interests in growing, and they aren't always benign. But defenders of human rights—even socioeconomic human rights—need not be fans of big government socialism. Friedman himself favored the guaranteed annual income approach discussed here not only because it would save the free market system from poverty-induced resentment and violence but also on the moral principle that there's something wrong with letting a human being collapse into such desperate circumstances when we can all readily, together, do something ameliorative about it.

Far from being conceptually biased in favor of any conventional political ideology, human rights seem compatible with most major, influential political doctrines, at least in the West. Their very plausibility and minimal focus make this understandable. Human rights appeal to conservatives in that they are an important and honored part of our civilization's heritage. Liberals like human rights because they are entitlements for each and every individual, regardless of group membership. They express, and protect, individualism in political life. And socialists appreciate the solidarity that goes with the universality of the human rights idea, as well as the more concrete material benefits it promises to the worst off.

Responding to the Second Objection

Before we can know whether socioeconomic human rights are affordable, we need to return to the issue of "fair shares," that is, with what we are genuinely duty-bound to do in connection with human rights. Up until the late 1970s, the duties correlative to claims of human rights were largely seen as being *either* negative *or* positive. For each human right, it was thought there correlated exactly one duty, and it was either negative or positive. The difference between negative and positive was seen solely in terms of whether or not the duty bearer had to perform an action. A negative duty was one of strict factual inaction. It was a duty of omission, of *refraining from doing something*. A positive duty, by contrast, required factual action. It demanded *providing something* or otherwise doing something beneficial for the right holder. Frequently, it was contended that the rights correlative to such duties should, in fact, be named after them: hence, the rights correlative to negative duties were "negative rights," and those correlative to positive ones were "positive rights."

It was often argued, on the basis of these assumptions, that the duties correlative to civil and political rights were wholly negative. It was thought, for example, that all others have to do for one to enjoy one's right to free speech is simply to refrain from interfering with one's speech. Civil and political rights, thus viewed, appear to have only costs of forbearance in this regard and, as a result, seem quite affordable. It was often thought, by contrast, that the duties correlative to socioeconomic rights were wholly positive. To enjoy a right to material subsistence, for example, would require that other people and social institutions go out of their way to supply one with the object of one's right, namely, a subsistence income or a bundle of vital goods. By this convenient conceptual linkage, older rights theorists such as Maurice Cranston were quick to pronounce on the utter illegitimacy of socioeconomic rights. Such rights, they said, really are not worthy of the name, due to the supposedly immense costs that their correlative positive duties mandate.[16]

Henry Shue, among others, formulated a devastating counterattack to this highly rhetorical conception of human rights and their correlative duties. Using the same understanding of the distinction between "negative" and "positive," he pointed out that some very traditional civil and political rights require the performance of duties that are not simply negative ones of forbearance. Consider, for example, the basic set of due process rights, such as the right to a fair trial by one's peers within a reasonable time period. To enjoy the substance of this right, is it true that other people and institutions need only to refrain from treating oneself in certain ways? The answer, clearly, is no. The right to a trial by peers within a reasonable time frame requires that a whole slew of positive duties be performed: it requires the presence, selection, and participation of jury members and officers of the court, a place to hold the trial, and so on. In fact, the right requires the positive construction and maintenance of an entire well-ordered judicial system charged with expediting one's case. It is clear that these positive actions do, in fact, come at a substantial cost.[17] Shue concluded that the sharp split between civil and political rights and socioeconomic rights is fallacious. The critics of socioeconomic human rights turned out, on their own terms, to be mistaken. *There is no sharp cleavage within the heart of human rights; such seems, rather, to form a unified and coherent whole.* One such unified and integrated understanding of human rights was developed briefly, in previous sections, focusing on fulfilling vital human needs.

Shue's alternative understanding of the duties correlative to human rights runs thus. His conception is not twofold but rather threefold. Shue still relies on the traditional conception of the difference between a negative and a positive duty. He contends, however, that correlative to any single human right is not one single duty, which must be either negative or positive, but rather multiple duties, which mix both negative and positive elements. Specifically, he says that correlative to any single assertion of human right are three correlative duties: (1) negatively, not to deprive the right holder of the object of his right; (2) positively, to protect the right holder in his possession of the object of his right; and (3) positively, to aid the right holder, should someone still manage to violate his right.[18]

But why these three kinds of duty, expressed in this manner? The answer, in Shue's mind, is straightforward: the performance of these three kinds of duty is, in fact, required to supply everyone with the objects of their human rights. Human rights, we have seen, exist to ensure a certain baseline level of decent treatment for all persons, usually by providing for them certain freedoms or benefits and by protecting them from standard, serious threats to the enjoyment of such freedoms and benefits. Shue contends, powerfully, that such protection from standard threats is ensured *only* when the relevant actors and institutions fulfil the following duties: (1) all persons and institutions refrain from violating the right; (2) effective institutions exist to protect the object of the right; and (3) all those in a position to do so come to one's aid in case such protection fails. This threefold structure, or what Shue calls "the waves of duty," is called for because it holds the greatest promise in terms of actually ensuring that everyone can enjoy reasonably secure access to the objects of their human rights.[19]

I think this is excellent, but I wish to make one amendment, which deals with Shue's reliance on the old understanding of the distinction between negative and positive. Shue's account fails to pay enough respect to the fact that many—perhaps even most—people persist in the belief that negative duties are more important than positive ones. I suggest that we can both keep this belief and retain Shue's essential elements, if we make the following adjustment: we redefine the meaning of "negative" away from factual inaction and toward the norm of not inflicting harm. A negative duty thus becomes a duty not to inflict grievous and unjust harm on another, whereas a positive duty becomes a duty to do someone some good, such as being polite to them. Let us call this redefinition the normative, or *prescriptive*, understanding of negative and positive, as opposed to the older *descriptive*, or factual, understanding. When apprised, and approving, of this redefinition, we can see how it squares with Shue's efforts: for it may well be part of one's duty not to inflict harm that one must both refrain from performing some act and perform some further action. For example, it may well be part of one's negative duty not to inflict harm on a person that one should both refrain from injuring that person and vote on election day for sound policies of law and order. To the extent to which one fails to do either, one has harmed that person—that person suffers harm as a result of one's free choice.

So what does satisfying human rights—including socioeconomic human rights—mean in this conception? First, if the right holder *already has* the object of the human right in question, then all persons and institutions *must not deprive* the right holder of that object, be it an aspect of security, subsistence, liberty, equality, or recognition. Second, full realization of human rights requires not merely that right holders *possess* the objects of their rights but that, additionally, they need to be *secure in their possession* of those objects. They need to be able *to count on having* such objects at their disposal as they go about living their lives. Non-deprivation is not enough: reliable protection against future non-deprivation is also required. The duty of establishing such a secure context falls, in the first instance, on social institutions. With their power and scope, they are the most capable of achieving the secure society-wide conditions sought after. Even though the duty of protection falls in the first instance on social institutions, this does not utterly unburden individuals, who must take secondary responsibility for doing their part to ensure that the social institutions they share have adequate resources to provide such protection and, indeed, are structured with the aim of achieving such protection in the first place. This secondary responsibility requires of all persons some degree of social engagement, political participation, and reasonable sharing of the tax burden required to fund such institutions. I think we as North Americans might ask ourselves sharp questions in this regard. Third, if the right holder *lacks* the objects of her human rights, then she *must be aided* in this regard, indeed *provided* the objects in question. This requirement of aid and provision assumes, significantly, that the objects can be provided at reasonable cost. If they cannot be so affordably provided, the requirement dissolves. This duty should likewise be seen as falling in the first instance on institutions, and only secondarily upon individuals. Why? The answer is that institutions can more effectively and efficiently provide such objects to people and can do so at a cost that can be intelligently and fairly spread out among all members of society, indeed over time. Having such cost fall on the shoulders of an individual would run a much greater risk of both failing to ensure that the right holder gets her object and imposing potentially ruinous costs on the duty bearer. Individuals do not make good providers for more than a very small number of people, such as parents for their children. But when individuals pool resources, delegate authority, and establish effective social institutions authorized to facilitate such provisions, widespread success is much more likely to result.

How can human rights be made affordable? The answer probably lies in an analysis of the social structures of those societies where human rights have already been more or less realized on a mass scale. What do they have in common?

- First, a shared moral culture that enshrines respect for the worth of each person. Simply providing a decent moral education that develops a sense of basic humanity can go a long way toward developing a rights-respecting culture.

- Second, rights-respecting societies allow people, in the first instance, the freedom and opportunity to secure the objects of their human rights for themselves. Most people, given the chance, will be able to find for themselves the means needed to live a minimally good life.
- Third, such societies are ruled by law and order, providing a social context secure enough that it makes sense for people to strive after what they want, not having to worry constantly about the security of themselves and their possessions. Human rights violations, moreover, get punished.
- Fourth, rights-respecting societies make it clear that the provision of human rights objects will be available *only* to those who genuinely cannot provide for themselves. This is a reasonable measure to take to reign in costs, because it sends out the appropriate incentives in favor of self-reliance, yet also humane in guaranteeing to the unfortunate that they will not be left to fall below the minimally decent standard of living denoted by human rights. This implies the presence of some social security assistance in the midst of an otherwise free society that allows and rewards effort and industry. Such assistance seems readily affordable. We are, again, talking about providing *only* that finite set of objects of vital human need to those who do *not* already have such objects *and* who genuinely cannot provide such for themselves. When one thinks of everything else contemporary governments lavish resources on, in addition to vital social programs, the affordability of such minimal welfare state protections becomes crystal clear. *The facts on the ground show that existing human rights deprivations*—such as dire poverty, homelessness, severe malnutrition, dangerously shoddy health care, and high rates of crime and violence—*have much more to do with a lack of political will than a genuine lack of resources. It is more a failure to prioritize what is truly most important.*
- The fifth quality that rights-respecting societies share is institutional accountability. Because social institutions play such an important role regarding whether or not people enjoy the objects of their human rights, it follows that there must be some mechanism for holding them accountable for fulfilling that function. Different societies differ here, but prominent options include the following: a division of power between institutions, designed to get them to serve as checks and balances on each other; efforts to keep the overall size of the total set of such institutions under control; and a system of democratic entitlements, allowing people to vote for and against those people with ambitions to run social institutions.[20]

The fact that so many societies have used these five principles to move toward success, in this regard, demonstrates the affordability of human rights, and manifestly so in countries as wealthy as America and Canada. The moral case has already been made that the costs are well worth absorbing, for the enormous payoff is ensuring that every human being can both have and lead a minimally good life in the modern world. Against the cost of realizing rights, we have to weigh the severe costs of failing to do so: the moral cost of inflicting brutal harm on people and the prudential cost of damaging the peace and stability of our societies as a result of such infliction.

Conclusion

The two major objections to socioeconomic human rights fail to persuade: they are not inconsistent with the very concept of human rights, nor are they impossible to afford—especially in North America. Together with civil and political rights, socioeconomic rights form a unified core of human rights, and strategies for realizing them at affordable cost have here been sketched. The strength of the justification of these rights inspires us for this ongoing task and convinces us of its abiding value.

Chapter 2
International Law of Economic, Social, and Cultural Rights
A U.S. Perspective

David Weissbrodt

The first part of this chapter traces the history of the U.S. approach to international law, particularly in regard to economic, social, and cultural rights and notes the important role that the United States has played in the development of relevant international human rights treaties and institutions. The second part shows that the United States has been, nonetheless, extraordinarily reluctant to submit itself to legal obligations under those treaties, related standards, and institutions. The third part reflects how U.S. judges have occasionally used international human rights law, including economic, social, and cultural rights. The chapter concludes that the United States and Canada share a legal tradition of protecting human rights, but the United States has more steps to take in bringing its human rights ideals into law and practice—particularly as to economic, social, and cultural rights.

Historical Approach of the United States to the Development of International Human Rights Law

In its early days, the United States needed international law as a means of protection from European powers. The prevailing approach to international law for most of its history has been focused on the obligations of sovereign governments among themselves. The legal position of individuals was largely a matter within the domestic jurisdiction of their states. Gradually, humanitarian concerns in the nineteenth and early twentieth centuries about slavery, suffrage for and other rights of women, the protection of wounded combatants during armed conflict, the rights of workers, self-determination, and the rights of minorities eroded the entirely state-oriented approach to international law.[1]

Prompted initially by the horrors of World War II and the Holocaust, the latter half of the twentieth century witnessed a new and increasingly broad strand of international law in which intergovernmental organizations, nongovernmental organizations (NGOs), and individuals have a more explicit role to play as participants in international human rights law. In his 1941 State of the Union address, President Franklin D. Roosevelt set out "Four Freedoms," which became the war aims of the Allies. President Roosevelt's third freedom established the basis for economic, social, and cultural rights: "The third [freedom] is the freedom from want, which, translated into world terms, means economic understandings which will secure to every nation a healthy peace-time life for its inhabitants everywhere in the world."[2]

Later during World War II, President Roosevelt's State of the Union message on January 11, 1944, more specifically addressed the freedoms he had previously enumerated.[3] They included the right to a job; the right to enough money for adequate food, clothing, and recreation; the right to a decent home; the right to decent medical care; the right to protection in the event of old age, sickness, accident, and disability; and the right to a good education. President Roosevelt, of course, presided over the New Deal, a series of programs by which the federal government combated the effects of the Great Depression of the 1930s. After World War II, the international community began to focus on the rights discussed by President Roosevelt. Several international instruments issued during the post-war period protect economic, social, and cultural rights to some extent. Notably, Article 55 of the UN Charter prescribes, "[T]he United Nations shall promote higher standards of living, full employment, and conditions of economic and social progress and development; solutions of international economic, social, health, and related problems; and international cultural and educational co-operation; and universal respect for, and observance of, human rights and fundamental freedoms for all without distinction as to race, sex, language, or religion."[4] As members of the United Nations, the United States and Canada have pledged, under Article 56, "to take joint and separate action in co-operation with the Organization for the achievement of the purposes set forth in Article 55."[5]

The first task of the newly created UN Commission on Human Rights, under the leadership of Eleanor Roosevelt, with an influential secretariat headed by Canadian law professor John P. Humphrey, was to draft the Universal Declaration of Human Rights and thus to define the general human rights obligations established by the UN Charter.[6] The Universal Declaration was adopted by the UN General Assembly in 1948, including Article 25(1) of the Universal Declaration that sets forth the seminal protection of economic, social, and cultural rights: "Everyone has the right to a standard of living adequate for the health and well-being of himself and of his family, including food, clothing, housing and medical care and necessary social services, and the right to security in the event of unemployment, sickness, disability, widowhood, old age or other lack of livelihood in circumstances beyond his control.7" The Universal Declaration also proclaims that everyone has the right to social security (Article 22), work and join trade unions (Article 23), rest and leisure (Article 24), education (Article 26), and to participate freely in cultural life (Article 27).

Following adoption of the Universal Declaration, the UN Commission on Human Rights drafted the remainder of the International Bill of Human Rights, which contained the International Covenant on Economic, Social and Cultural Rights,[8] the International Covenant on Civil and Political Rights, and an Optional Protocol to the Civil and Political Covenant. The two human rights Covenants elaborated upon and rendered as treaty obligations the principles proclaimed in the Universal Declaration. The two Covenants and the Optional Protocol were adopted by the General Assembly in 1966 and entered into force in 1976. The International Bill of Human Rights comprises the most authoritative and comprehensive prescription of human rights obligations that governments undertake in joining the United Nations.

The two Covenants distinguish between implementation of civil and political rights, on the one hand, and economic, social, and cultural rights, on the other. Civil and political rights, such as freedom of expression and the right to be free from torture or arbitrary arrest, are immediately enforceable obligations as States Parties must "respect and ensure respect" for the rights guaranteed by the Civil and Political Covenant.[9] Article 2 of the International Covenant on Economic, Social and Cultural Rights, however, provides that states should take steps within available resources to achieve progressively the full range of protected rights.[10] In other words, governments that ratify the Covenants must immediately cease torturing their citizens, but they are not immediately required by the provisions of the Covenant to feed, clothe, and house them. These latter obligations are generally to be accomplished progressively as resources permit. The difference in the texts of the two Covenants does not diminish the objective of the Covenant on Economic, Social and Cultural Rights, but rather reflects the reality that the achievement of economic, social, and cultural rights depends on the availability of resources and societal structures rather than state abstention. One should note, however, that ensuring certain civil and political rights, such as the availability of interpreters to assist criminal defendants, may require planning and expenditure. As to economic, social, and cultural rights, States Parties must begin immediately to work toward the obligations, even if they cannot be achieved instantaneously. Under both Covenants the obligation of States Parties to forbid discrimination as to civil, political, economic, social, and cultural rights is immediately applicable.

The Committee on Economic, Social and Cultural Rights was established to implement and interpret the Covenant. The committee has further interpreted the obligations of States Parties under Article 2: "While the full realization of the relevant rights may be achieved progressively, steps toward that goal must be taken within a reasonably short time after the Covenant's entry into force for the States concerned. Such steps should be deliberate, concrete and targeted as clearly as possible toward meeting the obligations recognized in the Covenant."[11] This principle places the burden on States Parties to show that they are "taking steps" to implement the Covenant and making progress. Hence, to "take steps" seems to entail more of a "guarantee" than anything else. The phrase "by all appropriate means" conveys the flexible approach of the Covenant. It allows States Parties discretion in the action that they will take; however, the final determination as to whether a measure is "appropriate" is left to the committee.[12] While some states have limited resources, this provision mandates that a government must use whatever means are available.

"Progressive realization" of rights generally means that the rights need not be achieved at once. Concern over emphasizing that the realization of the rights is not to be put off indefinitely is illustrated in General Comment No. 3: "The fact that realization over time, or in other words progressively, is foreseen under the Covenant should not be misinterpreted as depriving the obligation of all meaningful content. . . . [T]he phrase must be read in light of the overall objective . . . of the Covenant which is to establish clear obligations for States Parties in respect of the full realization of the rights in question."[13] The General Comments issued by the Committee on Economic, Social and Cultural Rights explain that the failure to meet minimum core obligations cannot generally be justified by lack of resources. As expressed in General Comment No.3, it is a prima facie violation of the Covenant when a state fails to provide for the basic subsistence needs of its people. Minimum core obligations are assessed as outlined by the Committee in General Comment No. 3: "In order for a State party to be able to attribute its failure to meet at least its minimum core obligations to a lack of available resources it must demonstrate that every effort has been made to use all resources that are at its disposition in an effort to satisfy, as a matter of priority, those obligations."[14]

The Committee on Economic, Social and Cultural Rights has further indicated in General Comment No. 9 that the provisions of the International Covenant on Economic, Social and Cultural Rights are justiciable and has rejected the idea that civil and political rights are justiciable, whereas economic, social, and cultural rights are not: "[T]here is no Covenant right which could not . . . be considered to possess at least some significant justiciable dimensions. . . . The adoption of a rigid classification of economic, social and cultural rights which puts them, by definition, beyond reach of the courts would . . . be arbitrary and incompatible with the principle that the two sets of human rights are indivisible and interdependent. It would also drastically curtail the capacity of the courts to protect rights of the most vulnerable and disadvantaged groups in society."[15] The Committee on Economic, Social and Cultural Rights has also summarized its experience in reviewing states reports and issued several instructive General Comments providing authoritative guidance as to the meaning of several substantive provisions of the Covenant, for example, on such subjects as the right to adequate housing, persons with disabilities, rights of older persons, the right to adequate housing and to be free from forced evictions, plans of action for primary education, the right to adequate food, the right to education, the right to the highest attainable standard of health, and the right to water.

The Changing Attitudes of U.S. Administrations to International Economic Human Rights Standards, Particularly Economic, Social, and Cultural Rights

Despite the leading role of the United States in establishing human rights standards and institutions, it has been extraordinarily reluctant to submit itself to legal obligations under these treaties and related standards. Aside from the UN Charter, the United States has only ratified four of the most important human rights conventions (International Covenant on Civil and Political Rights [1976], International Convention on the Elimination of All Forms of Racial Discrimination [1969], Convention against Torture and Other Cruel, Inhuman or Degrading Treatment or Punishment [1987], and the Convention on the Prevention and Punishment of the Crime of Genocide [1948]), while the great majority of other nations have become States Parties to a much greater number of treaties. One critic noted, "In an attempt to ensure that the treaties effected virtually no change in domestic law, the United States ratified . . . subject to a series of reservations, understandings and declarations . . . and declared them 'non-self-executing.'"[16] In contrast, Canada has ratified without reservations all the major human rights treaties, including the International Covenant on Economic, Social and Cultural Rights.

The attitude of the U.S. government toward economic, social, and cultural rights has varied considerably over time. As discussed earlier, President Franklin Roosevelt (1933–45) inspired UN provisions protecting economic rights. Under the administrations of Roosevelt and Truman (1945–53), the U.S. government accepted important protections for economic, social, and cultural rights in the UN Charter, the Universal Declaration of Human Rights, and the early drafts of the two human rights Covenants. Despite its active participation in the drafting of those early UN human rights instruments, the Eisenhower administration (1953–61) in the 1950s found itself unable to participate actively in drafting and ratifying human rights treaties because of congressional opposition. Several members of Congress, including notably Senator Bricker, feared that the Genocide Convention and various instruments then in draft (which later became the two Covenants, as well as the Racial Discrimination treaty) might lead to international scrutiny of United States practices, particularly racial discrimination, and might infringe on prerogatives of state governments.[17] As a result, a series of proposals known as the Bricker Amendment were introduced to amend the U.S. Constitution by restricting the government from entering into treaties that might infringe on the powers of the states or be applicable in domestic courts without implementing legislation.[18]

One version of the Bricker Amendment failed in 1954, by only one vote, to pass the Senate. To secure defeat, Secretary of State Dulles was moved to promise that the United States did not plan to become a party to any human rights treaties or present any such treaties for consideration by the Senate. He also indicated that the United States would neither sign the Convention on the Political Rights of Women nor seek ratification of the Genocide Convention.

The Kennedy administration (1961–63) sought to relax the Dulles doctrine by submitting three minor human rights treaties to the Senate. Only one, the Supplementary Slavery Convention, was approved.[19] During the presidency of Lyndon Johnson (1963–69) the United States ratified the Protocol Relating to the Status of Refugees, which guarantees to refugees several economic, social, and cultural rights.[20] In campaigning for the presidency, and then in office, Jimmy Carter (1977–81) emphasized human rights. On October 5, 1977, President Carter signed the International Covenant on Economic, Social and Cultural Rights and the International Covenant on Civil and Political Rights, submitting them to the Senate for advice and consent as to ratification.[21] The Carter administration recognized three categories of rights: rights of personal integrity, other civil and political rights, and economic rights.[22]

With the enactment of major civil rights statutes, the efforts of courts to eradicate the worst injustices of racial discrimination, a decrease of reliance on states' rights, and an increasing interest in international human rights, the climate for ratification of multilateral treaties gradually improved. In 1976, the United States ratified the Inter-American Convention on Granting of Political Rights to Women and the UN Convention on the Political Rights of Women. In 1986, at the urging of the Reagan administration, the United States finally ratified the Genocide Convention and thus broke a forty-year impediment to the ratification of the principal human rights treaties. At the same time, however, the Reagan administration (1981–89) declared that it did not believe in economic rights, but only in economic needs. For example, in the UN General Assembly, the Reagan administration cast the only negative vote against the Declaration on the Right to Development,[23] while several other developed countries abstained. By the later Reagan period and certainly during the first Bush administration (1989–93), however, the United States government began to accept the idea of economic rights and joined consensus on some UN actions relating to the right to development. During the first Bush administration, the United States also ratified the Civil and Political Covenant and the Convention against Torture.

Only five and a half months after being installed, the Clinton administration (1993–2001) announced at the World Conference on Human Rights in Vienna that it intended to ratify the American Convention on Human Rights, the Convention on the Elimination of All Forms of Discrimination against Women, and the International Covenant on Economic, Social and Cultural Rights.[24] Ultimately, the 1994 elections secured the Republican Party a majority in both houses of Congress, making the ratification of the three treaties politically untenable. During the Clinton period, however, the U.S. government did join consensus on a number of relevant UN resolutions on economic, social, and cultural rights and ratified the International Convention on the Elimination of All Forms of Racial Discrimination, which forbids racial discrimination in regard to economic, social, and cultural rights.[25] The Clinton administration was also a proponent of a rights-based approach to development; for example, U.S. Ambassador Betty King told the UN Economic and Social Council on October 14, 1998, that the United States supports "a human rights-based approach to development, supporting government policies that promote the progressive achievement of economic, social, and cultural rights."[26] The U.S. government under the Clinton administration also advocated for "expanding UNICEF's use of a human rights-based approach to development."[27] Further, the Clinton administration acknowledged a person's "right to a standard of living adequate for the health and well-being of himself and of his family, including food, clothing, housing and medical care and necessary social services," but it did not particularly encourage the recognition of specific economic, social, and cultural rights, such as the right to adequate housing or the right to food.

In contrast to the Clinton administration, the George W. Bush administration (2001–present) has been more inclined to support freedoms rather than rights, and opportunities rather than entitlements. This inclination is evident in the language that the administration employed to refer to issues surrounding what is commonly known as human rights. President Bush often spoke of both human dignity and basic rights but frequently failed to invoke the much more commonly used term "human rights." In fact, in certain situations and contexts, the Bush administration evaded standard human rights language, instead preferring ambiguous terms that carry uncertain legal force.[28] President Bush employed an arsenal of terms that are arguably interchangeable with human rights. In regards to the general reluctance by the United States to use the standard language of human rights, Harold Koh, the former assistant secretary of state for democracy, human rights, and labor in the Clinton administration, remarked, "In the same way [that the United States has] long resisted adoption of the metric system of weights and measures, we regularly fail to use the universal language of international human rights law."[29]

In addition to the *language* used by the Bush administration, the *reasoning* behind the Bush administration's rejection of a rights-based approach to economic, social, and cultural rights also supports the notion that the administration endorses freedoms rather than rights, and opportunities rather than entitlements. For example, in June 2002 the Bush administration announced to the UN Food and Agriculture Organization that "the United States believes that the attainment of the right to an adequate standard of living is a goal or aspiration to be realized progressively that does not give rise to any international obligation or any domestic legal entitlement, and does not diminish the responsibilities of national governments toward their citizens. Additionally, the United States understands the right of access to food to mean the *opportunity* to secure food, and not guaranteed entitlement."[30]

The Bush administration has put forth at least four different justifications as grounds for its rejection of a rights-based approach to economic, social, and cultural rights. First, the administration has posited that an emphasis on economic, social, and cultural rights is misplaced and that a more reliable path to the realization of these rights is through the vehicle of civil and political rights and free trade. Second, the administration has argued that the rights-based approach conflicts with

United States sovereignty and states' rights, respectively. Third, the administration has contended that the rights-based approach is not concrete and that economic rights are therefore not justiciable. Fourth, the administration argues that the ambiguity of economic, social, and cultural rights preclude more "evidence-based"[31] means to obtaining economic, social, and cultural goals.

The Bush administration frequently argues that civil and political rights and free trade—not economic, social, and cultural rights—are the surest means to attaining economic, social, and cultural goals. During a statement that the United States gave before the 59th Commission on Human Rights (March–April 2003), the U.S. delegation pointed out that the proponents of the communist system of governance viewed economic, social, and cultural rights as being superior to civil and political rights but that, contrary to this prioritization, history has shown that governments that protect civil and political rights are more likely to attain economic, social, and cultural aspirations than governments that pursue economic, social, and cultural rights as the primary means to attaining their economic, social, and cultural objectives.[32] President Bush believes that one of the key factors affecting development is "the extent to which they enjoy good governance . . . which allows them to speak and associate freely with one another, and which allows them to regularly choose their representatives in government."[33] In short, the key factor is the degree to which governments grant their citizens civil and political rights.

Another key factor for the Bush administration seems to be free trade. Indeed, the Bush administration has heralded free trade as the primary solution for a wide range of economic, social, and cultural problems ranging from political oppression and poverty to low employment rates and poor health. Bush has called free trade "the best weapon against poverty, disease, and tyranny,"[34] arguing that it "creates new jobs and new income,"[35] improves "the lives of all people, applying the power of markets to the needs of the poor,"[36] and provides a "real freedom, the freedom for a person—or a nation—to make a living."[37] The president also talks as though economic, social, and cultural rights naturally flow from free trade and civil and political rights: "Historians will note that in many nations, the advance of markets and free enterprise helped to create a middle class that was confident enough to demand their own rights."[38]

Instead of focusing on legislation that would create entitlements to economic, social, and cultural rights, the Bush administration argues that free trade is the surest mechanism for helping governments guarantee the economic, social, and cultural well-being of their people.[39] But the Bush administration believes that free trade is much more than a practical necessity; indeed, in the same manner that some nations view the entitlement of economic, social, and cultural rights as a moral principle, the Bush administration views free trade as a moral principle: "The concept of 'free trade' arose as a moral principle even before it became a pillar of economics. If you can make something that others value, you should be able to sell it to them. If others make something that you value, you should be able to buy it."[40] Notwithstanding claims about the moral and practical necessity of free trade, President Bush has undermined free trade by approving the largest farm subsidies in the history of the United States. Some have compared these subsidies to tariffs, pointing out that "[l]ike tariffs[,] . . . subsidies raise barriers to foreign agricultural producers and the developing nations for which agriculture is the primary export"[41] and that "[b]y keeping United States prices artificially low on the type of agricultural goods that developing countries produce, Bush renders toothless U.S. trade agreements."[42] Mari Alkatiri, prime minister of the Democratic Republic of Timor-Leste, has pointed out in a speech before the fifty-eighth session of the UN General Assembly (2003): "It is neither ethical nor moral for the rich countries to preach democracy, human rights and the dogma of a free market, while practicing protectionist policies that condemn hundreds of millions of human beings to perpetual poverty and dependency. It is less than ethical when they teach the rules of the free market while subsidizing their farmers with billions of dollars, making the products of our countries, which have a greater comparative advantage, increasingly less competitive."[43] Somehow, the $15 billion in annual foreign aid that the United States intends to spend on Africa seems less generous when one considers that these monies directly compete with the $19 billion given to American. farmers each year.[44] Muna Ndulo, a Cornell University law professor and director of the Institute for African Development, has pointed out that given the competition between U.S. subsidies and aid, the United States "doesn't even need to give aid . . . [it needs] to reduce subsidies."[45] Developing nations have joined this critique of the Bush administration, as evidenced by Nepal's comment before the UN General Assembly that "[i]ncreasing development assistance . . . will do little to help developing countries unless rich nations dismantle their farm subsidies and pull down their tariff and non-tariff barriers to products from the South."[46]

These Bush administration perspectives are in some ways consistent with the historical reluctance of the U.S. government to embrace economic, social, and cultural rights, but the Bush position reflects such a profoundly rejectionist approach that it is out of step with U.S. traditions—particularly established by Democratic presidents since Roosevelt—and the evolution of views in Canada, Europe, and the rest of the world. It is likely that hard-line Bush opposition to economic, social, and cultural rights will be rectified by future United States administrations. But the overall United States approach to applying international human rights law in the United States, described in the following section, may be more enduring.

Reticence of the United States to Apply International Human Rights Standards

The U.S. Constitution places treaties in a quite prominent place in the United States legal order, identifying them, together with federal laws and the Constitution itself, as "the supreme Law of the Land."[47] The classic view of the U.S. Supreme Court has sought to integrate treaties into the domestic legal order. For example, the Supreme Court has consistently held that "an Act of Congress ought never to be construed to violate the law of nations, if any other possible construction remains."[48] Further, in *The Paquete Habana,*[49] the Supreme Court has addressed the power of courts to enforce customary international law. In invalidating the wartime seizure of fishing vessels as contrary to the law of nations, the Court observed, "International law is part of our law, and must be ascertained and administered by the courts." Where no treaty or other legal authority is controlling, resort must be had to the customs of nations.[50]

Nonetheless, U.S. judges have, with a few exceptions, generally exhibited great reticence in making use of international standards in their decisions and have even appeared ignorant as to the application of international law. Former U.S. Supreme Court justice Harry Blackmun criticized the Court's opinions as showing "something less than a decent respect to the opinions of mankind" and that "at best, the Supreme Court enforces some principles of international law and some of its obligations some of the times."[51]

While the record of the Supreme Court is encouraging in some respects,[52] defective in others,[53] and far from impressive in general, there are some lower court judges in the United States who have found international human rights law, including economic, social, and cultural rights, to be useful if not dispositive. For example, in 1979, the West Virginia Supreme Court in *Pauley v. Kelly*[54] cited the Universal Declaration of Human Rights in holding education to be a fundamental right under the West Virginia Constitution.[55]

In *Moore v. Ganim,*[56] the Connecticut Supreme Court refused declaratory and injunctive relief against Bridgeport, Connecticut, to prevent it from terminating general assistance benefits. The fundamental premise of the plaintiffs' claims was that the state has an obligation under the

Connecticut Constitution to supply them with subsistence level resources irrespective of the availability of food and shelter from family, friends, charitable organizations, religious institutions, and other community sources. Chief Justice Peters concurred in the result of the four-judge majority, because the plaintiffs had not shown they were entitled to injunctive relief, but on the merits of the claim stated, "Contrary to the view of the majority, I am persuaded that the Connecticut constitution includes a governmental obligation to provide a minimal safety net to our poorest residents. As all of our historical sources indicate, the framers of our constitution believed that the government that they were establishing would not be permitted to stand idle while people, without food, shelter, clothing or medical care, were left to die in the streets."[57]

Justice Peters found support in the historical background of the Connecticut Constitution, as well as an "impressive array of contemporary sociological, economic and legal texts [that] support the recognition of such a governmental duty":[58]

These contemporary economic circumstances and contemporary conceptions of democracy already have led the international community to incorporate a right to subsistence into the international law of human rights. For example, Article 25(1) of the Universal Declaration of Human Rights declares that "[e]veryone has the right to a standard of living adequate for the health and well-being of himself and of his family, including food, clothing, housing and medical care and necessary social services, and the right to security in the event of unemployment, sickness, disability, widowhood, old age or other lack of livelihood in circumstances beyond his control." (Universal Declaration of Human Rights [1948])

Justice Peters continued by referring to Article 11(1) of the International Covenant on Economic, Social and Cultural Rights:

Although the United States is not a party to the International Covenant, and although no right to subsistence may yet apply to this country as part of customary international law; . . . the wide international agreement on at least the hortatory goals identified in the human rights documents strongly supports the plaintiffs' claim. . . . In sum, our constitutional framers, the contemporary academy, and the international community all support the conclusion that the government may not stand idle while its poorest residents die in the streets because of lack of food, shelter, clothing or medical care. The government has wide discretion in implementing its constitutional obligation and in imposing reasonable conditions on the provision of minimal support. The government, nonetheless, has a constitutional obligation to provide minimal subsistence.[59]

Associate Justice Berdon, with Associate Justice Katz, dissented saying:

It is clear to me that the preamble to our state constitution establishes an implicit right of destitute persons of Connecticut to receive those things necessary for minimal subsistence—minimal shelter, food and essential medical care. . . .

The concurring opinion of the Chief Justice, on the other hand, concludes that there is a state constitutional right to minimal subsistence. Although I agree with much of the scholarly constitutional analysis contained in the concurrence, I disagree both with its formulation of the extremely limited quality of this right and with its conclusion that there is an insufficient record . . . to sustain the appeals of these poor plaintiffs.[60]

In *Boehm v. Superior Court*,[61] the California Court of Appeal cited international law in concluding that a county was required to include clothing, transportation, and medical care when dispensing minimum subsistence grants.

The U.S. Court of Appeals for the Ninth Circuit has also cited the International Covenant on Civil and Political Rights and related treaties in concluding that the right to live with one's family is fundamental and, accordingly, that a state violated due process rights by denying foster care funding to children who live with close relatives.[62]

From these cases one can conclude that some lower court judges have found international human rights law to be useful in interpreting such broad federal and state constitutional provisions as "due process" and "equal protection." Nonetheless, in general, United States judges are either reluctant to use or ignorant of international law in making decisions. Such judicial reluctance to use or ignorance about international human rights standards is inconsistent with the status of the United States as a powerful and influential nation, which at the beginning of the twenty-first century became the world's sole superpower. The failure of the United States to ratify and apply human rights standards within its borders is also inconsistent with U.S. legislation that established in the Department of State a Bureau of Democracy, Human Rights, and Labor and that requires the bureau to issue a yearly report on the state of human rights in the world, based on submissions from United States embassies.[63] In addition, the U.S. Congress has also adopted legislation conditioning the granting of security, development, and international financial assistance to countries on their adherence to human rights standards.[64]

The economic and political influence of the United States has inspired other governments and peoples to emulate its democracy, its economic system, and its methods for protecting human rights. Its prominent position in the world community and dominance of the world's media both have made the United States the most visible nation—even as to its human rights problems—and at the same time has allowed it to ignore most international criticism. At the same time, United States officials, judges, and residents have been very slow to open this nation's human rights conditions to international criticism. Canada has, in contrast, subjected itself to nearly all of those international procedures.[65]

Conclusion

The United States shares with Canada commitments to the rule of law, democratic principles, and the protection of human rights. Those commitments draw their origins from the Magna Carta, the English Bill of Rights, the American Declaration of Independence, the French Declaration on the Rights of Man and of the Citizen, and the United States Bill of Rights. Based on their common legal traditions, both the United States and Canada have helped to establish a substantial body of international human rights standards for the rule of law and democracy.

While both Canada and the United States retain a basically dualist approach to international law in which treaties are the basis of relations among states, they have in varying degrees incorporated some aspects of international human rights law into their domestic practice. Having ratified all the principal human rights treaties (including the International Covenant on Economic, Social and Cultural Rights) and having incorporated human rights within the Canadian Charter of Rights and Freedoms, Canada has made significant progress in incorporating human rights law into its national law.[66] The United States has ratified a few of the main human rights treaties, including the International Covenant on Civil and Political Rights and the International Convention on the Elimination of All Forms of Racial Discrimination (containing several protections for economic, social, and cultural rights), has accepted the Protocol Relating to the Status of Refugees (protecting economic, social, and cultural rights for refugees), and is subject to the American Declaration of the Rights and Duties of Man, but has not ratified the International Covenant on Economic, Social and Cultural Rights. Even regarding these few treaties and instruments, there is an evident tension between the obligations of the United States as a nation vis-à-vis other nations, on the one hand, and the willingness of United States courts to apply international standards to activity within the country, on the other.

The United States has played a central role in the development and promotion of human rights standards in the modern world yet needs to take more steps to bring its human rights ideals into law and practice.

Chapter 3
On the Margins of the Human Rights Discourse
Foreign Policy and International Welfare Rights

David P. Forsythe and Eric A. Heinze

The International Covenant on Economic, Social and Cultural Rights (ICESCR) has always been the stepchild of international human rights law, drawing much less attention most of the time than the companion covenant on civil and political rights—at least in the West. If we look at the antecedent 1948 Universal Declaration of Human Rights, its provisions concerning international welfare or subsistence rights (to food, clothing, shelter, and health) have likewise usually drawn less attention than the provisions pertaining to civil-political rights—again, at least in the West.[1]

The studies that exist about the secondary status of international subsistence rights have mostly been undertaken by those with a strong legal bent. They have focused on legal issues such as treaty wording, legal obligation, what constitutes a violation, whether welfare rights can be adjudicated, and the effect of treaty monitoring mechanisms that emphasize the role of independent experts.[2] Almost no studies exist regarding state foreign policy and international welfare or subsistence rights. Virtually no one has asked which states have shown the most interest in these rights, and why; which states have opposed these rights most strongly and persistently, and why; what political strategies might be tried to increase state interest in these rights; and what are the prospects for success concerning such efforts.

This chapter represents a first step in addressing international welfare rights from an emphasis on foreign policy. As such, it ultimately argues two points: the current status and influence of the ICESCR is not likely to change in the near future; at the same time, other developments pertaining to socioeconomic conditions are more encouraging. In particular, many states increasingly emphasize ideas such as human security, sustainable human development, right to development, rights of the child, women's rights, and minority rights. This may compensate to some degree for state inattention—of a concrete and practical nature—to the ICESCR. However, if human rights are to be put in the mainstream of policy debates, a step endorsed in numerous international fora, it may be that a certain diminution of human rights as *rights* may be inherent in that process. If there is an increase in policy attention to socioeconomic conditions, the cost to the rights discourse may be accompanied by some practical advantage to persons. The human rights discourse is not the only moral or progressive discourse. The development discourse and/or the foreign assistance discourse can also be moral or progressive, with benefit to the socioeconomic welfare of persons.

General Overview of Foreign Policy on Welfare Rights and the ICESCR

We do not lack for publicists arguing for the importance of international welfare or subsistence rights.[3] Perhaps more important, as of July 22, 2005, 151 states have ratified the ICESCR, almost as many as for the companion civil-political Covenant (154). Welfare rights are repeatedly endorsed by the UN General Assembly as on a par with civil and political rights. But subsequent action in this and other fora belie that assertion to considerable degree.

When states are censured in the UN Human Rights Commission, for example, it is never for violation of welfare rights but rather always for violation of civil-political rights. When China or Ethiopia or North Korea adopted policies that led to massive starvation, they were not censured in that body.[4] When states consider adjusting foreign assistance for human rights reasons, it is almost always because of violation of civil or political rights and almost never because of violation of subsistence rights. States do not terminate foreign assistance to governments because the latter spend too much on military equipment, thus taking away from what they are, legally speaking, obligated to spend on maternal health care. When states consider the use of military force abroad, at least partially, for human rights reasons, the antecedent condition almost always pertains to civil and/or political rights, not welfare rights. The case of Somalia in the early 1990s aside, states do not consider humanitarian intervention in response to starvation that damages and kills on a massive scale.

In the early 1990s, in providing an overview of the United Nations and human rights, a leading expert on international welfare rights, Philip Alston, wrote: "In relation to certain issues, very little progress has been made: they include most notably economic, social and cultural rights."[5] There is little reason to second-guess his picture of the status of subsistence rights.[6] Particularly as found in the ICESCR, these rights have never met with biting, concrete, practical, follow-up by the global international community. In some respects, it is clear how the international community arrived at this double standard, but in other cases it is not.

The United States: Strong Opposition

The United States has always had a significant impact on international human rights. The human rights language in the UN Charter came initially from the United States, even if nongovernmental organizations (NGOs) and Latin American states made some contributions. That wording was not expanded or made more specific primarily because of U.S. resistance, even if Britain and the Soviet Union were only too happy to follow Washington's lead. The fight for the 1948 Universal Declaration was led by the United States. The United States has been opposed to the welfare rights found in the ICESCR most of the time since the conclusion of that treaty.[7] This opposition is especially manifest in modern Republican administrations, as was true for Ronald Reagan and is true for George W. Bush.

It was not always so. Coming out of the Great Depression of the late 1920s and the 1930s, and led by Franklin D. Roosevelt and Harry S Truman, the United States was sympathetic to welfare rights. Freedom from want was one of FDR's fundamental Four Freedoms. His New Deal represented a commitment by the public sector to compensate for the defects of private markets. Truman proposed, and fought for, a plan for national health insurance—recognition of a right to health care for all United States citizens.[8]

We do not know all the details of the fundamental shift in United States policy to opposing international welfare rights. The reasons remain historically unclear, despite American commitment to the Universal Declaration of Human Rights and Eleanor Roosevelt's chairing the UN Commission at that time.

By Eisenhower's first administration, big business, the Republican Party, and the other sectors of American society (such as the medical profession) that had opposed Truman's plan for national health insurance mobilized effectively against international welfare rights. The intensity of the Cold War gave subsistence rights a bad odor in Washington, D.C., smelling as they did of the socialism favored by the Soviet Union. Moreover, growing American prosperity after World War II was widely understood to mean that private markets could provide basic human needs if citizens would only take individual responsibility for their welfare and compete in the marketplace.

It is well-known that, early in the Eisenhower administration, the executive branch promised congressional elements that it would back away from all human rights treaties, in exchange for abatement of the effort to pass the generic Bricker constitutional amendments intended to reduce the authority of the chief executive concerning treaty law. From that time until today, no president has championed international welfare rights as found in the ICESCR, and some have strongly attacked them. Although the United States had helped negotiate the socioeconomic covenant, Eisenhower's deal with Senator Bricker effectively undercut United States activity on international welfare rights.

Some two decades later, Jimmy Carter signed the ICESCR and occasionally spoke in favor of international welfare rights, but he never invested any political capital in trying to secure its ratification. Bill Clinton likewise endorsed the ICESCR but never made ratification a priority of his administration. As the Republican Party became the normally dominant party, and as Republican ultra-nationalist and unilateralist politicians, personified by Jesse Helms as chair of the Senate Foreign Relations Committee, came to exercise great influence, the question of ICESCR ratification became a dead letter. Presidents like Ronald Reagan and George W. Bush, with their views of a divinely blessed role for the United States in world history, needed no encouragement from the likes of Helms to oppose international welfare rights that were at variance with the traditional American view of fundamental rights. Reagan was a master of using the bully pulpit of the White House to stress individual competition at home and American leadership for rights abroad; however, much of this mythology flew in the face of the real history of both Reagan and the country.[9] The dominant societal emphasis was certainly not on a need for big government at home or international standards from abroad.

Since the early 1950s, international welfare rights have been presented by important American circles as decidedly un-American—a threat to individual freedom and limited government, a socialistic intrusion from abroad inconsistent with the proven virtues of traditional American society. Social democracy has never been a consistently powerful force in American society; unlike most other Western democracies, the United States manifests no Social Democratic political party.

The United States, at both federal and state levels, manifests a welfare state reflecting some concern for the poor and those otherwise marginalized. Federal and state authorities provide some financial and other assistance to those not doing well in competitive American society. But these welfare policies are optional public policies undertaken at the discretion of authorities. If provided, they must meet civil standards of equality and equity. But the welfare policies do not exist because persons have a fundamental, basic, human right to them. United States opposition to the ICESCR is consistent with this dominant tradition.

Other Affluent Democracies: Other Priorities

It is usually the case that policy experience at home greatly shapes foreign policy abroad. Thus we find that, among the rich democracies, those with the largest welfare states at home have the most generous development assistance programs abroad, measured as a percentage of resources.[10] In other words, the developed countries showing the greatest compassion at home for the poor and marginalized also show similar compassion, relatively speaking, for the less fortunate in other countries through development assistance. That being so, we would expect countries such as Canada and the Netherlands, among other rich liberal democracies, to show great interest in international welfare rights, given that they pride themselves on constructing a humane society at home. And thus it is quite ironic to find that both the Canadians and the Dutch have shown only slight interest in international subsistence rights, although both have ratified the ICESCR. We expected indifference, indeed opposition, from the United States, given its competitive libertarian liberalism at home. We expected active and concrete support for international subsistence *rights* from the Canadians and the Dutch as representative of the social democratic version of liberalism. But broad and energetic support is largely absent.

As for Canada, a large part of that country prides itself on being different from the United States, particularly in recognizing a fundamental right to basic health care, and other socioeconomic rights, leading to a less competitive, more humane society.[11] Despite this, one searches in vain for policy statements from high Canadian officials stressing the importance of welfare rights in international relations. A rather lengthy 1997 statement on human rights in Canadian foreign policy by Lloyd Axworthy, then minister of foreign affairs, failed to mention socioeconomic rights.[12] This overview did mention human security, development, and poverty among other subjects. A 1995 speech by Raynell Andreychuk, senator from the West (Saskatchewan), on human rights and Canadian foreign policy also failed to mention subsistence rights.[13] There was approving mention, however, of women's rights, Aboriginal rights, and minority rights, among other subjects.

Analysts of Canadian foreign policy and human rights, whether or not they agree on the importance of human rights in Ottawa's foreign role,[14] note that subsistence rights receive short shrift.[15] One author conducted a study of Canadian food aid policy without mentioning human rights.[16] Beyond discussion of rights, it should be stressed that Canada sees itself as playing a constructive role in the world concerning such matters as foreign assistance and development and recognizing the socioeconomic sources of various problems such as political instability. The primary point is that Canadian policy toward these foreign issues is not often framed in the discourse of internationally recognized welfare rights.

As for the Netherlands, the pattern is similar to Canada. Few states do more to implement socioeconomic rights as fundamental human rights at home than the Netherlands. But subsistence rights do not figure prominently in Dutch foreign policy. The situation is well summarized in the following excerpt:

Classical and social human rights are considered of equal importance "in the sense that an existence worthy of human dignity is only possible if both categories of rights are enjoyed." Therefore, working for human rights should be seen as combating not only political oppression, but also economic exploitation and social discrimination. Such were the principles. In practice, however, human rights were usually interpreted as the promotion and protection of civil and political rights, as almost all the cases—China, Nicaragua, and El Salvador in particular—bear out.

In the latter case, the Dutch parliament raised the question whether the freedom to form and operate trade unions, land reform processes, and a policy of more evenly distributed income and wealth were part of a human rights evaluation project, because it wanted to include economic and social rights in the government's evaluation. Only in the case of Turkey (labour rights) did the Netherlands criticize a foreign government for the violation of the economic and social rights of their citizens. Furthermore, the Netherlands government has for a long time refused to endorse the idea of an Optional Protocol to the International Covenant on Economic, Social, and Cultural Rights for an individual right of complaint.[17]

As in the case of Canada, there is reason to regard the Dutch as manifesting a relatively progressive foreign policy on many aspects of development, status of women, fate of other marginalized groups, and so forth. But placing these concerns within the framework of general socioeconomic rights is not the preferred approach in The Hague, anymore than it is in Ottawa.

The same pattern is evident in most of the other core states of the Organisation for Economic Co-operation and Development (OECD) with a strong tradition of social democracy at home. In Norway, as early as the late 1970s, the government issued a white paper on international human rights indicating that "[t]his report will deal with all aspects of human rights in accordance with the enlarged human rights concept. When it comes to a question of what Norway can do, the emphasis will be laid on its civil and political rights aspects. Norway's contribution toward strengthening the economic, social and cultural aspects of human rights is principally channeled through the Norwegian policy on development assistance."[18]

If we look at the foreign policy of member states of the European Union (EU), and if we then look at the issue of EU conditionality because of human rights considerations, we find that EU conditionality of various types has been mostly linked to democracy. The focus—to the extent that there has been a serious and systematic focus at all—has been on the civil and political rights making up democracy, and on major interruptions in the movement toward democracy such as through coups d'état. Little attention has been given to subsistence rights.[19]

It is true that there has been some renewed attention to social rights, especially labor rights, through the Council of Europe and its European Social Charter. But to date this renewed interest by European states in the Social Charter had not led to major reorientations in state foreign policy on human rights. The primary focus of foreign policy by European liberal democracies concerning human rights remains on civil and political rights.[20]

Developing Countries: Also Other Priorities

State recourse to the international human rights discourse is often expedient if not cynical, greatly affected by the attempt to use international human rights norms for purposes other than the advancement of human dignity without discrimination.[21] The United States has used human rights standards to criticize Cuba but not Saudi Arabia, Iran after 1978–79 but not Kuwait.[22] But even the Canadians were more likely during the Cold War to criticize strategic enemies rather than allies on matters of human rights.[23] All states are inconsistent with regard to human rights in foreign policy, falling short of the goal of addressing human rights issues as a matter of moral or legal principle centered on the pursuit of human dignity without negative discrimination.[24] States may be prisoners of insecurity in the nation-state system and/or prisoners of domestic pressures pushing them toward pursuit of national advantage. In foreign policy, national governments traditionally exist primarily to pursue a non-cosmopolitan or narrow national interest whether defined in security, economic, or other terms.

Thus it is not very surprising that, in general, developing countries, while many of them have ratified the ICESCR, have followed up mostly by trying to turn welfare rights into a means to do something about the goals of a new economic world order, debt relief, protection for migrant workers, a condemnation of unilateral economic sanctions, and other subjects benefiting themselves or their citizens in particular. It is also the case that state reports by developing countries under the ICESCR have been, to give them the benefit of the doubt, just as late, incomplete, formal, superficial, and self-serving as any other category of states. So while many developing countries, particularly authoritarian ones with poor records on many civil and political rights, may be inclined to stress subsistence rights in their foreign policy semantics, there is little if any evidence to suggest that most developing countries give principled and serious attention to these welfare rights in their major foreign policy initiatives. Unfortunately, space considerations preclude detailed consideration of this evidence.

Are there differences in developing countries whose constitutions codify welfare rights, where a principled emphasis on subsistence rights might require their national legal system to treat these as fundamental rights? An examination of India, prepared in an earlier, lengthier version of this chapter, shows long-standing concern for human rights that carried over into its foreign policy. New Delhi's emphasis on the right to development, it seems fair to say, is both principled and expedient, that is, consistent with a genuine view of what advances human rights and consistent with what benefits India as a developing country.

Summary: The General Situation

Why is it, then, that despite broad ratification of the ICESCR (146 out of 191 states), most national officials—at least in the powerful West—have not given very much serious and principled attention to international welfare rights? We think there are four main reasons.

First, the idea that human rights means civil and political rights has proved durable in many intellectual and political circles, especially in right-of-center political parties. These circles believe in the broad goodness of an economic liberalism[25] that is only minimally restricted and that often translates into an opposition to welfare rights. This view not only is completely dominant in the powerful United States, but also has led to important attacks on subsistence rights, especially the right to adequate health care, in places such as Canada and the United Kingdom, where there is strong criticism of those existing rights. The argument of Nobel Laureate Amartya Sen, that a person without adequate health care, among other rights, is not really a free person, has never made much impact on these circles of opinion.[26] Freedom is still widely understood in civil and political terms, with great emphasis on the freedom to own and/or manage private property as a key civil right. Especially in the United States, political and economic "freedoms" have been understood in a way inimical to welfare rights. A related emphasis in international relations on the benefits of economic globalization, on the policy guidelines for economic growth known as "the Washington consensus," and on the demands for structural readjustment by the leading international financial institutions has had the effect of weakening international welfare rights. We should not underestimate the power of certain ideas to shape behavior.[27]

Second, linked to this is the fact that Western-based NGOs with considerable saliency among Western governments stressed civil-political rights rather than welfare rights. This was true for a long time for Amnesty International (AI) and Human Rights Watch (HRW), the two human rights NGOs that probably generate more statements read in Western governmental circles than any others. Moreover, when Human Rights First (formerly the Lawyers Committee for Human Rights), based in New York, wrote a policy primer for the George W. Bush administration, there was no mention of welfare rights (although there was great attention to labor rights).[28]

On some international issues, such as banning antipersonnel landmines or creating the international criminal court, there was a broad-based movement of support made up mostly of like-minded governments and NGOs. This has not happened with regard to welfare rights in part because a broad and often influential NGO community has not mobilized on their behalf. There are some NGOs that focus on subsistence rights, and some of these organizations are based in the West. Still, the salient NGOs such as AI and HRW were slow to see the relevance of welfare rights for their traditional mandate, much less to see a broader significance to subsistence rights in and of themselves. In 2001, AI issued the following statement:

After much debate it was agreed that the statute which defines AI's mandate should be changed to say that AI's work is focused on preventing and eliminating grave abuses of the rights to physical and mental integrity, freedom of thought and expression, and freedom from discrimination, within the context of promoting all human rights. This unanimous decision clearly lays the basis for responding to a much broader range of rights concerns than it has in the past. It enables us to tackle some abuses of economic, social and cultural rights and to focus more effectively on the main human rights concerns in different countries, unconstrained by the limits of the previous mandate.[29]

Likewise, in December 2002 HRW adopted the following policy: "Human Rights Watch considers that economic, social and cultural rights are an integral part of the body of international human rights law, with the same character and standing as civil and political rights. We conduct research and advocacy on economic, social and cultural rights under the same methodology and criteria as civil and political rights, namely, where it is possible to identify a violator, a rights violation, and a remedy to address the violation."[30]

If it is true that progress on internationally recognized civil and political rights since about 1970 came about, at least to considerable extent, because of the influence of NGOs, but the same influence has not been generated for international welfare rights.[31]

Third, fear of a zero-sum game in discussions of international welfare rights has also impeded serious attention to these rights. When, during the Cold War, the Soviet Union and its allies made reference to subsistence rights, the NATO countries suspected, with reason, an effort to distract attention away from violations of civil and political rights. Likewise when, after the Cold War, Cuba or China gave great diplomatic attention to international welfare rights, analysts suspected, again with reason, that more attention to socioeconomic rights might mean less attention to civil-political rights. After all, if Cuba had a reasonably good record on at least some rights found in the ICSECR, would it not be more difficult to mobilize international pressure on Castro's government because of violations of civil and political rights?

Finally, many officials in national foreign policy establishments are pragmatic rather than legally oriented, more interested in the facts on the ground than legal theories of obligation. When it comes to addressing issues such as starvation, malnutrition, potable water, effective sanitary systems, better agriculture, reducing the damage from HIV/AIDS, and so on, these national functionaries were more comfortable with pragmatic policy considerations than with a controversial treaty framework. Rather than spend time on debates about the meaning of "progressive implementation" of international legal standards, or the precise meaning of international legal phrases such as "to the extent possible" because of "available resources," many national officials preferred a non-legal discourse stressing development assistance as evaluated according to measures of practical achievement.

Especially in the United States, why stir up theoretical or ideological controversies about the legitimacy of welfare rights, when one could address issues like food and health care abroad in less controversial ways?[32] This view is reflected in what Harold Koh, former head of the State Department's Bureau of Democracy, Human Rights, and Labor, has written about U.S. non-ratification of the rights of the child convention: "But once one weighs in the unfavorable alignment of pro-ratification votes in the Republican-controlled Senate, and considers the amount of political capital that United States activists would require to obtain the sixty-seven votes needed for ratification any time soon, one soon concludes that the children's rights advocates are probably better off directing their limited energies not toward ratification, but rather, toward real strategies to reduce the exploitation of child labor."[33] Moreover, development assistance per se was often controversial enough in parliaments and public opinion, without adding as well a layer of controversy about welfare or subsistence rights.

In fact, the ICESCR was not a very good framework for foreign policy. Once a state ratified the Covenant, the review process focused on implementation of the treaty in that state's jurisdiction, not whether the treaty had great impact on that state's foreign policy. Logically, once Ghana ratified the ICESCR, the United Kingdom might choose to take up that matter in British policy toward Ghana, or vice versa. But nothing in the ICESCR required it.[34]

Contemporary Debates on Welfare Rights at the United Nations

Against this general background, we raise the question of whether contemporary state foreign policy shows any new and striking developments in behalf of international welfare rights. We look for evidence in UN proceedings. A focus on states and their policies channels us toward the UN General Assembly and Human Rights Commission rather than toward the UN Office of the High Commissioner for Human Rights and other UN agencies staffed by independent experts.[35]

General Assembly: Third Committee and Plenary

The documentation of the UN General Assembly and its Third Standing Committee on Social Affairs, where human rights preliminary debates occur, tells us very little that is new and important. Using 1999 as our point of reference, there were several debates and resolutions about international welfare rights—and about related subjects such as special protections for women, children, and minorities. Most of these debates and resolutions covered well-traveled ground. Almost all of the resolutions had numerous sponsors; it was obviously agreed in certain caucusing groups to advance particular draft resolutions. Many of the resolutions were worded in a very general way, creating little or no controversy, and leading to adoption without vote. These developments did indicate broad if abstract endorsement of such ideas as special emphasis on the health needs of women and girls. No new enforcement mechanisms or other matters of direct consequence were approved. No new conventions were proposed, in order to parallel the various conventions that exist for particular civil and political rights. On a few resolutions there was a north-south split in the voting, as on measures pertaining to unilateral economic sanctions as an impediment to implementation of human rights in developing countries, or on interpretation of the right to development as favoring transfer of resources to developing countries.

One of the main things states do at the United Nations is to legitimize certain ideas over time. This is as true for human rights as for development, ecological protection, security, or any other field. This process of producing collective endorsement and legitimization goes on in the Third Committee and Plenary General Assembly and may (or may not) be important for the long-term evolution of international politics, including human rights. Repeated collective endorsement of welfare rights might have the effect of changing United States policies toward these rights over time, although that change is nowhere in sight. Repeated attention to women's equal rights might help change the policies of most Muslim states on these issues, although broad change is not yet evident on that question either. At the same time, endorsement of abstract ideas without enhancement of political and legal mechanisms to transform those abstract ideas into concrete practice does little to bring about behavioral change in the short term.

The same trends were evident in the corresponding plenary session of the General Assembly. We made a cursory review of other recent years, concluding that 1999 was highly typical. States do direct foreign policy attention to many welfare rights and to related rights for women and minorities that have been the traditional targets of socioeconomic discrimination, but the short-term significance of this foreign policy in the General Assembly is highly questionable.

Human Rights Commission

The foreign policy game is played essentially the same way in the UN Human Rights Commission as in the General Assembly. It makes little difference that there are 53 states in the game instead of 191. There are draft resolutions introduced about international welfare rights, with many states as cosponsors, and with vague wording often allowing adoption by consensus. A few roll call votes indicate a north-south split, but even these resolutions remain general. None of these resolutions creates programs or establishes budgets designed to change behavior in the short term. None of these resolutions proposes new conventions on particular welfare rights. This leaves us with the fact that the Civil-Political Covenant is buttressed by follow-up treaties such as the one on the political rights of women or on prohibition of torture. We do not have a series of treaties specifying the legal obligations contained in the ICESCR, such as on rights to adequate nutrition or health, in general or for women.[36] A few states go to the trouble of making statements explaining their vote or why they joined in the consensus adoption. Most of these statements lack broad significance. The entire exercise remains focused on abstract wording. The game is about collective legitimization of ideas, not about concrete programs or authoritative agencies designed to implement, much less enforce, subsistence rights in the short term. The game may have significance for social learning in the long term, or it may not.

The only exception to this pattern came in the period 2000–2002, when the commission established Special Rapporteurs on Right to Food, Right to Adequate Housing, and Right to "The Highest Attainable Standard of Physical and Mental Health." While some human rights lawyers attribute great significance to these developments, it can be recalled that such individuals have virtually no authority or power at their command, that their visits to a particular country often go unreported in the national press, and that the behavioral impact of their reports is often not very evident.

Most of the resolutions from the UN Human Rights Commission about subsistence rights are eventually rubber stamped by the Economic and Social Council (ECOSOC). The game being what it is, we did not find it necessary to review ECOSOC approval in detail.

Developments Concerning Socioeconomic Conditions

It is perfectly obvious that much state foreign policy about international welfare rights continues to be pro forma. This is so not only because the ratification of the ICESCR exceeds the political will to take it fully seriously but also because the ritual adoption of general statements about these rights has little evident impact on anyone's behavior in the short term. Even the reports of Special Rapporteurs seem to do little more than keep an idea alive pending more decisive developments. Nevertheless, we would be remiss not to mention the growing attention that states are giving to socioeconomic conditions. It is a parallel development to, or perhaps even a substantive substitute for, attention to subsistence rights. This contemporary emphasis takes several forms.

Increasingly, states and other actors use the concept of human security. This notion has a socioeconomic component.[37] Adequate food is clearly part of human security, for example, whether in situations of peace, war, or unstable post-conflict transitions.[38] To take another example, states have increasingly accepted the idea that dealing with poverty, not just managing political conflict, is part of human security.[39]

Likewise, states have agreed at the United Nations on certain goals of development for the new millennium. These UN Millennium Development Goals (MDGs) clearly direct attention to vulnerable and marginalized groups in the poorest societies.[40] It is noteworthy that states have accepted, through the MDGs, specific targets for action as well as a follow-up evaluation procedure, designed to guarantee progress on improving the lives of the poor and otherwise marginalized in world society.[41]

The UN MDGs parallel state agreement on the meaning of "sustainable human development," the previous catchword for the UN Development Program and indeed for the United Nations' focus on economic growth with a human face, broadly speaking. Of course, international civil servants have been active in pushing this new notion of development through the United Nations, but state foreign policy is another reason for the new consensus.[42] The meaning of sustainable human development is specified by the MDGs.

It is increasingly clear that the United Nations' endorsement of MDGs and likewise of "sustainable human development" overlaps significantly with, and may be essentially the same as, the right to development. As one author noted, "Although the contours of this right [to development] are vague, it undoubtedly encompasses many economic, social, and cultural rights."[43] Another author argues that the right to development includes certain principles (focus on humans, incorporation of all human rights, stress on participation, reaffirmation of legal obligations, empowerment particularly of marginalized groups) that make clear the overlap with the other developmental ideas endorsed by states at the United Nations.[44] If the right to development is essentially a redundant emphasis on all codified international human rights, then obviously it includes welfare rights.

Moreover, we have already mentioned that most states now endorse renewed attention to women's rights, children's rights, and the rights of various minorities. All of this diplomacy touches upon the socioeconomic conditions of groups traditionally marginalized and exploited in most societies.

It may even be the case that for those states that would prefer to emphasize civil and political rights, their own practical experiences will compel them to recognize the importance of at least socioeconomic goods and services, if not welfare rights. For the United States, for example, when dealing with occupation or post-conflict involvement in Iraq, Afghanistan, Bosnia, Kosovo, and so forth, it should be perfectly clear that socioeconomic disruption is counterproductive to the effort to build stable liberal democracies based on civil-political rights. This experience should confirm the insights about some past situations, for example, that economic dislocation contributed greatly to the downfall of democracy in Weimar Germany and the rise of extremist political movements. And all of this fits with growing evidence in social science that one of the greatest barriers to establishment of stable liberal democracy is economic crisis.[45]

Now all of this diplomatic consensus on behalf of the importance of basic human needs of a socioeconomic nature should not lead us into a Pollyannaish position. If we look at the reality on the ground in, say, the Democratic Republic of the Congo in 2003, we find massive human suffering along with a very meager international response to it. All of the fine words in New York, Geneva, and elsewhere have not been translated into an adequate international effort to deal with profound human insecurity, lack of the most basic elements of "development," and so on. Chronic poverty, infant mortality, child malnutrition, and other forms of deprivation continue, whether exacerbated or not by armed conflict, and are regularly recorded on a global scale by the World Bank and the United Nations Development Program (UNDP).

Skeptics might say that the new diplomatic consensus on behalf of socioeconomic basic human needs is no different from the consensus that produced the ICESCR and that what we have is lip service to an idea followed by hypocrisy. That is possible. But we think there are at least two reasons for some optimism. One is that the World Bank and UNDP are part of the new consensus, and so we will see funded programs on the ground to implement the new thinking.[46] The second reason is that the Bush administration seems prepared to put new monies into things like the Millennium Account for development and a special development account for dealing with HIV/AIDS in Africa. At Monterrey, Mexico, the Bush administration publicly agreed that it had a responsibility to help the poorer countries develop. If Congress goes along, we will see new, concrete efforts for welfare rights by whatever name that will be added to the bilateral and multilateral assistance already extant. In 2001, Congress instructed a cooperative Clinton administration to oppose any World Bank or International Monetary Fund loan that required user fees for access to primary education or health care.[47]

Finally, we do see the clear beginnings of awareness in international relations that it is foolish to speak of meaningful civil and political rights without serious attention to socioeconomic context. Whether a pragmatic approach driven by ethics and politics is inferior to a rights approach driven by notions of legal obligation is an interesting question. In the meantime, the pragmatic approach seems to moving forward (no doubt not fast enough) while the rights approach seems to be treading water—at least regarding welfare rights.[48]

Conclusion

While we bemoan the lack of serious attention to international welfare *rights*, we may overlook the growing awareness by states (and other actors) of the importance of socioeconomic conditions that overlap with welfare rights.[49] We think that many objectives of the ICESCR are being addressed in non-legalistic fashion through diplomacy that uses notions such as human security, MDGs, sustainable human development, the right to development, and various specialized rights pertaining to women, children, and minorities.

We do agree that what is lost in some of this diplomacy is the notion of entitlement inherent in rights: that states *must* adopt certain policies because of personal rights. But in international relations, where state security is not ensured, human rights will not be treated as trumps most of the time anyway. National security traditionally defined will be trump. The best that can be achieved for now, we think, is to emphasize non-legal notions such as human security as being on a par with national security, or perhaps a component of national security. These political arguments are likely to be more compelling than the legal arguments. For example, the United States can be brought around to seeing the importance of socioeconomic conditions in Iraq and Afghanistan, among other places, for reasons of political stability if not democracy promotion. But Washington is not going to change its legal conception of human rights anytime soon.

We should not let a focus on legal rights and duties, and legal mechanisms, blind us to the increasing attention to the poor and marginalized that is occurring in contemporary world affairs. Of course, diplomatic agreement among states (and other actors) about what should be done is not the same as translating that agreement into effective action that actually improves lives in the short run. But ideational agreement is a useful (if overdue) first step, and the MDGs do create precise standards to evaluate practical action.

Part II
Poverty

Chapter 4
Homelessness in Canada and the United States

Barbara Wake Carroll

Section 11.1 of the United Nations International Covenant on Economic, Social and Cultural Rights (ICESCR) recognizes the right to shelter. Yet in both Canada and the United States more and more people are homeless. Even though it is a not a signatory to this Covenant, in the United States, the Fourteenth Amendment, which could provide for the "right to housing," has consistently been interpreted narrowly by the Supreme Court.[1] In Canada, which is a signatory, the Hellyer Report of 1969 affirmed the right to decent housing,[2] but it has not been acted upon by successive governments. This could arguably be extended by Section 7 of the Canadian Charter of Rights and Freedoms, which gives the right to "security of the person."

For the purposes of this chapter, homelessness is the lack of adequate housing or shelter. It can be considered as a continuum. At one extreme is absolute homelessness, in which persons live in temporary shelters or on the streets. At the other end are those at high risk of homelessness, often referred to as the "hidden" homeless. These are individuals who live in overcrowded or substandard conditions, live temporarily with extended family or friends, or are at risk of eviction.

This chapter argues that there are three sets of rights surrounding homelessness. The first is the right to shelter, an essential need in climates such as that in North America. This is the economic/social right that has concerned the United Nations' Committee on Economic, Social and Cultural Rights. The second involves the right of free will and the ability to make informed decisions. To be more explicit, many are homeless owing to mental illness and the process of "deinstitutionalization," which has been popular in North America from the 1970s to the present. The deinstitutionalization movement was intended to be accompanied by strong community support systems, but governments in both countries used it as a simple money-saving strategy, to put those with mental illness into the community without support. The right of these individuals not to take their "meds" has been established.[3] But when they don't, they lose the ability to make decisions about their physical needs—in this case, their need for shelter. This becomes a clash between individual rights and socioeconomic rights. The third is the right to choose to be homeless. Although very few homeless want such a choice, it is important when one views the issue in terms of rights. By exercising this right they should not, but often do, lose their rights to other services such as health services, which are more widely considered to be a right of citizenship—at least in Canada.

This chapter begins with an introduction to the nature and causes of homelessness, including the economic and social costs, with special reference to the particular problems of homeless women and children, and a history of the "right to housing." This is followed by a discussion of why this right has not been—and as has been argued by some, should not be—acted upon, and a brief history of housing policy in both countries. I suggest that the United States has been more proactive than Canada in dealing with homelessness. This would appear to be the result of institutional differences between the two countries rather than differences in the argument of "rights" in the two countries. But it also may indicate that ratification of international treaties is not a good predictor of state behavior.

How Many Homeless, and Who Are They?

The question of how many people are homeless, and who the homeless are, is fraught with problems.[4] Mark Maier, for example, outlines a number of definitions and indicates how the difference in definition could change the estimates of homelessness in the United States in the 1980s to range from 192,000 to 3 million.[5] In estimating the number of homeless in Canada, with one-tenth the population of the United States, Jack Layton uses a very expansive definition that puts the numbers at 500,000.[6] A more reasonable number based on estimates of "core need" would be in the range of 150,000–200,000 in Canada.[7] What we do know, however, is that the number has been increasing. In a survey of hunger and homelessness carried out for the United States Conference of Mayors in December 2002, 88 percent of the twenty-five cities surveyed reported an increase in requests for emergency shelter in the previous year. The average increase was 19 percent but reached as high as 64 percent in St. Louis.[8] For the purposes of this chapter, a homeless person or family is one who does not have permanent accommodation with security of tenure, cooking, and sanitary facilities. This includes those living in temporary shelters, on the streets, doubled up with family or friends (referred to as the hidden homeless), or families in temporary accommodation such as motels paid for by Social Security. It does not include those who are living in sub-standard housing or those living in housing that is more expensive than they can afford.

How do people become homeless? Most studies assume that the homeless are quite undifferentiated.[9] In its pilot study on counting the homeless, the Canada Mortgage and Housing Corporation (CMHC) eliminated several types of shelters for methodological reasons, including those for battered women, and only studied the homeless in the largest centers of the country.[10] Yet, the CHMC claims that this is a methodology that can be used for all homeless. The same is true of prescriptions for dealing with the problem. The assumption is that all homelessness is an economic problem and that the same solutions are suitable for all homeless individuals or families, usually prescribing more "social" housing, that is, government subsidized housing.

Talmadge Wright is an exception and gives an excellent outline of the various causes of homelessness.[11] Being able to differentiate among types of homeless is important not only in looking for solutions to the problem but also in understanding what "rights" each group might reasonably claim. There are those who are homeless for economic reasons, because either there is no housing available that they can afford or they have had to leave their previous home for economic reasons. In some cases, these are people who are employed but still cannot afford adequate housing. This group becomes larger in times of economic slowdowns, when unemployment rates go up. It has also become larger due to reductions in social spending and spending on housing programs and to changes in the economy, which have seen the loss of moderate paying jobs for the unskilled or semiskilled. A subset of this group is those— mainly youth, but also battered women—who have become homeless due to family problems. (For youth who are in school, this may be a problem of no hostels that are convenient for traveling to school.) This group has become larger as governments in both Canada and the United States, as a cost cutting measure, have made it more difficult for single persons to collect social welfare benefits. Both of these groups are what I consider to be the "economic homeless." They simply cannot afford housing in the market in which they are living.

The second group of people who are homeless—historically single men, but increasingly women and youth—are those who are homeless due to substance abuse or mental illness. This latter group has grown in the past thirty years as a result of policies of deinstitutionalization pursued in both Canada and the United States.[12] Indeed, some analysts argue that this, not the lack of shelter per se, is the key to homelessness and argue for greater funding of mental health programs.[13] The people in this category are not homeless for purely economic reasons, but for social and psychological reasons. Landlords are reluctant to rent to them, as they are frequently abusive or disturbing to other tenants. They are also often unable to make rational decisions about seeking, or staying in, shelter.

Finally, there are those who are homeless by choice. These are individuals who for their own reasons choose an itinerant lifestyle. They are a very small group, estimated to be less than 1 percent.[14] I suggest that this group has different rights from the other two. By being homeless, they are denied some of the basic rights of citizenship.[15] They are often unable to obtain Social Security or health benefits because they do not have a permanent fixed address. They are very frequently under-enumerated in the census and do not appear on voter enumeration lists. There is a question of the extent to which governments should be obliged to redesign services to accommodate them.

Housing Policy in Canada and the United States since World War II

Housing policies in Canada and the United States have followed somewhat similar patterns.[16] After the end of World War II, there was a period of what I have referred to as "economic development" responding to the pent-up demand of the war and returning veterans.[17] This was followed by a period of social development in the 1960s and 1970s, in which there was considerable government intervention in housing markets to provide social housing, that is, government subsidized housing, for those who could not afford housing in the private market without assistance.[18] In the 1980s, under the Reagan administration in the United States, and the Mulroney administration in Canada, there was a period of restraint and, in the case of Canada, disentanglement as the federal government devolved housing to the provinces and the federal government ceased to fund new housing programs and capped its financial obligations for existing programs.[19] This effectively closed down federal intervention in housing markets. In the United States, although the programs were downsized, they remained active.

Today, in the United States, there remains a myriad of programs, many of them federally funded, some federal-state funded, and some federal-municipally funded, as can be seen by the survey carried out by the Conference of Mayors.[20] The most striking thing about these programs is that there are so many different variations. Housing and Urban Development (HUD), under its Homeless Families Program, however, is able to fund a wide array of programs meeting the individual needs of cities or states. The big national programs, such as Section 8—primarily a housing voucher program similar to the food stamp program, where vouchers can be spent as cash—remain in existence although it has been greatly scaled back.[21] In 2002, it was proposed to replace Section 8 and a number of other programs by the Community Partnership to End Homelessness Act, which would place the onus on community planning boards to deal with homelessness, but with federal funding. This represented a major initiative to deal with homelessness, particularly as there had been proposals in the mid-1990s to eliminate HUD altogether.[22]

This has not been the case in Canada. By 2000, all of the federal programs, except for a small program for housing rehabilitation, had been closed to new funding. There were some sporadic programs in the provinces, but only Quebec and Alberta were actively funding housing programs.[23] In 2002, the federal government announced a willingness to fund new programs, but not all provinces were able to reach an agreement on the terms of the new program.[24] The notable difference between the United States and Canada, which is important for dealing with homelessness, is that in Canada all housing programs must be national in scope, and federal funds must flow through the provinces. Only projects funded under Section V of the National Housing Act (the research section) can be funded directly, and this is restricted to short-term, experimental projects.[25] There is no capability to provide long-term sustained financing to municipalities from the federal level.[26]

The visibility of housing in Canada, and the issue of homelessness, fell even lower in 1998, when the responsibility for homelessness was taken from CMHC and given to the federal department of Human Resources Development. Homelessness became redefined not as a problem of housing but as a social welfare problem. This move produced some limited programs addressing one-off, one-time community projects and research initiatives such as the National Homelessness Initiative Program and the Supporting Communities Program Initiatives (SCPI). The latter has been the major federal initiative in this area, and is viewed by some as a major presence, but is not specifically targeted to combat homelessness. The funding has been modest, but it is an attempt to bring together different initiatives at the community level to deal with issues of youth, Aboriginal, and mainstream "at-risk" clients. The funding is for only a three-year period. It is not directly for homelessness but is addressed to those "at risk" for a variety of reasons. The implementation and awarding of funds has been idiosyncratic and bureaucratically rather than needs driven.[27] Thus, there are no federal assistance programs for the homeless, and only a limited number of small-scale provincial programs.

What Is Being Done and the Implications of Homelessness

In the United States, most of the funding for programs to alleviate homelessness comes from the federal government and from municipalities. Surprisingly, given the tradition of private philanthropy in the United States, there is limited private funding other than the United Way. Many local housing agencies are acting in partnership with support service providers to create supportive housing solutions for some of the most difficult clients: the mentally ill, former prison inmates, and those with drug or alcohol dependency problems. Studies of such programs cover cities in many states, including New York, Ohio, Vermont, Texas, and Washington.[28] In Seattle, there is even a property tax surcharge agreed to by the voters to provide funding for housing programs, particularly for the homeless.[29] But what is striking is the similarity in the problems and the form of the solutions.

In Canada, there has been considerable research on homelessness carried out by the CMHC. Most programs and projects in Canada have taken their lead from projects in the United States, a practice which has been common in the housing field since the 1960s.[30] A survey of best practices shows that provincial programs for the homeless exist only in Quebec and Alberta, which have well-designed frameworks for dealing with this problem.[31] In the other provinces there is some funding, usually in the provision of support services, but it is mostly municipal and private. There is a very small federal presence through a Homelessness Initiative, which is mainly for research, and the SCPI program discussed earlier. The tenuous nature of the funding and the resultant precariousness of the various projects and programs are evident in all of the reports. What seems to work best is a continuum of programs addressing each of the types of homeless, including programs such as "out of the cold," which aim at getting shelter during severe climatic crises for that very small number of people who choose to live outdoors and function moderately well without what most people would call permanent housing.[32] The other main conclusion of this research is that programs work best that involve the clients themselves in both design and implementation.[33] Involvement of the former homeless in delivery of programs has been particularly effective.

Homelessness is a particular problem for women and women with children.[34] And women with children is the fastest growing group among the homeless.[35] Increasingly, too, homeless women are having children who are more likely to have low birth weights and are highly at risk. Many are taken into care within months of their birth. Older children, who are living with a homeless parent, have problems with schooling and with homework. The lack of kitchen facilities results in nutritional problems, which in turn lead to learning problems and later health problems.[36] This is a particular problem when homeless women and children are housed in units, such as motels, which were not intended either for children or for long-term occupation. Ironically, this form of housing is considerably more expensive than simply finding, and subsidizing, long-term, permanent rental housing. For many years, it was claimed that this was a necessary expedient because of low vacancy rates of less than 1 percent in most major cities. This is no longer the case in many cities, with vacancy rates now hovering in the 3–5 percent range, including Toronto, which has the highest proportion of homeless in Canada. But the policy is still in place because of a lack of long-term funding availability. Most of the money for this form of accommodation comes from mandated social service budgets rather than budgets for housing.

There are also well-documented cases of much higher levels of assault against both women and children who are homeless. Unlike the stereotype of "domestic violence," in these cases the assailant is not necessarily known to the victim, there is much more randomised victimization, and considerable concern is expressed that these problems are not dealt with well by law enforcement agencies.[37]

In conclusion, what is being done, if often innovative, is sporadic and disjointed. In nearly every study, in both countries, the difficulty of coordinating of the many agencies involved and the lack of long-term funding are cited as problems.[38] To date, there has been no government commitment to attempt to alleviate the problem of homelessness, much less the root causes of economic homelessness; to provide supportive services for the incapacitated; or to redesign programs for the "hardcore" homeless, often the least understood.[39] As Dowding and King conclude, major changes in attitudes are required if endemic homelessness, or what they refer to as "rooflessness," is not to be a condition of post-welfare states.[40]

The Evolution of Housing as a Right

The ICESCR was drafted in 1966, based on the Universal Declaration of Human Rights.[41] It recognizes economic, social, and cultural rights. But despite this recognition there has been a failure on the part of most countries to take any steps to entrench these rights, adopt any legislative or administrative requirements to implement or protect them, or provide any effective redress for their lack. Canada is a signatory to the ICESCR, and the United States is not. Yet their approach to housing rights and housing policy has generally been very similar; neither country has accepted in its policies the principle of a right to shelter. In Canada, a statement of the "right to housing" was provided in the 1969 Hellyer Report,[42] and in the United States a statement of "the right of every family to a decent home" was made in the 1944 State of the Union address by Franklin Roosevelt as part of a call for a "second bill of rights."[43]

In 1991, the ICESCR extended the right to housing beyond simply a "roof over one's head" to the right to live in security and dignity. In doing so, it also introduced the criteria stated in the following list:

a) legal security of tenure, i.e. legal protection against forced eviction, harassment and other threats;
b) availability of services, materials, facilities and infrastructure, i.e. water, energy, sanitation, food storage, refuse disposal, site drainage and emergency services;
c) affordability;
d) habitability, i.e. adequate space and protection from the elements;
e) accessibility for disadvantaged groups;
f) location, i.e. access to work, health care, schools, child care and social services;
g) cultural adequacy, i.e. the method of construction, building materials used must be consistent with cultural identity and diversity . . . and a National Housing Strategy which would "reflect extensive genuine consultation with, and participation by, all of those affected including the homeless, the inadequately housed and their representatives."[44]

In 1997, these requirements were extended further by an elaboration and extension of the definition of "forced evictions."[45]

There has been almost no action on this extended right in Canada or the United States except in the state of New York. I would suggest that one of the reasons for this is that the criteria developed by the committee to implement the ICESCR exhibit a lack of appreciation of the economic, social, and cultural "bundle of goods," which Larry Bourne has characterized as constituting housing.[46]

There are a number of limitations on rights that relate to housing and, by extension, to homelessness. The first is resource constraints; this limitation is generally recognized. It is more often thought of as applying to developing countries, but it also pertains to developed countries. While there are immense economic and social costs to housing, what might be called the "Cadillac" policy advocated by the committee would be a financial drain on any country, even the most wealthy. The second issue is justiciability: whether the courts can and will provide a remedy. Can there be a right if there is no redress via the courts to ensure it is upheld? In the case of housing, decisions by courts to intervene in the housing of prisoners would seem to indicate that they have no inherent difficulty with intervening on the issue of the quality of shelter.[47] North American courts have not indicated an unwillingness to rule on this issue, but I find little evidence that the issue of homelessness has come before the courts except in New York State. No one seems to have claimed that the state has an obligation to provide anyone with a roof over his/her head or to make it unnecessary for people to sleep under bridges.

A third problem is non-discrimination. Housing programs are, by their very nature, discriminatory. Integrated housing programs in both countries have been designed to discriminate positively on some basis, in the United States by race, in Canada by income.[48] Indeed, the non-profit housing program that, since the 1970s, has been the major vehicle for funding publicly subsidized housing in Canada did, and continues to, discriminate on the basis of culture, ethnicity, and religion. Most of the projects funded under that program through private rather than public non-profit organizations for seniors, and many for families, are restricted to people of a particular ethnic or religious background or, in the case of one cooperative in Toronto, aged actors. Thus there are senior citizen homes for Italians, Jews, and Japanese, and cooperative and non-profit family projects for Chileans and other national and ethnic groups. These criteria have never been tested in the courts and, I suspect, would not withstand a court challenge.

There are a number of reasons why the concept of economic and social rights is opposed by many observers. I will briefly review these as they apply to housing. The first is that rights to food, clothing, or housing are not individual rights but are instructions to government about government policies. Thus, G. Vierdag has called the introduction of such rights "regrettable," because they are not really rights at all.[49] This argument, I believe, is valid for housing. In climates in which it is impossible to live out-of-doors through many months of the year, it would seem that a minimal right to be in heated shelter could be an acceptable limitation.[50] It is easy to envisage court-mandated "out of the cold" programs to prevent death by hypothermia. This is consistent with the pre-1991 principle of the ICESCR of simply a "roof over one's head."

The second reason for opposing such rights involves the decision calculus of the courts. Proponents of this perspective, such as Bakan and Schneiderman, argue that entrenching social rights will result in courts' engaging in social policy making, a process that they are "institutionally incompetent" to carry out because they are inherently undemocratic.[51] In addition, Bakan[52] argues that when courts become involved in "social rights" they entrench existing conditions and tend to undermine attempts to solve the causes of social inequality. This is an echo of the argument made by Morton and Pal[53] on the decision calculus of the courts leading to "bad" public policy. This may be true. But no one seems to have told the judges this, because in both countries they have shown willingness to involve themselves in social issues.

There appears to have been nothing in the debate on economic and social rights that would seem to preclude the "right to housing" becoming an active right. When one looks at the 1991 extension of the right to housing by the committee, it becomes clear why this is a right that has not been taken seriously by governments in Canada or the United States.

The first two of the committee's criteria, security of tenure and availability of services, are quite reasonable. If the committee had stopped there, it arguably would have had a viable program for protecting shelter rights. Security of tenure is a question of property rights and is generally accepted within the tradition of English common law, wherein the right to property has been upheld without a written constitution.[54] The second criterion, availability of services, is relevant to public health concerns, and most countries would strive to attain these standards.[55] Certainly, in Canada and the United States, the provision of essential infrastructure services is considered an entitlement, which is why it is illegal in many jurisdictions to turn off utilities, even in the event of unpaid bills, during the winter months.

The remainder of the criteria and, in particular, the requirement for a consultative national strategy are problematic. Five of them—affordability, habitability, accessibility, location, and cultural adequacy—are relative terms that are determined by culture. The standard of affordability, for example, varies widely across Western cultures. An affordability level of 30 percent of gross income spent on housing is the norm in North America. In Western Europe it is far more likely to exceed 50 percent. Differences in norms of affordability can vary due to tenure (with families preferring to pay more for homeownership), form of land tenure, and the treatment of housing costs for income tax purposes. The requirement of "habitability," which is defined as adequate space, also raises the questions of what constitutes adequate and how to define people's right of choice. In the 1970s, in Canada, there was a debate as to whether "adequate" family housing required two bathrooms.[56] Municipal maintenance and occupancy bylaws restrict the number of people who can share a bedroom, but this again is a culturally determined standard. Accessibility for disadvantaged groups raises questions about the definitions of "access" and "disadvantage." The criterion of "location," which requires access to work, health care, schools, child care, and social services, ignores the existence of zoning codes that preclude the coexistence of residential, institutional, and industrial land uses. The stipulation of cultural adequacy, which requires that building materials and methods of construction must be consistent with cultural identity and diversity, presumably means that the Inuit must remain in their igloos! The requirement of a national strategy probably constitutes for most governments an unacceptable limitation on the sovereignty of the state. The requirement of widespread public participation would not be accepted by many policy makers and analysts. There is considerable debate about the effectiveness of public participation in the making of public policy in terms of the legitimacy of the participation, the expertise of those participating, and their accountability.[57] Most important, however, is that the drafters exhibit a lack of understanding of housing, housing markets, and the policy making process in Western developed states. Proponents of extended "shelter rights" do not seem to spend much time considering the obstacles to the implementation of these rights.[58]

In the first place, housing is not merely shelter. It is a market commodity that is often the main family asset.[59] As Bengdesston has put it:

Housing is not free but distributed in the market. Though the relations between state and market is at the core of both the political and scientific debate about housing, housing researchers seldom confront explicitly what is common about housing in all modern welfare societies, i.e. the fact that it is *at the same time* defined as an individual market commodity and as a public good demanding state involvement. Since housing is always provided through markets, analogies with other welfare sectors, where state allocation is the main mechanism of distribution, are often misleading. Housing policies in most Western countries are best perceived as *the state providing correctives to the housing market.*[60]

Bengdesston goes on to argue that this would mean that the state has an obligation to provide only some form of minimum right to shelter, as the first two requisites of the ICESCR would involve. In another sense, he argues that to the extent that the state makes correctives for the market, the right to housing becomes a selective social right rather than a universal right. This distinction between individual and collective or universal rights is echoed by R. C. Ellickson.[61]

It is clear that neither governments nor courts in the United States (with the exception of New York State) or Canada have accepted the proposals of the committee. I would suggest that this is in large part because the requirements of its criteria are far too broad and would be economically and politically unfeasible, and probably impossible, for any government to achieve. In the United States, if there were a right to housing, it would likely fall under the "equal protection" clauses of the Fourteenth Amendment. But, even under the expansive Warren court of the 1960s, in the United States the Supreme Court has been unwilling to designate poverty as a suspect category like race and religion. "Suspect" categories are those that the courts consider very carefully, under the presumption that any law that discriminates on the grounds of that category is unconstitutional. Even gender, which arguably could be used as a category because there is ample evidence that economic homelessness is a problem that affects women more than men, has only achieved the level of "intermediacy" or middle ground as a suspect category. Thus, a "right to shelter" has not been supported as a constitutional issue in the United States.[62]

In Canada, any such right would fall under Section 15 of the Charter of Rights and Freedoms, the provision for equality before and under law and equal protection and benefit of law, or possibly Section 7, the provision for security of persons. The courts have, however, been reluctant to interpret these sections in such a way. One case using Sections 7 and 15 against an eviction from public housing was rejected by the Canadian courts.[63] The right to security of person was rejected on the grounds that it did not apply to economic benefits. The equality right was rejected on the grounds that it did not apply to people receiving social benefits.

This unwillingness to intervene is not, however, because the courts are unwilling to become involved in public policy or to make decisions that mandate spending. This has occurred in both countries. The Eldridge case in Canada required hospitals to hire "signers" for deaf patients.[64] A 2003 Supreme Court of Canada ruling gave mentally ill patients the right to not take their medication, resulting in their need to remain in state-run institutions.[65] In the United States, a similar case involving a prisoner on death row, also centered on the relationship between medication and sanity and was wending its way through the courts in 2003. In the United States, the courts have been active in mandating prison spending for housing,[66] as they have done in Canada.[67] The difficulty in implementing such court-mandated policy is well documented in the case of disability legislation in the United States.[68]

The exception of New York State, however, is worth considering. In 1979, in *Callahan v. Carey*, it was argued that the New York constitution gave a right to welfare.[69] Callahan represented a class-action suit of ten thousand who alleged that there was a lack of shelter space and that much of the space available was sub-standard. The courts agreed. Subsequently, the courts upheld the obligation of the city to provide shelter for the homeless, including women and children. This began a twenty-one-year fight over the right to shelter in New York, particularly New York City. Mayor Rudy Giuliani tried to make shelter assistance a form of welfare assistance rather than an absolute right. This would have required recipients to meet conditions of welfare assistance, such as workfare. He lost.[70] Mayor Michael Bloomberg, in 2002, announced his intention to appeal this decision. He wanted to evict shelter residents who were not actively seeking permanent housing. The reasoning from other court challenges over the last twenty-one years suggested that he too would lose.

If so, this will establish a precedent for the "right to shelter" in the United States. The willingness of courts to accept judgments from other states, however, is not as well established as it is in Canada.[71]

Conclusion

The UN standard for refugee camps requires 4.5 to 5 square meters per person, yet homeless shelters in Toronto, Canada, routinely accommodate four people within such an area.[72] Homelessness and the loss of productivity and dignity that follow from it cost Canadian and American society dearly in social and economic terms. Services such as short-term hostel rental for families with children are more costly than permanent housing, and they are more of a burden on the health care system. Children from homeless families do less well in school, are less likely to graduate, and are also more likely to develop substance abuse problems—all factors that are highly correlated with criminal activities as adults. At the same time, the homeless are less likely to participate in the formal labor force or pay taxes. Most importantly, our willingness to tolerate high levels of involuntary homelessness represents a serious loss of social capital in our society. Yet as citizens we do little to push our governments to try to alleviate these problems. Why?

It could be argued that we have become less caring societies in Canada and the United States over the past two decades. But there is enough everyday evidence of altruism in both countries to contradict this.[73] Instead, the answer may be an institutional one. In the first place, homelessness is largely an urban problem. Electoral systems at both the national and sub-national level are highly biased toward rural, and to a lesser degree suburban, voters in both countries, who are less aware of or concerned with this issue.[74] Second, the level of government that has the de facto responsibility for dealing with the homeless is the municipal level, which has the least financial resources to develop and sustain assistance programs. The homelessness problem has also been exacerbated by devolution of policies, such as deinstitutionalization and social assistance reform, by senior levels of government. More importantly, very few people have suggested viable resolutions to the problem. In Canada, the most common prescription offered is to build more non-profit social housing, the form of housing that was built between 1973 and 1985.[75] This program was very expensive because it subsidized not only the poor but also those who lived in the same buildings with the poor. The latter group paid only the "low end market rent" for new housing units, which had been built at twice their economic rent; this at times resulted in subsidies in excess of $1,000 per month for families earning as much as $50,000 per year.[76] As a result, the program benefited land developers, builders, and consultants far more than it benefited the poor or homeless.[77] In the United States, where more experimental and small-scale interventions have been attempted, there appears to have been more success.

In the opinion of some legal rights experts interviewed as part of this research, it is only a matter of time before shelter is brought before the Canadian courts as an issue of basic rights, particularly as those cases that have been decided on these grounds[78] have been decided on very narrow margins.[79] Finlay was the case of a welfare recipient who, through an administrative error, received overpayments of his benefits. When this was discovered, the provincial welfare authorities began to withhold part of his benefits. He claimed that welfare was a basic right. He won at the Appeal Court level but lost at the Supreme Court by a four to three decision, with the deciding vote cast by the last of the justices appointed by the Conservative Party. A change in one judge could change the outcome for the next case. If this is true, it would be worthwhile for those advocating such an approach to clearly distinguish between the different forms of "rights" that I have outlined in this chapter. For those few who choose to be homeless, there may be a right to services. For those who are mentally ill, there may be a right to supportive services, and even an obligation on the part of the state to ensure that they either are able to make rational decisions or are in care. For those who are homeless due to economic circumstances, it would be best for the state to recognize that it is more efficient for the state to alleviate these problems. If this does not happen, it is quite possible that the courts will make the decision in this latter case. It will be interesting to see what will result, as from a public policy point of view the outcome will almost certainly be less than satisfactory and not in line with the recommendations of the committee.

Chapter 5
Welfare Racism and Human Rights

Kenneth J. Neubeck

Poverty and the Limitations of United States Welfare Policy

The United States is among the most affluent of Western industrialized nations in per capita terms. However, it possesses marked inequalities in its distribution of income and wealth. Not only is the proportion of the United States population living in poverty high in comparison to other industrialized nations such as Canada, France, Germany, the Netherlands, Sweden, Finland, and Norway,[1] but also the gap between the most affluent and the poorest members of United States society has been growing.[2] In 1990, the poorest fifth of United States families received 4.6 percent of the nation's aggregate income, while the most affluent fifth received 44.3 percent. By 2001, their aggregate income shares had shifted to 4.2 and 47.7 percent, respectively.[3] This extreme economic inequality has produced a persistently high rate of poverty, a rate that averaged more than 13 percent in the 1990s.[4] Periodic economic downturns exacerbate the poverty rate due to increases in unemployment and greater competition for low-wage jobs.[5]

According to annual statistics issued by the United States Bureau of the Census, the poverty rate in 2002 was 12.1 percent for the United States population overall. However, the rate was significantly higher for those persons living in female-headed families. While the poverty rate that year was 5.3 percent for married-couple families, the rate for female-headed families was 26.5 percent.[6] This fact helps to account for the high rate of poverty among children in the United States, almost 17 percent in 2002.

While the overall poverty rate was 12.1 percent in 2002, nearly 5 percent of United States population experienced "severe poverty," defined by the census bureau as an annual income below 50 percent of the poverty line. The severely poor made up 40.7 percent of the total poverty population that year.[7] Women and children—especially those of color such as African Americans, Latino/a Americans, Native Americans, and members of some recent immigrant populations—are disproportionately represented among those living in both poverty and severe poverty. Census data show that the average dollar amount by which people who were poor fell below the poverty line was higher in 2002 than in any year since 1979 (the first year such data were available).[8]

It is not as if the U.S. government has never viewed impoverishment of many of its citizens as a human rights issue. In 1944, President Franklin D. Roosevelt advocated an "Economic Bill of Rights" in his State of the Union address to Congress.[9] Roosevelt commented that while political rights were important, "true individual freedom cannot exist without economic security and independence." His economic bill of rights included the right to a job and earnings enough to provide adequate food, clothing, and recreation; the right to a decent home, a good education, and adequate health care; and protection from economic fears due to problems over which one had no control. Roosevelt advocated "a new basis of security and prosperity for all—regardless of station, race, or creed." Yet, as it would turn out, Roosevelt's call for the recognition of economic human rights within the United States would never be seriously pursued.

In line with the spirit of Roosevelt's thinking, in 1948, the United States did join with other nations around the world in voting for the Universal Declaration of Human Rights (UDHR), a document that includes provisions addressing poverty as a human rights issue. However, in the sixty years since its inception, the United States government has notably and visibly failed to recognize and take action to respect the social and economic human rights that are alluded to in Article 25 of that document, including the right to an adequate standard of living and necessary social services for mothers and children.[10]

In 1977 President Jimmy Carter—sometimes called "the human rights president"—signed the International Covenant on Economic, Social and Cultural Rights (ICESCR), an international treaty that spells out in more detail human rights such as those addressed in Article 25. As of July 22, 2005, 151 nations have ratified this treaty. However, the United States Senate has never ratified it, and the United States does not consider itself subject to the Covenant's human rights provisions, which have assumed the status of customary international law.[11]

Generally speaking, the United States government does not treat social and economic human rights violations as phenomena that even exist within the United States.[12] When human rights are addressed by national-level political elites, their principal focus is almost exclusively on civil and political rights and on the availability (or lack thereof) of those human rights in other nations.[13] Even among major human rights nongovernmental organizations (NGOs; e.g., Amnesty International, Human Rights Watch), the issue of social and economic human rights violations within the United States has historically been given short shrift. Today, with the exception of a small number of United States welfare rights and antipoverty groups, economic inequality and poverty in the United States are rarely framed in human rights terms.[14]

Continual high rates of severe impoverishment among female-headed households with children are in part an expression of the failure of United States political elites to conceive of poverty as a human rights issue. One must bear in mind that how problems are thought about and framed has a great deal to do with the solutions that are likely to be considered. If human beings have a right to an adequate standard of living as posited in the UDHR and the ICESCR, then government bears the responsibility of taking whatever steps it can to address the needs of those who struggle in poverty. Yet, instead of treating poverty as a human rights issue, United States political elites have increasingly framed poverty as a matter of personal responsibility. United States welfare policy reflects this. Today, no family in the United States is "entitled" to economic assistance as a matter of right. In United States society, people have the right to be poor, but have no right to receive help in confronting their poverty.[15]

U.S. political elites' rejection of the notion that people who are poor have a human right to an adequate standard of living was underscored in the mid-1990s with the passage of federal legislation aimed at "welfare reform."[16] This landmark legislation removed any vestiges of entitlement by female-headed families to what had been historically meager, and often grudgingly granted, means-tested public assistance or "welfare." Joint federal/state-supported public assistance had been relied upon by millions of impoverished families since Franklin D. Roosevelt's New Deal. As part of Roosevelt's Depression-era economic recovery program, the first-ever federal provision for such assistance was included in the Social Security Act of 1935.

In an act of bipartisan political cooperation, the Republican-dominated Congress passed and Democratic president Bill Clinton signed the Personal Responsibility and Work Opportunity Reconciliation Act of 1996 (PRWORA). This act effectively abolished the sixty-one-year-old guarantee of a minimal economic safety net for the nation's poorest families, largely leaving decisions as to whether and to what degree to aid such families up to the individual states. Since the passage of this act, the number of impoverished families receiving welfare has dramatically fallen even as their rates of poverty (including severe poverty) remain high. By 2003, the number of recipient families had dropped to just over 2 million, a decline of 53.7 percent since PRW-ORA's passage in 1996.[17]

Explaining the Gap between U.S. Welfare Policy and Human Rights Ideals

Public assistance eligibility has always been greatly restricted in the United States, and the welfare benefits available to poor female-headed families with children have always been extremely meager in the face of their substantial need.[18] Recent "welfare reform" legislation simply ratcheted up to a new level the long-standing federal policy of helping few with little. How does one explain the gap between such welfare policy and the ideals held by Article 25 of the Universal Declaration?

U.S. welfare policy is sometimes said to be shaped by a dominant ideology that extols the existence of equal opportunity for individuals to achieve and thus places the burden of escaping poverty on the poor themselves. Public opinion polls show, for example, that people in the United States are far less prone to hold to the idea that the state should intervene to help the poor in comparison to those in European nations such as the United Kingdom, Sweden, and West Germany.[19] Scholars often point to the individualistic values that hold sway in much of U.S. society, values that urge acceptance of the notion that "anyone can make it if they really try." If one is poor, there is only oneself to blame and no justification to complain. If one is wealthy, there must be good reason.[20]

Other explanations place less emphasis on ideology and more on social structural factors in making sense of U.S. welfare policy. Some scholars are prone to emphasize the lack of political organization on the part of the poor and the weakness of working-class organizations in electoral politics.[21] Others have noted that, while U.S. capitalism generates gross economic inequality and wide disparities in life chances, there is no viable socialist or labor party to advocate on behalf of the social and economic human rights of oppressed groups and others who are in need.[22] Still other scholars view the absence of government attention to the needs of the poor as stemming from certain features of the state in U.S. society.[23] The state is seen as limited by its decentralized structure, its failure to develop an organizational and fiscal capacity to adequately address poverty, legacies of previous debates and policies that do not support state intervention, state actors' own priorities and organizational self-interests, and the like.

Then there are scholars who stress the important role of class or, alternatively, gender relations in shaping U.S. welfare policy. For some, policy is seen as being shaped by the influential political role played by a "corporate-conservative coalition," made up of the capitalist class and its representatives.[24] Even in the face of class struggle on the part of the poor and the working class, the capitalist class is said to be generally successful in steering the state away from adopting welfare programs and expenditures that could increase taxes, undermine labor discipline, and slow capital accumulation.[25] In contrast to this emphasis on class relations, other scholars emphasize the significance of patriarchy in U.S. society. Patriarchal interests are said to be served by welfare policy that undermines mothers' abilities to adequately support their children on their own, thus encouraging women's reliance and dependence upon male partners. U.S. welfare policy is shaped by what is, in effect, a patriarchal state.[26]

One should not reject the salience of these various factors and their contribution to the gap between the reality of U.S. welfare policy and social and economic human rights ideals. This chapter, however, addresses the significance of yet another key factor to which most scholars of U.S. welfare policy have long been studiously blind: racism. More specifically, this chapter is concerned with "welfare racism," defined as "the organization of racialized public assistance attitudes, policy making, and administrative practices."[27] As will be explained, the social significance attached to race in U.S. society has had a great deal to do with the policy treatment of the nation's poor.

The Racialization of U.S. Society

The writings of historians and social scientists leave no doubt that the United States has been and is today a highly racialized society.[28] Slavery, Jim Crow segregation, institutionalized oppression, genocidal violence, and many years of civil rights struggles are a well-known part of this nation's history. While denial of the present-day salience of racism may be fashionable in many quarters,[29] there is ample evidence that the color lines established in the past have only partly been dismantled. Vestiges of racism continue to guide interracial relationships and promulgate serious racial inequalities in U.S. society.[30]

Sociologist Eduardo Bonilla-Silva has characterized present-day U.S. society as a "racialized social system," drawing attention to the fact that race remains an important organizing principle in social relations.[31] Modern science, however, tells us that there actually are no biologically distinct races.[32] While members of U.S. society are ever sensitive to so-called racial differences, "race" is clearly a social construction rather than a biological reality. But since many if not most people in the United States act as if race matters, it does.

Since the 1960s civil rights movement and its successes, experiences with racism have continued to plague African Americans and other people of color, and "white-skin privilege" remains very real in U.S. society.[33] People of color continue to face limits on their life chances due to entrenched patterns of school and neighborhood segregation, workplace discrimination, lack of access to adequate health care, income and wealth inequalities, political powerlessness, and victimization by the criminal justice system. Awareness of the historical and continuing racialization of U.S. society is central to a full understanding of the factors that have helped to shape the conception, formulation, and implementation of U.S. welfare policy.

Changing Expressions of Welfare Racism

The modern era of means-tested public assistance for impoverished mother-headed families began with the New Deal-era Social Security Act of 1935. But "welfare" existed in the United States even before that time, as did the impact of racism on U.S. welfare policy. Once set in motion, racialized public assistance attitudes, policy making, and administrative practices would continue throughout the remainder of the century.[34]

In the two decades prior to passage of the Social Security Act, many individual states adopted laws aimed at providing "mothers' pensions" to those impoverished mothers deemed deserving of aid. In actual practice, the mothers assisted were usually white widows, and only white women who were considered to be of impeccable moral standing in their local communities were approved for assistance.[35] In the prevailing climate of Jim Crow racial apartheid, women of color and their children——who on average suffered higher poverty rates and even greater levels of hardship than poor white families—were largely excluded from mothers' pension programs. Skin color was widely assumed to be an indicator of moral worth and thus a guide to whom among the needy was deserving of aid.[36] Such sentiments would continue to surface.

Mothers' pension programs established by individual states served as the precursor to the present-day national system of "welfare" for female-headed families with children. The Social Security Act of 1935 created the first federal/state welfare program, called at the time Aid to Dependent Children (ADC). While imposing certain guidelines on the states in return for the contribution of federal funds to state ADC programs, the Act did not set any minimum benefit-level requirements that states had to meet. Respecting "states' rights," the federal government also gave individual states a good deal of latitude in establishing standards of income eligibility for need-based ADC assistance.

Not surprisingly, as had been the case for mothers' pensions, similar patterns of racial exclusion from assistance quickly emerged.[37] In some states direct racial exclusion occurred, particularly involving African

American families. More commonly, states and localities developed ways to control access to ADC by such families without appearing blatantly discriminatory. Such practices included confining aid to households that caseworkers defined as providing "suitable homes," cutting off recipient families off from assistance whenever employers had need for seasonal low-wage labor, and declaring families ineligible on the basis of allegations that there was a man in a mother's life. Such practices were primarily and routinely aimed at poor African American mothers.[38] As a consequence of such exclusionary practices, the number of impoverished families of color receiving ADC was much smaller than the number of families whose level of economic deprivation should have rendered them eligible.

This situation changed dramatically in the 1960s, a decade in which both the welfare rolls and the proportion of the rolls made up of recipients of color increased sharply. ADC, renamed Aid to Families with Dependent Children (or AFDC), was the subject of successful class-action suits brought by legal services attorneys connected with the nation's War on Poverty, as well as the focus of protests by numerous welfare rights and civil rights organizations.[39] Together with the political pressures brought about by African American rebelliousness and rioting in cities across the United States, these suits and protests forced states and localities to loosen up AFDC eligibility restrictions. Court rulings in the 1960s outlawed many of the practices that had been used to prevent eligible families of color from exercising their entitlement to aid on a par with whites. The Social Security Act of 1935 had granted "entitlement" to aid to families meeting tests of need. It took more than thirty years for this entitlement to begin to become a reality for many impoverished families of color.[40]

As the 1960s came to a close, the color composition of AFDC began to more closely match the racial makeup of the nation's population of impoverished mother-headed families. That is to say, the welfare rolls grew darker. By the early 1970s, approximately half of those receiving AFDC were of color, primarily African American, but many were Latinos/as.[41] Concurrent with this darkening of the rolls, "welfare" began to serve as a national lightning rod issue for increasingly successful conservative white politicians.[42] The latter both stimulated and played upon white-backlash sentiments awakened by the changes in the oppressive racial order won by the 1960s civil rights movement. Welfare began to be used as a national political issue embedded with racial significance.

As more female-headed families began to receive AFDC, and as more of them were of color, a reaction against welfare and its recipients began that included taxpayer hostility to increasing cash welfare benefits. From 1970 to 1994, the median monthly benefit for a mother with two children dropped by almost half after adjustment for inflation.[43] The limited purchasing power of welfare benefits and the low wages of the jobs many mothers had to take left many poor families well behind the rising costs of living.[44] Thus, during the very period when impoverished families of color were finally gaining more equitable access to the need-based aid to which they were entitled under the Social Security Act of 1935, the dollar value of the aid on which they relied—never adequate—was progressively dwindling.

The electoral successes of white conservatives whose campaigns included harsh attacks on excessive welfare spending and undeserving welfare recipients were not lost on white liberals. By the 1980s they too had begun to include such attacks in their campaigns.[45] For conservative politicians in particular, the demonization of welfare recipients relied heavily upon subtle racist stereotypes that had been in use since the mothers' pension era to dismiss women of color as undeserving of aid.[46] Such stereotypes commonly alluded to the allegedly inferior work ethic, excessive reproductive proclivities, and immorality of African American women.

Politicians' campaign speeches and public utterances often left the erroneous impression, however subtly, that all welfare recipients lived in racially segregated ghettos. Mass media portrayals added to this impression of recipients by implying in its coverage that welfare was essentially a "black program" whose recipients were often abusing it. One analysis of survey data has shown that widespread beliefs in African Americans' alleged lack of a work ethic underlay much of the public's hostility toward welfare.[47]

This then was the climate within which the goal of "welfare reform" was pushed ever harder in the 1980s and 1990s by conservatives and liberals alike. Their objective of welfare reform was realized with the 1996 passage of the landmark PRWORA mentioned earlier. By the time PRWORA was passed, some two-thirds of AFDC recipient families were families of color, in large part a reflection of their overrepresentation in the severe poverty population. Such families, who for so many years had struggled to gain equal access with whites to the need-based aid to which the Social Security Act of 1935 entitled them, now found entitlements abolished under PRWORA. Aid was henceforth to be made available to families only temporarily and under highly restrictive and demanding new conditions.

"Welfare Reform" and Welfare Racism

PRWORA made a number of significant changes in AFDC:[48]

- AFDC was renamed Temporary Assistance to Needy Families (TANF) to reflect the limited duration of any assistance provided and to signal the end of the need-based, open-ended entitlement to aid that poor families previously had under AFDC. All states created a TANF program, although states were under no obligation to offer families aid, no matter how great families' financial need.

- Under TANF, individual states were permitted to tighten up their public assistance eligibility requirements as they saw fit. They could also implement practices that served to "divert" or shunt impoverished families away from TANF, and many did so. Diversion often rested upon the policy position that needy families should be self-supporting and should come to TANF only as a last resort after looking for help from private charitable and faith-based organizations.
- While there had been no time limit restrictions on receiving AFDC so long as recipients met need-based requirements, time limits for benefit eligibility were imposed under TANF. Now, for the first time, welfare recipients could receive aid for no more than five years in their lifetimes. Individual states were allowed to establish shorter eligibility time limits, and many did. For example, Arkansas, Idaho, and Indiana set twenty-four-month time limits. Connecticut set its limit at twenty-one months.
- Mothers had to meet compulsory, thirty-hour-per-week work activity requirements under TANF, work requirements that had never existed before. States were permitted to impose "sanctions" that included the loss of some or all of families' TANF benefits if mothers did not meet these work requirements. Families could also be sanctioned for TANF rule violations (e.g., a mother's quitting her job, failing to keep an appointment with her caseworker, or not sending paperwork in on time).
- Under AFDC, most states had provided a small cash supplement to families when a mother gave birth to an additional child while receiving AFDC benefits. TANF, however, allowed states to impose "family caps" on cash assistance that eliminated or reduced any additional cash assistance in the event of a new birth. Because existing assistance must then cover an additional family member, family caps translate into a per capita decrease in TANF benefits to a family when a new child is added.
- While AFDC benefits had never been available to illegal immigrants, legal immigrants could receive AFDC. Under TANF, their access to benefits was sharply restricted. PRWORA made legal immigrants arriving after August 22, 1996, ineligible to receive federally supported TANF benefits until they had been in the United States for five years. Individual states were permitted to provide immigrants TANF benefits on their own during this five-year period, but only twenty of the fifty states chose to do so.

Adopted in a racialized political climate, the provisions of PRWORA subtly reflect a preoccupation with combating the supposed sloth, irresponsibility, and excessive child bearing of African American women.[49] Key provisions of PRWORA not only subtly mirror stereotypical thinking about such women; the very substantive content of these provisions serves to stimulate and reinforce stereotypical thinking.[50] For example, the provisions calling for benefit time limits and mandatory work requirements, always linked in politicians' discourse to the need to put an end to "welfare dependency," cannot help but reinforce the already widespread view that AFDC mothers lack the motivation to leave welfare and become "self-sufficient." Likewise, the inclusion of family cap provisions in PRWORA automatically feeds into a common stereotype about welfare recipients' supposed immorality and irresponsibility: the notion that mothers receiving welfare seek to become pregnant and give birth to additional children simply to increase their cash benefits.

Besides African Americans and other native-born mothers of color and their families, others of color were impacted by welfare reform. Most immigrants to the United States in the 1980s and 1990s were people of color from Latin America, the Caribbean, and Asia. Many were poor or struggling financially. For some politicians, concern with keeping legal immigrants off the welfare rolls reflected a desire that the United States not become a magnet for immigration due to its "generous" welfare benefits. At times, this issue was linked to fears that this magnetism was leading to an undesirable change in the racial demographics of the predominantly white U.S. population.[51]

Ample evidence exists to suggest that contemporary welfare reform was—at least in part—race based or racism driven in its conception and formulation. But what about the implementation of welfare reform? To what degree and in what ways has welfare reform had adverse effects along skin color lines?

Racial Inequities under Welfare Reform

PRWORA is "race blind" in that it does not openly single out African Americans or other people of color for discriminatory treatment. And yet this legislation and the individual state TANF programs initiated under it have had disproportionately adverse effects on impoverished families of color.[52] Some of those effects are described here.

"States' Rights" and Bias in TANF Policies

The Social Security Act had long granted individual states leeway in setting cash benefit levels and in determining welfare program eligibility requirements. As has been discussed, PRWORA handed over even greater powers to the states in this regard. Research has underscored the racialized directions into which this present-day version of "states' rights" has recently traversed.[53]

Examining TANF programs in the individual states, political scientist Joe Soss and colleagues found that family caps, harsh sanctions for violating welfare department rules, and short eligibility time limits for TANF were most likely to be found in those states having higher proportions of African American and Latino/a residents.[54] Researchers are only beginning to firmly establish the link between a state's racial climate and the political processes that lead to this correlation between the color composition of a state's population and the harshness of its welfare policies. However, the outcomes are clear in terms of racial inequity. Families of color, by virtue of residential location, experience disproportionate rates of reduction, suspension, and loss of TANF assistance under "race-blind" welfare reform.

Employment Discrimination

A report by the Economic Policy Institute, issued during the economic recession of the early 2000s, underscores the difficulties that poor mothers have been facing in meeting TANF's mandatory work requirements: "Because of the weak job market, low-income single mothers are having a much harder time finding work than they did in the first four years of welfare reform [1996–2000]. The unemployment rate for low-income single mothers has risen more than the overall rate, and their real incomes—low to begin with—have fallen."[55]

Many low-income mothers lack high school diplomas, have little work experience beyond minimum-wage jobs, and in some cases have limited or even no English language proficiency. But it is not simply the dearth of human capital that contributes to employment difficulties for poor mothers of color.

Welfare reform mandates that all mothers receiving TANF go "from welfare to work." Yet it ignores barriers to employment posed by racial discrimination and other forms of employer bias. Non-profit service providers that help TANF recipients and former recipients find jobs have reported high levels of workplace discrimination on the basis of race, national origin, and citizenship status. These service providers have also found discrimination in hiring based on sex and on welfare recipient status.[56] All of these forms of discrimination have disproportionately adverse effects on poor mothers of color.

Workplace discrimination has no doubt contributed to the fact that white recipients have been leaving the TANF rolls at a more rapid rate than recipients of color. Moreover, data indicate that when white families leave TANF, it is likely to be because their incomes have risen to a level where they no longer meet program eligibility requirements.[57] This in part reflects the fact that white mothers generally have more success than women of color in gaining and retaining employment.[58] However, it must be stressed that most welfare-recipient mothers who find jobs, regardless of color, are in low-wage service positions that do little to move their families out of poverty.[59]

While many mothers of color do find jobs, families of color are much more likely than white families to leave TANF because they have been sanctioned off for rule violations, or have run out of eligibility for aid due to time limits.[60] However, those otherwise eligible who are sanctioned off for minor infractions usually return to the TANF rolls, as do many mothers who initially go "from welfare to work."[61] Mothers of color are more likely than white mothers to take low-wage jobs that turn out to be temporary, subject to layoff, or on inconvenient and difficult-to-manage workplace shifts. Together, these factors have contributed to the increase in the proportion of families on TANF who are of color.

Mistreatment by Welfare Agencies

Racial discrimination against people of color who are seeking employment, poor or not, has been well documented. But not only must TANF recipients who are mothers of color contend with employment discrimination,[62] but there are also reports of discrimination and other forms of mistreatment by welfare agencies that exacerbate the problems with which impoverished families must contend.

Agencies have been found engaging in questionable practices of "diversion" of applicants for aid, meaning that many eligible families—who, coming from severe poverty circumstances are disproportionately of color—have not been getting TANF assistance. In other instances applicants and recipients have not been fully informed as to what they may be eligible for. In some instances caseworkers have favored white mothers over mothers of color in providing information and assistance getting jobs and help with transportation costs.[63]

Language discrimination in welfare agencies has been found to be a particularly serious problem, with agencies often failing to provide forms and instructions in languages that recipients can understand, or interpreters and translators to help them. One survey of TANF recipients and others needing welfare assistance found that "People of color routinely encounter insults and disrespect as they seek to navigate the various programs that make up the welfare system. . . . People whose first language is not English encounter a serious language barrier when they

have contact with the welfare system. . . . Eligible immigrants and refugees are often told to go back where they came from when they try to
get help for themselves or their U.S. citizen children."[64]

Mothers who are diverted from receiving TANF, as well as mothers
who successfully gain entry to the TANF rolls, are not always fully
informed by caseworkers of benefits for which their families may be eligible. For example, low-income mothers may not be told that they and
their families are legally entitled to Medicaid and food stamps, whether
or not they receive TANF. These two government programs—which provide health care and food assistance to individuals and families that
meet low-income requirements—remain entitlements under federal
law.

After the implementation of TANF, there were significant decreases
in the numbers of people being served by these programs. For example,
the Center on Budget and Policy Priorities reported a nationwide
decline of 11 million people in the Food Stamp program between 1994
and 2000, a decline in part associated with welfare reform.[65] In major
urban centers, such as New York City, which have had a large number of
households impacted by welfare reform, decreases in Food Stamp and
Medicaid enrollment have been particularly notable among poor
female-headed families.[66] Unmet health care needs and hunger are
especially common among impoverished families of color, and they thus
bear a disproportionate burden of suffering from the failure of existing
programs to serve all those who are eligible.

Making Welfare Reform and Welfare Racism a Human Rights Issue

The human rights implications of PRWORA have not gone ignored by
advocacy and activist groups concerned with the shortcomings of the act
in addressing poverty. Indeed, there has been a growing movement to
define the U.S. government's punitive, paternalistic approach to those
needing public assistance as a human rights violation. However, some
groups have specifically singled out the act's disproportionately adverse
effects on mothers and children of color, both domestically and internationally.[67]

• The Philadelphia-based Kensington Welfare Rights Union (KWRU),
  a multiracial grassroots anti-poverty group, has filed a petition with
  the Inter-American Commission on Human Rights, citing human
  rights violations under PRWORA, including deprivations inflicted on
  families of color. KWRU is a leading force in the Poor People's Eco-

nomic Human Rights Campaign that is active across the United States (www.kwru.org). (See Chapter 6 in this volume.)

- The New York-based Urban Justice Center's Human Rights Project has been documenting human rights abuses under welfare reform, and the negative impacts it has been having on families of color, including immigrants. It has called for the United States and individual state governments to adjust their laws to respect economic human rights (www.urbanjustice.org).

- The Transnational Racial Justice Initiative (TRJI), a project of the California-based Applied Research Center, has singled out PRWORA policies as violating the International Convention on the Elimination of All Forms of Racial Discrimination. TRJI argued this point at the 2001 World Conference against Racism in Durban, South Africa (www.arc.org).

- Another California-based group, the Women of Color Resource Center, has criticized PRWORA not only as violating the earlier international convention on racism mentioned above, but also as being at odds with the concept of women's rights as human rights, addressed in the 1995 Platform for Action at the UN World Conference on Women in Beijing, China (www.coloredgirls.org).

Such groups have been outspoken in condemning the racialization of welfare and the disproportionately adverse effects of welfare reform on people of color. While they often do not use the term "welfare racism," the problems with which they have expressed concern are certainly manifestations of it. Their work has helped to spark and reinforce the interest of more mainstream organizations, leading in turn to broad support for bills that have been introduced into Congress. These bills have been aimed at providing at least some protections against racial inequities in the administration of welfare reform.

Welfare Racism and Racial Equity Legislation

As of mid-2004, the U.S. Congress was in the process of extending and perhaps modifying some of the provisions of PRWORA, which otherwise was subject to expiration. While a wide range of organizations lobbied fiercely for changes to reduce its draconian character and make it into a poverty-reduction program rather than a welfare-roll-reduction program, PRWORA was unlikely to undergo these kinds of changes in the near future. Indeed, President George W. Bush's administration, in concert with the Republican-dominated Congress, proposed that additional demands be imposed on mothers of families receiving TANF. Foremost was an increase in the mandatory work requirement for mothers receiving assistance, an increase to forty hours per week from the Act's original thirty-hour requirement. Republicans also proposed to divert $300 million per year away from TANF cash assistance to individual states in order to fund programs to promote marriage, programs portrayed as a solution to poverty.

On April 2, 2003, Democratic senators Russell Feinberg (WI), Edward Kennedy (MA), and Mary Landrieu (LA) introduced bill S770 into the U.S. Senate, entitled the "Fair Treatment and Due Process Protection Act of 2003" (www.senate.gov). S770 is a version of a bill previously introduced in the U.S. House of Representatives in 2002 by members of the Congressional Black Caucus. The Republican Party majority in the House was not in the least interested in supporting that bill and it died in committee.

S770 is quite modest in its objectives, given welfare racism's complexity, deep roots, and the seriousness of its effects. The bill would do the following:

- require local welfare department offices to provide appropriate interpretation and translation services to individuals who lack English proficiency;
- require that welfare offices assist those TANF applicants who lack English proficiency in identifying programs to address their language needs (e.g., English as a Second Language) and count participation in such programs as meeting TANF's mandatory work requirements;
- require welfare offices to take steps, before sanctioning an individual or family, to send notice (translated into their native language) of the reasons for the sanction, the amount of the sanction and its duration, ways to get assistance to come into compliance, and the procedures for appeal of a sanction;
- require welfare agencies to notify all applicants for and recipients of aid of their rights under the law and train welfare office personnel in respecting these rights;
- require each state to collect statistical data on its TANF applicants, recipients, and leavers so as to permit analysis by race, ethnicity or national origin, primary language, gender, and educational level. Data are to include reasons why applicants are not approved to receive TANF as well as reasons why recipients' cases are closed.

While it was unlikely to pass into law due to Republican resistance, the Senate bill gained the backing of a broad array of some forty national civil rights, labor, legal assistance, faith-based, women's, and anti-poverty organizations, including the Leadership Conference on Civil Rights, the National Association for the Advancement of Colored People, the American Federation of Labor-Congress of Industrial Organizations, the American Civil Liberties Union, the National Council of Churches, the National Council of La Raza, and the National Organization for Women. Such organizations have become attuned to the widespread racial inequities and disparities that have been occurring under welfare reform. From these organizations' perspectives, such inequities and disparities raise obvious civil rights protection issues for women, people of color, and legal immigrants.

On the surface, S770 addresses at least some of the recent expressions of welfare racism that have been discussed in this chapter. If passed and strongly enforced, the bill would make it difficult for individual states and localities to maintain racial inequities in the administration of their TANF programs. Such congressional legislation is certainly deserving of strong support for this reason.

However, the proposed legislation does not frame the problems to be addressed in human rights terms. Social and economic human rights are not advanced very far by providing racially equitable treatment under a welfare program that fails to provide an adequate standard of living to impoverished mothers and children. Poverty itself must come to be seen and acted upon by the U.S. government as a human rights issue, and its mitigation must be seen as an obligation under international human rights law. Until then, congressional legislation aimed at protecting impoverished families from racial inequities in the administration of public assistance, while desperately needed, will do little more than mask the fundamental failure of the United States to respect its poorest citizens' social and economic human rights.

Two decades ago, Robert Justin Goldstein commented that the United States had "an economic-social human rights record that in terms of distributive equity is perhaps the very worst in the Western industrialized world."[68] The U.S. government's treatment of impoverished mothers and children—among the most vulnerable and oppressed members of society—stands in stark contradiction to the principles of the Universal Declaration. U.S. welfare policy and the racism that infuses it undermine the credibility of the United States as a self-proclaimed champion of human rights.

Chapter 6
The Movement to End Poverty in the United States

Mary Bricker-Jenkins and Willie Baptist

By 1967, having led the United States in a non-violent struggle for civil rights against Jim Crow segregation laws, the Reverend Martin Luther King, Jr., saw clearly that the intertwined threats of militarism and poverty undermined the gains of the civil rights movement. In May, speaking to the leadership of the Southern Christian Leadership Conference, Dr. King asserted that it was "necessary for us to realize that we have moved from the era of civil rights to human rights."[1] With this assessment, he saw the need to build a movement to end poverty; the movement would be based in the leadership and unity of the poor across color lines. He said, "There are millions of poor people in this country who have very little, or even nothing, to lose. If they can be helped to take action together, they will do so with a freedom and a power that will be a new and unsettling force in our complacent national life."[2] In December 1967, Dr. King announced a Poor People's March from Mississippi to Washington, D.C., planned for April 1968, a march in which "waves of the nation's poor and disinherited [would] demand redress of their grievances by the United States government."[3] This proposal represented a fundamental shift in movement strategy.

Early on in the month of the planned march, he was assassinated. The Poor People's March took place as planned, but no sustained movement emerged from it. Certainly a dearth of leadership contributed to the evaporation of the energy that drove Martin Luther King, Jr., in this new organizing effort. In addition, many, if not most, of the remaining civil rights leaders were not committed to the shift in strategy. However, we contend that there was a more salient factor: the economic and political context of the period constrained the development of this movement. More importantly, we argue in this chapter that the conditions are finally and inexorably ready today for the emergence of a "new and unsettling force," to awaken a broad movement with the power to demand, and make fast, an end to poverty and its attendant conditions forever. We then describe the work of organizations directed at uniting those who constitute this force—the *new class* of the poor and economically vulnerable—the millions who have been rendered superfluous in the new, electronics-based, global economy.

We write from our perspective as members of the Kensington Welfare Rights Union (KWRU) and the national network of which it is a part, the Poor People's Economic Human Rights Campaign (PPEHRC). In taking up the mantle of Martin Luther King, Jr.'s vision, we are using economic human rights concepts and instruments to build a movement to end poverty. We have found that people have been drawn to the movement because the notions embedded in economic human rights express both the daily conditions and the aspirations of those for whom human survival and dignity are increasingly at risk. We will illustrate our use of economic human rights in organizing by describing two of the many interrelated initiatives we have undertaken to build a movement— one national and the other local.

Our Assessment of the Organizing Context

Standing in the Kensington section of Philadelphia we see, close up, the effects of deindustrialization on the daily lives of residents: crumbling housing, shells of factory buildings, corner commerce (both legal and illegal), police everywhere, children carrying their hopes and see-through backpacks through the metal detectors of sub-par schools, and—the image most emblematic of this moment in history—white, black, brown, and yellow-skinned people alike all sharing the conditions and conundrums of post-industrial poverty. Their jobs will never return. We are told that the jobs have gone offshore, and there is some truth in this. What we are seldom told is that, given the transformation from the industrial age to the electronics age, many jobs—and workers—are no longer necessary to produce essential goods and services. Substantially gone as well is the social welfare system that once provided temporary shelter in stormy economic times. In the new economy, the people of Kensington are castaways.

Purveyors of a contemporary "politics of hope" point to signs of neighborhood rejuvenation: large-scale removal of "abandoned" cars and houses, new low-income housing, government subsidies for microenterprise, and "engaged" community police officers. But when we adjust our lens to view the backdrop of this setting, disturbing details are revealed: people previously living in the "abandoned" cars and buildings are now homeless; the new low-income housing requires income earlier poverty level as well as considerable screening and surveillance of applicants by government-funded social agencies; funded entrepreneurial endeavors generally support few and lock those few into a service economy yoked to major corporations that dictate the terms of the enterprise; the friendly "beat cops" are using a combination of high-tech community mapping, psychological profiling, and the so-called war on drugs to build a sophisticated "snitch" network. These are some of the building blocks being used to dam the rage of the discarded, many of whom are quite aware of the nature of their plight and of the manipulations intended to keep them quiet and separated from one another.

Efforts to Reform

A similar assessment is shared by many community-based organizations both in Kensington and in comparable locales throughout the country, and both in the already de-industrialized North and the South where corporations are closing down in pursuit of even cheaper labor abroad. But this assessment *by itself* points primarily to two strategies that differ from ours: efforts to strengthen the elements of "civil society" at the local level, on the one hand and, on the other, efforts to strengthen the "loyal opposition"—meaning, in most cases, the Democratic Party—in order to restore or rejuvenate programs of the "new" social welfare state. Frequently these strategies are blended: for example, community-based organizations and, of late, faith-based organizations supported by local government, seek to purchase the party loyalty of a neighborhood's poor but relatively economically stable people by "revitalizing" a few targeted blocks, pushing the poorest into homelessness and the homeless into shelters and prisons.

Two things are particularly significant about this approach to organizing in response to the discontent of the discarded: first, by focusing on the mediating structures of civil society—local government, voluntary associations, churches, charities, and the like—attention and energy are diverted from the social, political, and economic institutions that are served by the mediating structures—institutions that can no longer meet the needs of increasing numbers of people, the new *class* of poor. Feeling energized and elated by a victory "to clear a drug-infested block of debris and dealers," for example, neighborhood residents are unlikely to notice, or care to notice, that the blight was created by capital flight and that the drug dealers were trying to support their families through whatever means were available. In other words, their analysis and action, however noteworthy, remain contained within an arc of legitimacy

defined by the loyal opposition. The fundamental structures and relations of society are left unquestioned and in place.

Second, the "new social welfare state" programs for which "progressive" people are fighting, such as retraining programs for the new economy, expansion of social capital, shelters and transitional housing, and
more, are *not based in rights and entitlements*. The loss of rights-based services and entitlements—not the design, content, or target populations
of the programs—is the single most significant fissure in the landscape
of the new social welfare state (terribly akin to a "soft cop" state) for
which most activists are fighting today. Into this void slips the very sense
of the possible; scattered around the edge are the corpses of cutback
programs and politicians' promises. Almost imperceptibly, the very *right
to rights* is disappearing from view and, with that, the primary tool
needed in the construction of a new society.[4]

As we craft our organizing strategy, we acknowledge the value of
strengthening both opportunities to participate in decisions that affect
our lives and "safety net" social welfare programs. But we see these as
necessary but not sufficient for the ultimate security of our neighbors and,
indeed, the people of this country. These strategies are insufficient
because they assume an economy—a primary mode of production and
distribution—that no longer exists, as well as upon social and political
structures that have yet to evolve to accommodate new economic realities. In other words, efforts to reform are no longer sufficient to meet
human needs; we must have a transformational strategy. As Dr. King
said, "We have moved into an era where we are called upon to raise certain basic questions about the whole society. We are still called upon to
give aid to the beggar who finds himself in misery and agony on life's
highway. But one day, we must ask the question of whether an edifice
which produces beggars must not be restructured and refurbished."[5]
We have affirmed that the day has come. In the next section, we will
explain why.

Informing Our Effort to Transform

To develop a transformational strategy, we need an assessment that takes
yet another step back to study a broader topography—the structural
changes in the economic mode of production, which in turn have given
rise to structural dislocations in social organization. These, in turn, create opportunities to fashion new political alignments and structures
both within the United States and, given the global and interconnected
nature of the changes, among the poor and displaced across national
boundaries. These are the conditions that make the realization of Dr.

King's dream possible—conditions that did not exist thirty-five years ago.

As we have suggested, the economic shift that has taken place—the term "economic revolution" would not be too strong—is the transition from industrial to electronic production of goods and services.[6] Despite the incessant rhetoric of scarcity and the need to downsize, we are actually in a state of overproduction[7] and most likely have, or soon will have, the capacity to meet the basic needs of the world's population. That is, we can guarantee everyone's economic human rights in the twenty-first century. The impediment to doing so is political will, not economic scarcity. Our organizing efforts address the political dimension, the hearts and minds of the people who must be united in political motion. But these devolve from our understanding of who they are and how they can be organized.

Therefore, it is important to sketch in "flesh and blood" detail what we see as we look at the fallout of the economic transformation from labor-intensive industrial production to labor-replacing electronic production. First and most obvious is not simply unemployment but the absolute loss of jobs. For what is being protected through such mechanisms as free trade agreements, gutting of labor rights, fiscal and tax policies that work to the advantage of rich individuals and corporations, and so on are not employment opportunities but opportunities for enhanced capital accumulation and concentration among those who control most of the activity in world production and markets. The growing worldwide mass demonstrations at the gatherings of the captains of "free trade" are indicative of a growing awareness of the *class* nature of the issues at hand, and that class interests cannot be reconciled through the policies and programs being proffered at these gatherings, which result in a permanent loss of job-related income for millions of families.

What this means to American families on the ground is substantial in terms of economic well-being, family functioning, and psychological distress. The decline in real wages of U.S. workers intersects with the introduction of the light, cheap, energy-efficient, mass-produced microprocessor in the early 1970s.[8] Families that have maintained their real incomes often have done so at the expense of family health and stability.[9] Of course, in single-parent (usually female-headed) households, increasing work effort is often not an option. Moreover, as the "middle class" collapses and the gap between the rich and everyone else increases, the psychological impact is substantial.[10] For many, despite a national propensity for optimism (or, perhaps, denial), the American dream has proved to be a nightmare, as college-educated people are on the food lines and fully employed people are seeking shelter on grates and under bridges.

Beyond the loss of jobs and income is the loss of the welfare state. Since its beginnings in the nineteenth century, welfare-state programs have served at least three functions: they have quelled the unrest of dislocated workers, they have maintained a relatively stable and educated labor force in reserve for expanding and contracting economies, and they have served a limited redistributive need to ensure a market for goods and services.[11] Given these functions, the dismantling of the welfare state would seem to defy logic. However, the combination of increasing political surveillance and the erosion of civil rights serves the control function of the welfare state, electronic production requires fewer workers having different skills than mass public education produces, and the redistributive function is now served by a new form of public-private alliance—public policy that forces people into "McJobs," where they make just enough to create a market for cheap goods but not enough to jeopardize the corporate profits of their employers. In short, from the perspective of capital, there is probably no need for the welfare state. The new needs of increasingly mobile and global capital investment are best served by a contingent labor force and a militarized state, not a welfare state.

In fact, given the real concessions that governments have had to make to the market in order to allow it to pursue its destiny unfettered, states can no longer afford a robust welfare state. Neil Gilbert, long a champion of social democracy, conducted a multiphase comparative study of modern welfare states' adaptation to the exigencies of the global economy. He concluded, with resignation, that capitalism had triumphed, forcing governments into a headlock to serve market interests, and that the best we might hope for would be more "family friendly" policies in the private sector.[12]

To summarize, the dissolution of the welfare state affects not just the very poor and temporarily unemployed. It not only heralds a loss of programs, but—even more insidious—constitutes an attack on the very notion of rights and entitlements for all residents of the United States. It also has a wage-suppressing effect that has created a level of economic vulnerability among the so-called middle class that has not been felt since the Great Depression. Among millions, it has become a truism that we are all one accident or illness away from the soup kitchen or homeless shelter.

Just as the mechanical cotton picker created the conditions for the civil rights movement, the microchip has created the conditions for a new movement to end poverty. Electronic production has downsized and dislocated a whole section of the population that has considered itself "working class" and even "middle class"; it has produced a new class—a class with no stake in the economic status quo—and a system that is destroying its livelihoods and security. This new class is much larger and, in its superfluity to the new mode of production, has a different character from the "poor and dispossessed of the nation" to which Dr. King referred in his day. However, his assessment of the potential for unifying people around their class interests is even more relevant today than it was in 1967: the new class's members "have very little, or even nothing, to lose. If they can be helped to take action together, they will do so with a freedom and a power that will be a new and unsettling force in our complacent national life."[13] Our organizing goal is to unite this *new* class of poor—a class whose economic vulnerability is now starkly revealed—to act on its own behalf.

A key element of our organizing strategy is also drawn from Dr. King's assertion in his 1967 speech to the leaders of the SCLC that "we have moved from the era of civil rights to the era of human rights."[14] He urged support for a mass movement that would claim the rights to decent jobs, homes, and quality education, but received only lukewarm support for the shift in strategy. At KWRU, and now in the nationwide network PPEHRC, we have taken up the banner once held by Martin Luther King, Jr., not only out of respect and inspiration but also because our assessment of the organizing context for our work is that there is a convergence of forces and objective conditions that make possible—and necessary—a movement to guarantee the fulfillment of economic human rights. In the next section, following a brief overview of our understanding of some requirements for a social movement, we will illustrate our use of human rights—and *economic* human rights in particular—in our organizing.

Building a Movement to End Poverty

First and foremost, to build a movement, the objective conditions must be right, and we have argued that they are.[15] Second, there must be a clear overarching strategy informing the organizing effort that is consistent with the goal. Third, certain structural elements must be developed; these will differ as the movement evolves.

The overarching strategy of the movement to end poverty is encapsulated in the mission statement of the PPEHRC: "The Poor People's Economic Human Right's Campaign is committed to the unity of the poor across color lines as the leadership base for a broad movement to abolish poverty. We work to accomplish this through advancing economic human rights as named in the Universal Declaration of Human Rights—such as the rights to food, housing, health, education, communication and a living wage job."[16]

Parsing this statement reveals the campaign's motivations and methods. As we have suggested earlier, the *unity of the poor* is the sine qua non of the movement, and here we are talking about the entire new class of poor as described in the previous section. We believe that people who have "followed all the rules"—as the vast majority of people in poverty have—can come to understand their economic vulnerability as the result of structural, not personal, characteristics and forces. With that understanding, employed and unemployed can make common cause. While we recognize that we are attempting to wrestle to the ground a giant of mythic proportions—one swelled and armed with racism, sexism, and xenophobia—and we believe that people's real material conditions can be the basis of their awareness and action. Thus, we actively involve ourselves in such organizations as the Labor Party, comprised largely of workers whose jobs are being eradicated in the age of electronic production, and we focus heavily on such issues as health care, a condition and concern that is shared across alleged "class boundaries" and reveals the inherent unity of interest between so-called poor, working-class, and middle-class people. We also concentrate on small- and medium-sized cities, which are disproportionately ravaged by the closure of plants moving "offshore" or adopting "labor-saving" (actually, labor-*replacing*) methods of production, where loyal families pursuing the American dream "by the book" suddenly find the book slammed shut and the mortgage note stamped "foreclosed."

Organizing and uniting the poor *across color lines* is, as Dr. King understood, strategically imperative. Not only are there more white people than people of color living in poverty, but the skillful use of racism to disunite people has vitiated class-based efforts throughout the course of U.S. history.[17] Thus, we place heavy emphasis on organizing among poor white populations, and our educational program focuses attention on the history of the use of race-based stereotypes, myths, and fears in the disruption of movements. We are finding that achieving unity across color lines is becoming increasingly possible as electronic production is resulting in a growing "equality of poverty." The character of the new period is most clearly expressed in the fact that poor whites are currently experiencing a more rapid rate of growth than non-white poor. The building of the unity of the poor across color lines is the starting point in the abolition of a system that creates both abundance and abandonment.

We believe that the *leadership base* for the movement must be the program of the poor as a united and organized force. As Dr. King said, the poor have no stake in a system that has abandoned them. Professional advocates—particularly those who make their living in the social welfare system—have a stake in "reducing, managing, or moderating" poverty, not in ending it. For business and industry, poverty is raw material in the productive enterprise. If we are to *end* poverty, the movement must be driven by a vision and a program fashioned from the experience of the poor—experience excavated and examined collectively to develop the kind of political consciousness that can inform action toward meeting everyone's basic needs.

A primary organizing tool we have adopted is the Universal Declaration of Human Rights (UDHR) and, in particular, those articles that encompass economic human rights: Articles 23, 25, and 26.[18] Article 23 guarantees everyone the right to work, Article 25 guarantees an adequate standard of living, and Article 26 guarantees the right to education. Given the requisite for communication in the building of a transformative movement,[19] and the contemporary threats to communication posed by the erosion of civil rights, we have recently incorporated Article 19 into our program. We were drawn to the *concept* of economic human rights because they reflect, in their absence, the daily conditions of increasing numbers of people in the United States and, in their fulfillment, the perceived promise of the United States to its people since the inception of the nation. We were drawn to the *instruments* of the UDHR, especially the International Covenant on Economic, Social and Cultural Rights, because of their legitimacy in world opinion and the ways they speak starkly and simply to people, creating a potential basis for unity of a common vision. In the next and final section, we will illustrate the use of these concepts and instruments in two of our organizing efforts.

Organizing: Key Elements and Methods

In our estimation, we are at an early phase of movement building; therefore, we must construct the scaffolding for the movement. Some of the required elements of that scaffolding are leadership, consciousness, relationships, and membership organizations.[20] Let us examine each in turn very briefly, and then illustrate them.

First, *leadership* is the sun around which the other elements orbit. We emphasize recruiting a core of *individual* leaders who can educate, organize, and consolidate the *class* leadership of the poor as a conscious social force. This class leadership is what Dr. King spoke to when he pointed out the need to help "the poor to take action together, [becoming] a new and unsettling force in our complacent national life."[21] Not all of the individual leaders must come from the ranks of the poor, but they need to identify with and promote the program of the poor. Key to this process and key to contesting anti-poor stereotypes—including those internalized stereotypes by the poor—is our "panning for gold" among people who are living in or at the edge of poverty, people who have authority and legitimacy among their peers. Leadership development is the first (and necessary stage) of building a broad movement, and we recognize that it cannot be truncated.

A primary tool in the development of a new *consciousness* is the use of the language of economic human rights. Our use of economic human rights speaks to core values in the United States personality, expressed in the founding creed of the nation: equality, inalienable rights, government responsibility for the common good, the duty of citizens to ensure the proper function of government. Moreover, the language of "poverty" is so tainted and toxic that it is difficult for people who are using it, particularly with reference to themselves, to conceive of the poor as worthy and, when united, able to participate in the decisions that profoundly shape their lives. The language of "rights," on the other hand, expresses a universal longing—a legitimate collective claim of humanity on the prerequisites for a life of dignity. The language of rights has particular potency in the United States, of course, where rights denied have historically moved people to action. Thus, in all of our educational work and materials, we have adopted the language of economic human rights, underscoring their indivisibility from other rights advocated in the UDHR.[22]

A third element in our scaffolding is the forming of new *relationships*, particularly among people living in poverty. This is very difficult to do because they have usually absorbed the dominant myths and legends about poverty and therefore often don't like or trust each other very much. However, new relationships among people living in poverty permit and foster the emergence of new leaders from their ranks. We also seek new relationships between people living in poverty and those who are not who can come to understand and accept the need for the program of the poor to prevail.

The fourth element is *membership organizations*. In order for people to act collectively, they need collectives or associations in which they can participate in the decisions that affect the group. Not all of the nearly one hundred organizations in the PPEHRC have the same structure or type of program, nor do they all focus exclusively or even primarily on economic human rights. They are all, however, membership organizations. They are the incubators of the collective leadership of the poor.

The following section illustrates the ways we are implementing our analysis and constructing the scaffolding of the movement with reference to two of our many campaigns—one national and the other local.

The New Freedom Bus Tour of 1998

In the winter of 1997–98, the War Council (policy-making body) of the KWRU made a difficult but enormously strategic decision: they decided to use the scarce resources of the organization to fund a nationwide organizing bus tour.[23] With so many members of KWRU desperately needing resources for themselves and their families, the decision reflected a high level of understanding and commitment to the goal of building the movement. A great deal of reflection on their collective struggles in recent years, as well as their study of the nature of poverty and social movements, led to the decision.

The "New Freedom Bus—Freedom from Hunger, Homelessness, and Unemployment" departed Philadelphia in the summer of 1998 in pursuit of two goals: building a national network of groups organizing, in one way or another, around the issues of poverty, and "panning for gold," or identifying indigenous leaders in impoverished communities and organizations concerned about poverty. The New Freedom Bus visited thirty-five towns and cities in thirty days, participating in local actions, press conferences, and other events organized by local groups. Reflecting the character of the conditions of poverty today, the locales ranged from small towns to large cities, covering all geographic regions of the country; the people were young and old, employed and unemployed; and they were people of all colors, often working together in the same organizations.

The New Freedom Bus tour marked our first large-scale use of the instruments of economic human rights. Drawing language from the UDHR, the organizers created a "documentation form"—a questionnaire used by the bus riders and local organizers to interview people all over the country about their circumstances, casting their narratives in a human rights framework. Those who were willing appeared at "truth commissions," that is, hearings at which the *patterns* of economic human rights violations were dramatically evidenced. The month-long bus tour culminated in a march across the George Washington Bridge, through the streets of Manhattan, to the United Nations. At a church across from the United Nations, the final truth commission of the tour was held. People from organizations across the country sent representatives to bear witness to endemic violations of economic human rights in the United States. The report of a panel of jurors was presented to Mary Robinson, the UN High Commissioner for Human Rights, who referenced the findings in her annual report later that year.

The power of the principles of economic human rights for validating the commonality of experiences and creating a common vision among disparate groups cannot be underestimated. That fact was evidenced by the overwhelming response to a call for a poor people's summit that went out to the groups that we met on the bus tour and others. Held in October 1998 in Philadelphia, the summit drew approximately three hundred representatives of groups from forty states and Puerto Rico. In their work, these organizations were addressing a range of issues—homelessness, health care, and the needs of contingent workers and the unemployed, battered women, immigrants, and more—from many theoretical perspectives and strategies. At this summit, the PPEHRC was born under a banner that encompassed all the concerns represented and provided a framework for a unifying analysis and action.

The Economic Human Rights—Pennsylvania Campaign

In the spring of 2002, HR 473, the "Curry Resolution," was introduced to the Pennsylvania House of Representatives. The resolution called for the establishment of a select House committee to study the feasibility of integrating economic human rights principles into the laws and policies of the commonwealth. A few months later, it passed unanimously and the select committee was established.

The Economic Human Rights-Pennsylvania (EHR-Pennsylvania) campaign resulted from a convergence of serendipity and strategic thinking. For a variety of reasons, some elected officials have supported our work; one of the more consistent supporters—a Democrat from a heavily Republican district north of Philadelphia—was Rep. Larry Curry. Trained as a historian, Rep. Curry understood the importance of social movements. He also had particular interests in the United Nations and in Pennsylvania's significance as a wellspring of rights-based democracy. When one of our members was asked to take a leadership position in the Pennsylvania chapter of the National Association of Social Workers (NASW-PA), she called upon Rep. Curry to craft a joint legislative economic human rights agenda. He agreed, and KWRU and NASW-PA representatives began a collaboration that continues today.

The EHR-PA campaign uses legislative tactics to accomplish the strategic objectives of identifying and developing leadership, creating new consciousness, and building new relationships and organizations. We do not expect that a legislative solution to poverty is possible today; in general, legislative bodies represent the program of the rich, not the program of the poor. For this to change, the kind of mass social movement we are attempting to build is necessary. In the case of HR 473, we in KWRU actually did not want the resolution to pass because the appointing of and setting the agenda for the select committee would then go into the hands of the Republicans who controlled the legislature.[24] This could limit our opportunity to travel around the state with Rep. Curry having hearings on the resolution—that is, to organize in small towns and cities around economic human rights—and the introduction of the resolution was enough to accomplish that. In fact, even before the resolution was introduced, Rep. Curry had begun to hold hearings under his authority as a member of the Democratic caucus' policy committee. These hearings were held in communities identified by KWRU as strategically significant, where NASW-PA had active divisions with strong leadership and where Rep. Curry could garner the support of his legislative colleagues from the area.

In preparation for these local hearings, NASW-PA divisions and social work educators organized training sessions on economic human rights and the movement to end poverty. These were conducted by KWRU members, including members of its social work strategy group. Trainees learned the core concepts of economic human rights, how to document rights violations, and how to organize hearings. The hearings then brought together social workers, other professionals and advocates, and the people with whom they were working as "clients" to bear witness to economic human rights violations, both personal and political, individual and institutional. We were able to capture the attention of the media in these small communities by personifying and punctuating esoteric analyses of socioeconomic forces and data trends with stories of local people's lives. In most of the communities, we were able to identify indigenous leaders and either strengthen or stimulate the development of local organizations.

Given the infrastructure we had built, both in our unusual coalition and around the state, we were able to maintain momentum and focus when the resolution passed and the select committee was appointed. The committee had time for only one hearing, which was held at the state capitol, before its report was due in November 2002. The committee voted unanimously to call for a new resolution, HR 144, mandating that the study continue another two years. HR 144 passed easily in the next legislature, and we are busily organizing more trainings and hearings around the state.

Conclusion

A summary review of the EHR-PA campaign illustrates the principal points of our chapter; it illustrates an application of our assessment of the contemporary organizing context and the requirements of this early stage in the building of a social movement. We concentrate efforts in small and medium-sized cities, where the new class of poor is growing rapidly out of the rubble of industries replaced by electronics-based global production. These are locales where the unity of the poor across color lines can be fashioned, because it is so clear in most of them that poverty today is an equal opportunity phenomenon. While we are not seeking legislative solutions to poverty, the legislative process still has enormous credibility in these communities, where the "American dream" is still very much alive. So while we are not seeking a legislative solution to poverty, we are using legislative tactics to organize a mass movement at the base of U.S. society, where legislative hearings can reveal the scope and nature of people's vulnerability and the language of economic human rights can contribute to a new consciousness about the roots of poverty and economic vulnerability.[25]

The EHR-PA campaign has four specific strategic objectives that derive from the need for new leadership, consciousness, relationships, and organizations. The first is to build a leadership committed to the struggle to unite and organize the poor across color lines. In the United States, this is a seditious notion. Martin Luther King, Jr., was assassinated when he tried to do this, because it threatens to erode the foundation of institutions and mechanisms used in this country to maintain the status quo. In order to create leadership of the poor as a class, we seek and develop individual leaders, primarily—but not exclusively—from the ranks of the poor. To confront, challenge, and change the stereo-types and racist dynamics that have been used deliberately to disunite the poor, we organize heavily in poor white communities.

To create new consciousness, we work to redefine poverty as a viola-tion of economic human rights and reveal its structural nature. Using the UDHR as our point of reference, we introduce new language and new concepts to provide an intellectual scaffolding for the construction of new ideas about poverty, rights, and, ultimately, the responsibility of government. We take documentation of economic human rights viola-tions through brief survey interviews, extended narratives, and formal testimony. In other campaigns, we also use art, music, photography, video and other forms of media to communicate the realities of poverty and the potential power of the people who can, in unity, lead a move-ment to end it.

A third objective is to facilitate new relationships. New relationships among people living in poverty permit and foster the emergence of new leaders from their ranks. In the EHR-PA campaign, we also seek new relationships between social workers and people living in poverty. Social workers often have more opportunities to interact with people living in poverty than people in poverty have with each other. However, for social workers to help build the movement, the relationship between social worker and "client" must change from one of "service" to one of soli-darity. The structure of the EHR-PA project promotes that change. Simi-larly, other advocates who commit to the movement must come to understand and commit to the program and leadership of the poor as its base.

The fourth objective is to develop new organizations. In the case of the EHR-PA campaign, we look for opportunities to create local economic human rights committees consisting of people who are directly affected by economic human rights violations as well as advocates and other allies who are indirectly affected. Opportunities are found particularly in small- and medium-size cities where economic dislocations are engulfing people who consider themselves middle class. Geopolitically and strategically, these people are our organizing edge.

We believe we are living at a juncture in history when it is particularly crucial to remember the words of poet Marge Piercy: "We make history or history makes us."[26] In this moment, we have the technology and abundance to ensure that all human beings on this earth have basic human needs met and all human rights promoted and preserved forever. The other road from this historic juncture leads to increased poverty and political repression. Standing in Kensington, it is easy to see clearly that poverty is not a by-product of production, but the essential raw material of production in our economic system, and that it can and must be ended. It is increasingly possible to see this from any other location in the United States as objective conditions crush illusions shaped in a different epoch. The work of the movement is to help people see this—and see beyond it—to the full realization of economic human rights.

Part III
Contentious and
Emerging Issues

Chapter 7
So Close and Yet So Different
The Right to Health Care in the United States
and Canada

Virginia A. Leary

"Is there a right to health care?" I asked the students in my human rights seminar at the University of Saskatchewan College of Law several years ago. I was teaching in Saskatoon that year, on leave from SUNY-Buffalo Law School, and had previously asked the same question of the students in my SUNY class. In Saskatoon, the students replied that there was a right to health care; in Buffalo, they had replied there was no right to health care.

Why such different responses from students in two similar, adjacent countries? Did the responses merely reflect the practical differences between the health care systems in the two countries, or were the responses, more fundamentally, an indication of the differing ideological bases of the two systems? The Canadian and U.S. health care systems differ considerably. Canada has a government-managed health care system referred to as a "single-payer" system: all residents are guaranteed basic health care and hospitalization regardless of ability to pay. In the United States, health care systems are (largely) funded through private insurance, and 40 million Americans have no health care insurance or hospital insurance.

Although both the U.S. and the Canadian systems are criticized by participants, the majority of Canadians, in contrast to the majority of Americans, express support for the fundamentals of their health care system. Polls reflect the dissatisfaction of substantial numbers of Americans with their health care system, but there is little agreement on what should be done to improve it.

Critical examination of the Canadian health care system is facilitated by the publication in 2002 of the extensive *Final Report of the Commission on the Future of Health Care in Canada*.[1] The commission was established by the prime minister and headed by Roy J. Romanow of Saskatchewan. The lengthy *Report* (hereafter *Romanow Report*) examines and criticizes numerous aspects of the Canadian health care system in detail, but concludes that, although there is much needed improvement, the universal, single-payer system should be retained.

The work of the commission may be compared—to its credit—with the abortive effort of the Clinton administration in 1994 to reform the U.S. health care system.[2] The failure of the Clinton effort, after great opposition from the insurance industry, demonstrates the difficulty of undertaking a fundamental reform of the U.S. system. Political and ideological obstacles, the complexity of the proposed reform plan, and the variety among the fifty states all militated against reform. Yet repeated expressions of dissatisfaction with the U.S. system have persisted and once again were emphasized during the 2004 presidential campaign.

Why do the two adjacent countries of Canada and the United States, with easy and constant communication, open borders, and mainly a common language, differ so fundamentally in their health care systems? What influences, history, and experience explain such different approaches? This chapter attempts to answer these questions.

The Canadian Single-Payer System

The Canadian system of basic health care and hospital insurance is a governmental program referred to as a universal, "single-payer" system.[3] It differs from the primarily privately funded system found in the United States. Each Canadian resident carries a health care card, similar to the Social Security card that Americans carry. When receiving health care from a freely chosen physician or for a stay in a hospital, the Canadian shows the card and is not required to make a direct payment. The system is financed by provincial taxes imposed directly on those who can afford to pay and by federal contributions. Because the programs are run by the provinces, but with considerable funding from the federal government, they may differ slightly, but not fundamentally, from one province to another. Persons with low income are provided with care even if they are unable to contribute to the system. A patient in a Canadian hospital is not aware that the person in the bed next to him might not contribute to the system. In the United States, welfare patients are often treated in special hospitals where the medical treatment may be good, but the hospital overcrowded.

To the surprise of many Americans, who speak disparagingly of "socialized medicine," patients in Canada freely choose their physician but do not pay the physician directly; the medical provider is reimbursed by the government. Medical associations negotiate with the government on the amount of compensation for the treatment of patients. In general, medical personnel in Canada have a lower income than comparable professionals in the United States. The higher income available to physicians practicing in the United States has had an effect on the Canadian systems. Canadian doctors are attracted to practice in the nearby U.S. system because of stress on the Canadian system.

In general, Canadians may freely choose hospitals for treatment. However, the same facilities are not available in all hospitals. Only a limited number of magnetic resonance imaging machines (MRIs) may be available in a geographic area; not every hospital has the same advanced facilities. Duplication and multiplication of necessary equipment (and extra costs) in a particular area is thus avoided. In the United States, nearly every major hospital or medical facility carries the most advanced equipment, duplicating what may be available in nearby facilities and adding to hospital expense.

A surprising aspect of the Canadian plan for Americans is the prohibition against Canadians buying private basic health insurance, covering the same benefits as the government plan but permitting the patient to jump over queues and have quicker access to care. The federal government withholds contributions to any provincial plan that permits "extra billing"—the purchase of private insurance for the same benefits the governmental plan provides. The prohibition of extra billing has proved a controversial but effective method of controlling the use of private insurance to receive quicker or perceived better care than the government plan. It emphasizes in a striking manner the equal treatment of Canadians regardless of income and would be very difficult to duplicate in the United States, in which the prevailing attitude is "I have a right to it if I can pay for it." The Canadian system covers basic health care—some pharmaceuticals and medical and dental procedures are not covered.

Criticisms of the Canadian System—The Romanow Report

Many Americans are aware of the criticisms of the Canadian health care system as a result of negative publicity, particularly by the medical profession, but are not always aware that, despite many criticisms of their system, the majority of Canadians do not wish to change to a fundamentally different (i.e., U.S.-type) system. In general, Canadians reacted positively to the conclusion of the *Romanow Report*, supporting the basic orientation of their system but also welcoming the numerous suggestions for improvements. The emphasis on the shortcomings of the Canadian system, without a perception of its valuable aspects, results in a failure by many Americans to appreciate the values of that system.

Canadians, nevertheless, continue to voice criticisms and the need for reform. The extent of the suggestions for improvement in the *Romanow Report* suggests that so many aspects of the system need to be changed or improved that one is entitled to wonder if it is a criticism of the system as a whole rather than simply a proposal for reform. In the next section, on values, I suggest that this is not the case—the Canadians remain strongly in favor of their system, but they nevertheless perceive much need for improvement.

The mandate of the Romanow Commission was to engage Canadians in a national dialogue on the future of health care and to make recommendations to preserve the long-term sustainability of Canada's universally accessible, publicly funded health care system. The *Romanow Report* is extensive, consisting of 375 pages and forty-seven detailed, costed recommendations, with time frames for implementation. It recommends the establishment of a Canadian health covenant to express the country's collective vision for health care and updating the Canada Health Act. It also recommends fostering collaboration among governments, providers, and citizens through a new Health Council of Canada. In the report, the relationship between the federal government and the provinces in financing health care appears to be a major problem in the Canadian health care system.

The *Romanow Report* recommends additional federal funding earlier than the current forecasts and the creation of five new targeted funds to address immediate priorities until the minimum federal funding threshold is attained: a rural and remote access fund, a diagnostic services fund, a primary health care transfer, a home care transfer, and a catastrophic drug transfer.

Other recommendations include making the system more comprehensive by integrating priority home care services within the Canada Health Act and improving prescription drug coverage, improving timely access to quality care through special initiatives to improve wait list management, and encouraging a national personal electronic health record system. The *Romanow Report* also addresses Aboriginal health care, culturally sensitive access, the impact of globalization, and applied research.

Romanow summarized the report by stating that the recommendations were premised on three overarching themes: that Canada requires strong leadership and improved governance to keep Medicare a national asset; that Canada needs to make the system more responsive, efficient, and accountable; and that Canada must make strategic investments over the short term to address priority concerns, as well as in the long term, to place the system on a more sustainable footing.

The Economist reported in the February 8, 2003 issue, that "When it comes to worrying about health care, Canadians seem to have a touch of hypochondria. Compared with Britain's struggling national health service or the lavish American system that leaves out millions of uninsured, Canada performs well; it provides good-quality care for its citizens in reasonable time and at moderate cost. Even so, Canadians fret about a shortage of doctors, rising drug bills, and lengthy waits for non-emergency treatment and diagnostic tests. And they worry whether the system will continue to care for them in the future."[4]

It was reported, as a follow-up to the *Romanow Report,* that the federal government would transfer an extra CAN$13.5 billion to the provinces over the following three years and create a new health reform fund to pay for changes in primary care, home care, and drug coverage and an extra sum for diagnostic treatment. *The Economist* stated that Romanow's proposals enjoyed huge popular support, in part because his commission solicited views from thousands of Canadians.

After the extensive re-examination of the Canadian health care system by the Romanow commission, the essential aspects of a publicly funded and managed system, the single-payer system were once again reaffirmed, but with multiple suggestions for improvement. However, one year after the publication of the *Romanow Report* in December 2003, a news item stated that not one of the almost fifty recommendations had been implemented despite widespread publicity and wide public support. It was also reported that Paul Martin, the new prime minister, appeared to be making health care a priority in his administration, giving hope for substantial health care reform.[5]

It was also reported that, as of June 27, 2003, Romanow's recommendations for four of the five funds (the diagnostic services fund, a primary health care transfer, a home care transfer and a catastrophic drug transfer) had been approved in principle, but there was no action on the rural and remote access fund, and there was foot-dragging and even opposition in three provinces for his suggestion of the formation of a Health Council of Canada, which was to have been in place by May 5, 2003.[6]

Despite general approval of the *Romanow Report,* less enthusiastic reactions were voiced in a colloquy on the report in the 2003 issue of the *University of Saskatchewan Law Review.* Summarizing the contributions published in the colloquy, the editors noted that the "underlying current of these articles is one of dissatisfaction; the authors recognize that in trying to review such a broad topic as 'Canada's health care system,' the [*Romanow*] *Report* not unexpectedly, comes up short on many issues."[7]

The U.S. Health Care System in Crisis

The health care system in the United States has been criticized in recent years by politicians and the public alike. Criticism and calls for improvement marked the presidential primary campaign in 2004. It was repeatedly noted, as it has so often before, that more than 40 million Americans lacked health insurance, and the poor and racial minorities had the worst health status and least health care.

Health insurance in the United States is largely provided by employers through a number of private insurance companies, and generally with employee contributions. Increasingly, however, employers are not providing health insurance, and it is usually not provided for part-time workers. Thus, many employed Americans, as well as the unemployed, lack health insurance. Those without insurance through employment may purchase it themselves, but usually at a prohibitive cost, and they often do not do so. Federal and state governments attempt to fill the gap through Medicaid programs for the very poor and the Medicare program for the elderly, but the figure of approximately 40 million Americans without health care insurance has held steady for more than a decade.

The health care system in the United States, apart from Medicaid and Medicare, is largely a privatized system with some governmental admixture and local efforts to improve coverage of the uninsured. Private insurance companies control much of the health care system. In recent years, companies have initiated efforts to control costs, most notably through health maintenance organizations (HMOs). These organizations employ physicians and other medical personnel and offer health services with strict financial controls. The HMOs are often run by insurance companies, and not by physicians, who may be employees. While initially regarded as a solution to the rising cost of health care and increasing the accessibility of patients to medical care, they are now frequently criticized. Patients complain that they are allowed too short a time with physicians—normally a fifteen-minute appointment. Doctors complain that they are no longer free to treat patients as they wish—cost takes precedence over necessary care; decisions are made by non-medical personnel. And at the same time, costs for health care in the United States continue to increase.

Most serious observers of the U.S. health care system believe it is a broken system, but there is little agreement on the remedy, as strikingly evidenced by reported statements of Democratic presidential primary candidates in Iowa in October 2003:

Most of the candidates struggled to explain their complicated [health care] programs in answers of less than 30 seconds or a minute. Mr. Gephardt touted his $228 billion health care plan and said Mr. Kerry's and Dr. Dean's proposals would encourage companies to drop health coverage for employees. Mr. Kerry said Mr. Gephardt was not being realistic. . . . Dr. Dean's plan cost $87 billion and his own cost $75 billion. "We're not going to be able to find $228 billion. . . . Mr. Kucinich and Ms. Braun . . . both repeatedly said they support a single-payer system of universal health insurance."[8]

Uwe E. Reinhardt of Princeton University has provided some of the most trenchant criticisms of the U.S. health care system—and has arrived at the pessimistic conclusion that little can be done to improve it—because, as he points out, the uninsured are largely a marginal socioeconomic class lacking in economic leverage. He maintains that about one-third of the uninsured have high enough incomes to be able to afford health insurance if it were offered to them at a reasonable price, but the private health insurance sector has never been able to service individual customers at affordable rates. The "majority of the uninsured, however, belong to families headed by the economically homogenous group that we might call 'low-income hard-working stiffs.' As such they represent for the most part a marginal socioeconomic class that has neither economic nor political leverage," writes Dr. Reinhardt.[9]

Reinhardt blames the U.S. employment-based health care system for the chronic problem of the uninsured: "If one thinks about it for a moment, it is unreasonable on its face to look to private employers, especially to small firms with a low-wage workforce, as the foundation for a nation's health insurance system. Use of the labor contract between private citizens and private employers as a source of health insurance has to rank as one of the oddest ideas in the development of modern social policy."[10]

Reinhardt points out that the uninsured receive medical and hospital care through various safety-net programs amounting to about 60 percent of the health care that similarly situated well insured Americans receive. Americans are concerned over the plight of the uninsured, and for many years there have been proposals for providing health care for them. These competing proposals, however, contain a condition in the minds of the proponents, namely, that the economic privilege of those who already have excellent health care not be reduced. Because that condition is difficult to meet, in the end the proposals all result in a second-best solution: namely, to do nothing. "Over the decades, no group putting forth proposals on the uninsured has been powerful enough to cram its ideas down the throats of other groups. . . . [W]e shall never have universal health insurance coverage in this country for the uninsured," observes Reinhardt.[11]

A number of state governments have proposed programs to extend and expand health care. Oregon is often cited as an example of an attempt to improve the situation. In 2002, Oregonians voted overwhelmingly against a ballot proposal for a system of universal health care after opposition and strong lobbying from the medical profession and concern about costs. The vote was far from close, with approximately 80 percent of votes against the proposal. A coalition of insurance companies blanketed the airwaves with negative ads, outspending by more than 30 to 1 the proponents of the measure.[12] It was reported that, in 2004, the Oregon health system remained inadequate, with almost as large a number of uninsured as before reforms were instigated in the state in 1986. The Oregon program and other state programs remain basically private programs with an attempt to alleviate some of the problems for the poorer populations.[13]

The most recent proposal for a radical change in the U.S. health system was published in the August 13, 2003, *Journal of the American Medical Association* (*JAMA*) under the title "Physicians' Proposal for National Health Insurance." The proposal was supported by 7,782 U.S. physicians, including two former surgeons general; it proposed a single-payer system, rejecting proposals for reform that would retain the role of private insurers. The physicians called for health insurance that would cover every American for all necessary medical care—"in essence an expanded and improved version of traditional Medicare." Under the proposed plan, patients could choose to go to any doctor or hospital, and hospitals and clinics would remain privately owned and operating, receiving a budget from national health insurance to cover all operating costs. Physicians would continue to practice on a fee-for-service basis or receive salaries from group practices, hospitals, or clinics.

The *JAMA* article pointed out that the United States spends more than twice as much on health care as most other developed nations, all of which boast universal coverage, yet more than 40 million Americans have no health insurance. Many more are underinsured. Confronted by the rising costs and capabilities of modern medicine, other nations have chosen national health insurance (NHI). The United States alone treats health care as a commodity distributed according to the ability to pay rather than as a social service to be distributed according to medical need, the physicians stated. In this market-driven system, insurers and providers compete not by increasing quality or lowering costs, but by avoiding unprofitable patients and shifting costs back to patients or to other payers. According to the physicians, this creates the paradox of a health care system based on avoiding the sick. It generates huge administrative costs that, along with profits, divert resources from clinical care to the demands of business: "We [the Physicians' Working Group for

Single-Payer National Health Insurance] endorse a fundamental change in U.S. health care—the creation of an NHI program. Such a program, which in essence would be an expanded and improved version of traditional Medicare, would cover every American for all necessary medical care."[14]

The program, according to the physicians, would be paid for by combining current sources of government health spending into a single fund with modest new taxes, offset by reductions in premiums and out-of-pocket spending. It would save at least $200 billion annually, the news release reported, by eliminating high overhead and profits of the private, investor-owned insurance industry. Administrative savings would fully offset the costs of covering the uninsured as well as giving full prescription drug coverage to all Americans.

The proposal was sponsored by the organization Physicians for a National Health Program (PNHP), founded in 1987 and headquartered in Chicago. The organization, headed by Dr. Quentin Young, a leading Chicago physician, has long campaigned unsuccessfully for a national health insurance program, but has had increasing public support in recent years. The publication of the proposal in *JAMA* received widespread attention. (The journal pointed out that its publication did not constitute endorsement.)

Negative reactions were not long in coming. It was alleged that the idea was a risky scheme that would result in longer waits for routine procedures, health care rationing, and price controls, according to Dr. Donald Young, president of the Health Insurance Association of America, a Washington-based industry group. Dr. Young further said that "[a]ll of us share in the desire to offer health insurance coverage to anyone who wants it, but private health insurance continues to give people better access to quality medical care, and greater control over health decisions affecting their families, than would the worn-out, one-size-fits-all proposal, put forward yet again today."[15]

The American Medical Association (AMA), representing 280,000 physicians, opposes a single-payer approach, according to AMA president Donald J. Palmisano, believing instead that a health care system based on private and public sector financing "will best benefit the uninsured, improve quality, restrain costs, and expand patient choice and individual purchasing power." He pointed out that the signers of the physicians' proposal account for less than 1 percent of the health personnel in the United States as of 2000.[16]

Does the recent plan proposing a universal, single-payer health care system in the United States signal a trend toward the adoption of such a system? In view of the failure of previous proposals and strong objections from private insurers, this appears unlikely. The prognosis for the U.S.

health care system appears to be more of the same: continued discussion of the deficiencies but failure to make any but incremental improvements, such as the recent addition of pharmaceutical benefits to the Medicare system.

A large number of working (and voting) Americans have excellent health care services, and, while being concerned for the many who do not, they cannot agree on a solution, especially if it might diminish in any manner their own benefits. Those without satisfactory medical care are less educated and less politically active and are not able to bring about changes. Short of a radical change in the economic situation of a majority of Americans, Reinhardt and many others remain pessimistic about any fundamental changes. In the meantime, more than 40 million Americans will remain without health care.

Values and Ideological Foundations of the U.S. and Canadian Health Care Systems

Are the differences between the U.S. and the Canadian health care systems solely practical differences based on historical developments or do they, as I believe, reflect fundamentally different approaches to the role of the state in social matters in general, and specifically in health care, making it difficult to envision the U.S. system evolving into a universal, single-payer system in the foreseeable future? Such a fundamental evolution in the United States may occur incrementally over time, but opposition to a pervasive governmental role in health care (and many other social matters) in the United States makes such evolution unlikely.

Values and the Canadian Health Care System

The present universal, single-payer Canadian health care system was adopted following recommendations in the 1964 report of a federal Royal Commission on the Delivery of Health Services, headed by Justice Emmett Hall of Saskatchewan.[17] Prior to that time, the health systems in most provinces were similar to the U.S. health care systems. The basic elements of the universal, single-payer system were reaffirmed by a second Emmett Hall-led Royal Commission report in 1980, and, most recently, in the 2002 report by Roy Romanow,[18] former premier of Saskatchewan. The 1980 report criticized extra billing and hospital user charges and recommended compulsory arbitration in determining physicians' fees. All three commissions have appropriately been headed by Saskatchewan residents, the province where the concept of publicly financed and run medical insurance had its birth.

The reports and conclusions of the three commissions followed extensive hearings and public consultation throughout the country, in contrast to the semi-secretive manner in which the Clinton administration began its aborted study of the U.S. system. The title of the 2002 *Romanow Report* on the Canadian system, "Building on *Values*: The Future of Health Care in Canada" (emphasis added), succinctly reaffirmed and emphasized the basic postulates of the health care system adopted in 1964: the values of *universality, equity,* and *solidarity. Portability*—the right to preserve one's health insurance coverage when moving to a different province—is also a basic characteristic of the Canadian system.

The *Romanow Report* emphasized that the health care system should cover basic health care and hospitalization for all residents of Canada, regardless of ability to pay, and proposed the establishment of a Canadian health covenant "as a tangible statement of Canadians' *values* and a guiding force for our publicly funded health care system," which would set out the major objectives of the health care system for the public, for patients, and for health care providers. The covenant would be a "mission statement" for the health care system, "supported by First Ministers, formally endorsed by the federal government and each of the provincial and territorial governments, and widely circulated to the public and health care providers." The proposed covenant would contain the following essential points:

- Our health care system is a public resource and a precious national asset. . . .
- Public health insurance must be accessible to all Canadians on uniform terms and conditions, regardless of where they live in the country. . . .
- Canadians . . . are entitled to health services based on health needs, not ability to pay.[19]

Although a universal, single-payer system was adopted at the federal level in Canada in 1965, it had been preceded by successful efforts in Saskatchewan to create a universal health care system prior to that date. The province of Saskatchewan, situated between Alberta and Manitoba, and just north of Montana and North Dakota, is not well known to Americans (or to many Canadians who frequently fly over it en route to British Columbia). Yet Saskatchewan's contribution to the development of the Canadian health care system is remarkable. The values underlying the Canadian system were first formulated in that prairie province.

Emmett Hall, chairman of the first two Royal Commissions on Health in 1964 and 1980, was an outstanding Saskatoon jurist and federal Supreme Court justice. Roy Romanow, the chairman of the commission that re-examined the Canadian health care system in 2002, was a former premier of Saskatchewan. But it is Tommy Douglas, premier of Saskatchewan from 1944 to 1960, who is entitled to major credit for the development of the Saskatchewan health care system, a precursor of the later Canadian health care system.[20] Despite this, Douglas is virtually unknown in the United States and even to many contemporary Canadians.

Douglas is remembered and honored because he pioneered the development of a universal, single-payer health system in Saskatchewan in the 1960s. "[T]he creation of a system whereby anyone could get the medical attention needed, regardless of personal wealth" was a promise he had made, and kept, to the electorate. Douglas's efforts created great opposition from the medical profession—as did later efforts to create a Canadian universal health care system. It led to a doctors' strike in 1962 and considerable turmoil in the province. The strike was broken when an airlift from Britain brought in replacement physicians.

In 1960, John Diefenbaker, the then Canadian prime minister and a member of the Conservative Party and not the Cooperative Commonwealth Federation (CCF), and also a native of Saskatchewan, announced that he intended to name a royal commission to inquire into the health needs of Canadians, with a view to establishing a national health plan. The commission was named, with Justice Emmett Hall, also a progressive Conservative, as its head. To the surprise of many, including the medical profession, the commission proposed the development of a universal, single-payer health plan—the plan that has remained in effect in Canada to date. The adoption of the Canadian universal health care plan at the federal level was the result of Conservative Party proposals and not those made by the CCF.

Dr. Efstathios Barootes, who had been one of the foremost opponents of the Saskatchewan health care plan and a leader of the doctors' strike in 1962, was interviewed, in 1996, about his opinion of the health care system adopted in Saskatchewan thirty-five years earlier. Barootes, who had continued to practice in Saskatchewan, explained the intensity of the doctors' original resistance to the Douglas health care plan, which the physicians had termed "compulsory state medicine." He referred to the doctors' strike, the bringing in of replacement physicians by the government and some concessions made to the physicians. In the interview, Barootes remarked, "I will tell you that today I support the universal health care program we have here. Our people are satisfied with it. Nobody that I know would be able to change it without a cataclysmic debate. Today a politician in Saskatchewan or in Canada is more likely to get away with canceling Christmas, than he is with canceling Canada's health insurance program."[21]

The values underlying the development of the present day health care system in Canada remain intact nearly forty years later. The final report of the 1964 Royal Commission on Health Service (vol. 1) stated, "What we seek is a method that will provide everybody in Canada with comprehensive coverage regardless of age or state of health or ability to pay, upon uniform terms and conditions."

Ideology and the U.S. Health Care System

As this chapter was being written, in March 2004, primary elections for the Democratic Party candidate for president of the United States were being held, and concern about the state of the U.S. health care system was a focus of candidates, closely following concern over the economy. The approaches of the candidates to improvements in the health care system provide a striking illustration of the manner in which social reform is normally proposed in the United States—with a focus on practical, incremental steps without emphasis on the social principles or ideology underlying proposals for improvements. Although no reference is generally made to the underlying ideology of the U.S. system—a privatized system with as little government interference as possible—the basic ideology is evident in proposals for change. The major Democratic Party candidates criticized the U.S. health care system but avoided radical criticism of the basic philosophy of the privately funded health care system.

The views of Senator John Kerry, who became the Democratic Party candidate for the presidency, are of particular interest. Kerry had long been interested in health care reform; his platform contained extensive, far-reaching proposals for improvement of the system, but these were deliberately phrased as incremental rather than radical. He proposed health care reform that would give every American "access to affordable health care through the same plan that the President and Congress give themselves," an astute argument easily understood by the electorate and focused away from any suggestion that a reformed health care plan could be viewed as "socialist" or contrary to American social policy. If the president and Congress have extensive health insurance, why not the rest of Americans?[22]

Surprisingly, however, Kerry's platform on health care began with the ideological statement that health care is a *right*: "Making health care a right and not a privilege is something worth fighting for." The concept of access to health care as a right is not a common approach among politicians in the United States and, even when voiced in terms of right, may be more rhetorical than a plea for fundamental reform.

Kerry's extensive proposals for reform of the U.S. health care system can be read in his published platform; the phraseology "universal health care" or a "single-payer" system—the essential aspects of the Canadian system—are avoided. Americans are often leery of referring to fundamental concepts that may give rise to controversy, preferring to work out reforms in practice and to avoid disputes over language. At a meeting organized some years ago by the Science and Human Rights Program of the American Association for the Advancement of Science (AAAS), a doctor noted for his care of underprivileged minorities voiced objection to the use of the concept as a "right to health care." Dr. H. Jack Geiger, M.D., was reported as stating, "The establishment of a right to health care is of no functional consequence in the U.S., and is diversionary from the important issues—determining a minimum adequate standard of health care, and addressing the needs of vulnerable populations. Recognition of a right to health care would require wildly redistributive policies."[23] Dr. Geiger's remarks illustrate the American tendency to avoid reference to ideologically stated values and are particularly striking because of his own dedication to medical service for the poor. The American approach appears to be better "to do" than engage in divisive ideological discussions.

In 1991, *Rights to Health Care* was published as one of a series of volumes on philosophy and medicine, with chapters by American medical practitioners and philosophers focusing on the right to health care.[24] This dated publication remains of interest today. Baruch A. Brody, Ph.D., then Leon Jaworski Professor of Medical Ethics at Baylor College of Medicine and Professor of Philosophy, Rice University, Houston, Texas, expressed doubts as to whether philosophical references to a "right to health care" had practical value. He wrote,

The rise in health care costs has indicated to us that our policy discussions need to focus on the question of how much health care we are going to provide to those who cannot afford to pay for it. It is . . . a question about the many diagnostic and therapeutic inventions that might be used with some benefit but at a considerable cost. These day by day decisions are far more important to shaping the structure of American health care than some much discussed esoteric decisions. I know of no discussion of the right to health care and the correlative social obligation that provides us with a framework for resolving these questions.[25]

The editors of the Bole and Bondeson volume also expressed their rejection of the right to health care: "After all, claims regarding justice in health care or about rights to health care limit the property rights of those whose resources will be used to provide care. The languages of rights to health care or justice in health care, if secured, lead to others having duties to give aid and to relinquish claims over their own time, money and resources. The languages of rights to health care and of justice in health care construe much of what is unfortunate as also unfair in the sense of supporting moral claims for particular allocations of health care."[26]

The answer of my SUNY-Buffalo students, that there is no right to health care in the United States, would not strike most Americans as unusual. It has frequently been pointed out that the rights-based approach of the U.S. Constitution is reflective of an individualistic, liberal tradition in which social rights have no real place.[27] In 1983, the President's Commission for the Study of Ethical Problems in Medicine and Biomedical and Behavioral Research published a report titled *Securing Access to Health Care*, in which the commission explicitly rejected the concept of a right to health care as an ethical basis for reform of the health care system. In its report, the commission stated that its conclusions were better expressed in terms of "ethical obligations" rather than rights. They concluded that society has a moral obligation to achieve equity in health care, but stated that they had "chosen not to develop the case for achieving equitable access through the assertion of a right to health care."[28]

Is John Kerry's reference in his platform to a *right* to health care indicative of a changing mentality in the United States, or is the negative reaction of the AMA to the proposal of the PNHP more indicative of the continuing dominant U.S. view? The United States appears to be moving cautiously toward extending health care benefits to more citizens, but without a fundamental ideological change of mentality that would logically lead to more drastic reform.

Conclusion

This chapter has focused on the health care *systems* of the United States and Canada, but a consideration of the health *status* of the populations—particularly minorities—in the two countries is an important, perhaps even a necessary, complement to an evaluation of the *systems*. An evaluation of the health care systems in the two countries appears unduly limited. In both countries, the health *status* of minority populations is far below that of the majority. Health *status* touches on many aspects of the health condition of populations beyond the provision, or lack of provision, of health *care*. The importance of the distinction between health *care* and health *status* is clearly brought out in the chapter of the *Romanow Report* on Aboriginal health.[29] "[T]here are deep and continuing disparities between Aboriginal and non-Aboriginal Canadians both in their overall health and in their ability to access health care services. The reasons for this are complex and relate to a number of different factors, *many of which have less to do with health and more to do with social conditions*" (emphasis added).[30] The references to "health" independently of the phrase "health care" emphasize that there is a distinction between health care and health status. It refers to the disparities between the health status of Aboriginal peoples and other Canadians: their life expectancy is shorter, and young Aboriginals are more frequently exposed to problems such as alcohol abuse and drug addiction. "Combined with pervasive poverty, persistent racism and a legacy of colonialism, Aboriginal peoples have been caught in a cycle that has been perpetuated across generations."[31] Aboriginal representatives in testimony before the Romanow commission emphasized the health disparities between other Canadians and Aboriginal peoples: growing rates of HIV infection, cardiac problems, high disability rates, and, especially, mental disabilities.

Even in a system that attempts to provide universal health care, disparities may thus remain in the health status of the general population and the disadvantaged, suggesting that factors other than the provision of health care are involved. In the United States, the problem of health status is even more striking than in Canada—the poor and minorities have the worst health status—but they are also among the many Americans that lack even the basic health care generally available to minorities in Canada.

The preamble to the World Health Organization (WHO) constitution[32] refers to the "highest attainable standard of *health*"; there is no mention of *health care* in the preamble, although other parts of the constitution refer to *strengthening health services* among a long list of WHO objectives. Internationally, the shorthand term *right to health* is used as a shorter version of the longer language of the WHO constitution: "the enjoyment of the highest attainable standard of health."

The use of the preferred expression "right to health" internationally has implications beyond the more limited concept of the "right to health care." It implies that health status is often determined by social conditions and not solely by the provision of health care. This chapter has focused on *health care,* but a more comprehensive follow-up study might usefully focus on the broader social conditions in the United States and Canada that affect the *right to health*—but that is a study for another day.

Chapter 8
International Labor Rights and North American Labor Law

James B. Atleson

A number of writers sympathetic to labor have recently argued that the humanitarian and justice concerns that should, even they often do not, underlie American labor law or American judicial and administration decisions should again be stressed.[1] Historian Nelson Lichtenstein, for instance, argues that "questions involving the dignity and the value of work" should return to the national agenda. The goal is to once again make a resolution of the labor question seem "synonymous with the economic and civil health of the society as a whole."[2] It is not uncommon for supporters of labor and unions in the United States to focus on the human principles supposedly underlying American labor law. These concerns have not been foreign to discussions and analyses of American labor law, and they motivate much of the progressive scholarship in the area. Overwhelmingly, however, the administrative and judicial approach in American law has been pragmatic, as if the only purposes of the National Labor Relations Act (NLRA) were merely functional or practical, for instance, based on economic efficiency.

Concededly, many of the bases of the NLRA of 1935, indeed of much of New Deal legislation, revolved around very pragmatic, utilitarian assumptions. Thus, the most common argument in favor of the statute proposed by Senator Wagner of New York was that it would reduce "industrial strife," which interfered with interstate commerce. This argument, stressed repeatedly in the statute's preamble, was no doubt framed with an eye to the likely constitutional hurdle the statute would face before the Supreme Court,[3] and yet this was certainly a useful and reasonable argument to make in a period of sustained labor warfare. It is likely that the outpouring of worker dissent created both the conditions for the statute's passage and the ultimate Supreme Court declaration that it was constitutional.

A second theme, mentioned explicitly in the statute's preamble, was that the economy would be strengthened by independent unions that would insist on a more equitable division of profits, thereby maintaining public purchasing power. The statute, therefore, viewed unions as antidepression devices. An influential group in FDR's government viewed the Great Depression as being caused by under-consumption. Unions, therefore, were seen as possessing positive social functions, and the state would support and encourage their growth while simultaneously restricting antiunion corporate power.

Closely related, the most important theme in all of Wagner's speeches was that the statute would create greater economic stability because of the creation of a better economic balance between conflicting forces. That is, unionization and collective bargaining would promote a higher level of real wages and a better distribution of the national income.[4] In other words, unions would serve a public function, as they would reallocate wealth.

There were also broader goals underlying the act. Thus, Wagner repeatedly argued that political democracy would be given deeper roots by encouraging democratic processes in the work life of employees. Industrial democracy, albeit vaguely defined, was important not only in its own right but also because it would strengthen attachments to the principles of political democracy thought to be threatened in the mid-1930s. The lights were beginning to go out in Europe, and many in the United States felt liberal democracy was threatened from both the Left and the Right.

The Supreme Court, however, has historically ignored all of the broader goals of the act, tending to rely only on the aim of reducing industrial warfare. This preference perhaps might explain why the overwhelming trend since World War II has been the narrowing of the act or at least decisions that did not expand its protective scope. Moreover, because the assumption is that the NLRA was solely enacted for instrumental purposes, it is not premised on any set of inherent worker rights. Thus, in the Supreme Court's *Emporium Capwell*[5] decision in 1975, the Court said in referring to NLRA, section 7, the source of all rights under the act, "These are, for the most part, collective rights, rights to act in concert with one's fellow employees; they are protected not for their own sake but as an instrument of the national labor policy of minimizing industrial strife 'by encouraging the practice and procedure of collective bargaining.'"

In other words, the reigning legal view is that workers have only those rights found in statutes or individual or collective bargaining agreements. Moreover, the assertion of worker rights often confronts values of property, often deeply held by decision makers. If worker rights are only granted because of their social utility, then their assertion can be overcome by stressing the greater social value of employer control over capital and property.

Thus, the notion that American law is or should be based on some set of inherent rights that employees possess apart from their economic or social value is not an easy one to make in the United States, a country whose history shows a pattern of hostility or indifference to worker rights. Although one could tease out concepts of justice, liberty, and freedom underlying the statute, one has to overcome the strong functional bias inherent in labor thought in the United States. This makes it difficult to try to use the corpus of international labor law. As my former colleague, Virginia Leary, has noted, labor lawyers and unions, at least in the United States, have generally not stressed international labor rights, and at the same time, international human rights groups have tended not to focus on labor rights, at least not collective rights.[6] The statute itself, however, uses concepts and even language that suggest that human rights arguments might have some traction. For instance, the preamble of the NLRA stresses the importance of guaranteeing workers "full freedom of association," including the right to pick "representatives of their own choosing," language closely paralleling international labor rights documents.[7]

International Labor Rights

Few American lawyers, I would venture to suggest, have any knowledge of the conventions and standards set by the International Labor Organization (ILO), a special UN agency, let alone relevant provisions of UN conventions and covenants.[8] It is true that many believe that the ILO, while perhaps useful in setting standards, can be ignored, because it has little ability to enforce them. Indeed, given that it has a tripartite representational structure, with each country sending a team consisting of representatives of labor, employers, and the state, there may be a close relationship between the protective standards that are set and the knowledge that they have no direct enforceability.

Nevertheless, when one looks at the content of ILO and UN conventions and documents, it seems surprising that these principles or standards are not better known and employed by unions and their supporters in the United States. For instance, in 1998, the ILO issued its Declaration on Fundamental Principles and Rights at Work. The ILO attempted to stress and specify which of the many work rights dealt with in numerous ILO conventions were "fundamental." Freedom of association and the right to organize and bargain collectively were recognized as critical rights.[9]

There are three international documents relating to collective labor relations apart from those produced by the ILO. First, the Universal Declaration of Human Rights of 1948 states that "everyone has the right of peaceful assembly and association" and "the right to form and join trade unions for the protection of his interests."[10] Second, the International Covenant on Civil and Political Rights, one of the few human rights documents ratified by the United States, states that everyone "shall have the right to freedom of association with others, including the right to form and join unions for the protection of his interests."[11] The International Covenant on Economic, Social and Cultural Rights obliges states to "insure the right of everyone to form trade unions and join the trade union of his choice . . . the right of trade unions to function freely . . . [and] the right to strike."[12] Finally, other documents illustrate the importance of freedom of association. For instance, the UN Sub-Commission on the Promotion and Protection of Human Rights recently issued a set of norms for transnational enterprises that, among other things, obligates these corporations to ensure freedom of association and the recognition of the right to collective bargaining. Transnational corporations are to implement the norms via internal rules of operation, and states should establish an appropriate legal and administrative framework for insuring that the norms are indeed implemented.[13]

As Human Rights Watch noted in *Unfair Advantage*, the International Labor Organization, "with nearly universal membership and tripartite representation by governments, workers, and employers, recognizes freedom of association and protection of the right to organize as core workers' rights. Over decades of painstaking treatment of allegations of violation of workers' rights, the ILO committee on Freedom of Association has elaborated authoritative guidelines for implementation of the rights to organize, the right to bargain collectively and the right to strike."[14]

The labor law world is probably more familiar with the products of the ILO. The relevant sections of the 1998 Declaration were based on two earlier ILO conventions, numbers 87 and 98. Convention 87 deals explicitly with freedom of association and the protection of the right to organize: "Workers and employers, without distinction whatsoever, shall have the right to establish and, subject only to the rules of the organization concerned, to join organizations of their own choosing without previous authorization." Convention 87 recognizes that workers have rights to establish functioning labor unions, and it obliges ILO member states to develop laws and regulations to protect those rights. Although Convention 87 is often referred to as the Convention on Freedom of Association, other important rights are also included, such as the right of employee organizations to draw up their own constitutions and rules, elect their own representatives, join federations, and formulate their own programs and goals without any interference by state authorities.

Convention 87 established principles and guarantees involving the right to organize in relation to the state, protects workers in their organizations, especially from employers, and Number 98 promotes voluntary collective bargaining to create conditions of employment. As Lee Swepston has noted, "The two instruments taken together contain the essential elements for the creation, administration, and functioning of employers and workers' organizations."[15]

Convention 98 also protects against anti-union discrimination. It bars conditioning employment on not joining a union and forbids any discrimination or prejudice because of participation in union activities. States are required to take those steps necessary to encourage and promote "the full development and utilization of machinery for voluntary negotiation between employers and workers' organizations, with the view to the regulation of terms and conditions of employment by means of collective agreements."[16]

Finally, the more recent Declaration on Fundamental Principles and Rights at Work provides that, as if clearly written with the United States in mind, "all members, even if they have not ratified the conventions in question, have an obligation rising from the very fact of membership in the organization, to respect, to promote, and to realize, in good faith and in accordance with the [ILO] constitution, the principles concerning the fundamental rights which are subject of those conventions, namely: (a) freedom of association and the effective recognition of the right to collective bargaining."

Although there are many conventions and standards issued by the ILO, the 1998 Declaration focused on four that it deemed fundamental: freedom of association and the effective recognition of the right to collective bargaining, the elimination of all forms of forced or compulsory labor, the abolition of child labor, and freedom from discrimination in respect of employment and occupation. The Declaration does not seek to impose any new obligations on member states, but reaffirms the obligations states have as members to respect fundamental rights. The assumption is that, by voluntarily joining the ILO, each member has endorsed the principles and rights set out in its constitution and the Declaration of Philadelphia, which either implicitly or expressly recognized the rights included in the 1998 Declaration.[17]

The United States supported the adoption of the ILO's Declaration on Fundamental Principles and Rights at Work, and according to the

ILO the United States is bound to respect general rules such as Conventions 87 and 98, even without ratification.[18] There are many other standards adopted by ILO that, rationally or not, after 1998, are not deemed "fundamental." The ILO has adopted 184 conventions and 192 recommendations. Among these are many relating to employment, wages, health and safety, social security, employment of women, migrants, and children, but I wish to focus only on those provisions which relate to collective worker action, that is, labor-management relations.

Although 122 of the ILO's 174 member states are bound by Convention 87, barely half the world's population live in countries that have ratified it, and few of the most populated countries have done so.[19] Nevertheless, as noted earlier, the ILO takes the position that all states that are members of the ILO, meaning virtually all states in the world, are covered by the 1998 Declaration and its follow-up.

One significant aspect of these documents is their collective focus. Although human rights are generally considered to be individual rights, both labor rights and human rights obviously have a collective dimension. Indeed, even rights initially considered individual rights, such as hours of work or social security, are in fact meaningful only when exercised in a collective manner.

Although the ILO has limited authority to enforce its standards,[20] there is evidence that the standards have some meaningful impact in some parts of the world.[21] Lawyers outside North America often cite these standards in their briefs, and they have been cited in some judicial decisions as well.[22] Even the United States has relied upon the ILO/UN standards. Thus, they are used to set the labor standards of the U.S. Generalized System of Preferences, as well as the Labor Side Agreement of the North American Free Trade Agreement.[23] Moreover, they are regularly used privately to create the standards in voluntary corporate codes.

The United States has been brought before the ILO's Committee on Freedom of Association twenty-seven times, ten times after 1982. Notable challenges were made to the doctrine that strikers can be permanently replaced[24] and to exclusion of many state and federal workers from collective bargaining.[25] These complaints were sustained by committee rulings, but the decisions have had no impact on U.S. law.

Interestingly, the number of claims, even successful ones against a country, is not intuitively indicative of its labor standards. Thus, more than sixty complaints have been filed against Canada since 1982, most of which have been "successful." The committee reached a conclusion in forty-nine complaints, finding freedom of association violated in thirty-five of the cases.[26]

The Weaknesses of Domestic Labor Law

The potential of using international human rights in the United States is significant. The weaknesses of the NLRA, stemming primarily from its interpretation rather than its text, are well known and need not be listed in depth. The following is a brief summary that suggests the scope of the problem. Workers in the United States cannot simply form a union and then require the employer to bargain with it, for, despite the apparent meaning of the NLRA,[27] employers may require that questions of representation are to be decided in NLRB-sponsored elections. In election periods, which usually last between a month and a half to two months, employers often mount vigorous campaigns to persuade employees to vote against the union. The referendum often focuses not on the willingness of employees to seek collective representation but, instead, whether they wish to maintain their employment. This means that for a period of at least a month or two the employer is permitted to state its view as to why unionization would be a bad thing. Employer views carry great weight, and it is clear that during this period unions generally lose support. Threats are not permitted, but interference and implied threats are difficult to prove, especially in the appellate courts, which, depending on your point of view, have historically been more supportive either of employers or their right to free speech.

In 75 percent of organizing campaigns, employers hire antiunion consultants, and 92 percent of employers force employees to attend antiunion meetings. Significantly, in 51 percent of campaigns, employers threaten to close the workplace if the union wins. Although this is generally unlawful, remedies are weak, and rerun elections rarely overcome the effect of a threat to move or close. For instance, employers in 71 percent of campaigns in manufacturing use this threat, and these threats to move overseas must be taken seriously.[28] A relatively new antiunion technique is to call in federal immigration agents.

The most effective weapon is probably the discharge of union supporters. During organizing campaigns, one-fourth of private sector employers fire at least one worker for union activity. Studies vary as to how many workers are illegally fired during organizational campaigns, and the percentages range from 1 to 10, 1 to 16 or perhaps 1 to 48. Because evidence indicates that employees believe that all discharges during election campaigns are discriminatory, the great incidence of discharges is serious.

Moreover, there has been a significant increase over time in the number and the percentage of employees discharged, the amount of back pay awarded by the National Labor Relations Board (NLRB), and the volume of unfair labor practices committed by employers in organizational campaigns. As Paul Weiler of Harvard Law School notes, "Perhaps the most remarkable phenomenon in the representation process in the past quarter-century has been an astronomical increase in unfair labor practices by employers."[29] For instance, from 1957 to 1965, unfair labor practices charges against employers increased by 200 percent while the number of certification elections increased by only 50 percent.[30] Between 1965 and 1980, unfair labor practice charges against employers increased another 200 percent. Moreover, the percentage of these charges found meritorious by the NLRB remained roughly consistent. As mentioned earlier, discharge of union supporters is common. In 1998, twenty-four thousand workers proved that employers had illegally discriminated against them for engaging in union activity (i.e., they received back pay). Thus, the conclusion is inescapable—"employers are increasingly violating employees' rights, especially the right to engage in union activities. Even the increase in back pay awards . . . has not stemmed the tide of employer lawlessness."[31]

Just as seriously, recent studies demonstrate that unfair employer labor practices do affect the outcome of representational elections. That is, the chances of a union victory in an election are reduced when employers engage in unfair labor practices. Finally, many unions, after successfully winning certification rights in board-sponsored elections, fail to secure a first collective bargaining agreement in one out of every four first contract negotiations,[32] and statutory violations during an election campaign are predictive of failure.

In short, studies demonstrate that the outcome elections and the securing of first collective bargaining agreements are critically affected by employer resistance and unfair labor practices. The law simply does not serve as a very effective deterrent to violations, and most important, the remedial measures of the board are not sufficient to overcome the value to employers of unlawful action.

There may be many causes of union weakness, but one clear example is this overt lawlessness. One cannot simply point to an assumed unwillingness of American workers to join unions, or their adoption of some form of rugged individualism. Indeed, in one poll, more than 40 percent of non-union workers stated that they would prefer to be represented by a union. Yet, in a Peter D. Hart Research Associates' poll in February 2003, employees stated that they believed their employers would oppose any attempt to form a union, and other polls indicate that most workers believe that organization would place their jobs at risk. A 1984 Harris poll of non-union workers indicated that 43 percent believed that their employer would either discharge or otherwise discriminate against union supporters in an organizing campaign.[33]

Another study indicated that 36 percent of workers who were opposed to a union said they voted "no union" because of management pressure. In the public sector, on the other hand, where managers rarely opposed unions vigorously, if at all, unions win more than 80 percent of representation elections, compared to about 50 percent in the private sector.

These election problems are avoided in most Canadian provinces and, under federal law, unions can secure recognition and bargaining rights through signed authorization cards. Five provinces require a certification vote, however, although the election period is short; that is, an election is held within five or seven days of a union's application.

Most discussions of the weaknesses of U.S. labor law, especially those dealing with the relevance of international labor law, have stressed the representation process and its adverse effect on the freedom of association. Yet, even if the NLRA provided significant and enforceable rights to employees, thousands of employees are excluded from the coverage of the act. For instance, not only does the act rationally exclude those covered by the Railway Labor Act—those not in interstate commerce or working for public entities—but agricultural workers, domestic workers, supervisors, and independent contractors, often defined broadly by the courts, are also excluded.[34] The United States, however, is not alone in excluding domestic and agricultural workers from basic labor legislation. Ontario does as well, and it also excludes hunters, trappers, lawyers, land surveyors, dentists, doctors, and architects.[35]

Another substantive problem, however, which surely involves the effective use of freedom of association or collective bargaining, is the limit to the right to take effective collective action. Limitations on the ability of public sector workers in the United States to take collective action has drawn international attention, but private sector workers face at least two serious problems. First, the clearest denial of the right to strike in the United States is a 1938 decision by the Supreme Court that to permanently replace strikers is not an interference with the right to strike.[36] What was an aside in the decision has now become settled law, despite the explicit protection for the right to strike in the statute. In addition, many countries, not only the United States, limit the type of collective action that unions can lawfully take, and this is especially true of sympathetic or secondary action, which is of increasing concern in a global world. Although the ILO's Committee on Freedom of Association has interpreted ILO conventions to protect secondary and sympathetic action, indeed, even political strikes, this type of solidarity action is clearly unlawful under the law of many states.[37]

The right to strike is generally protected by domestic law in developed countries, but strikes in particular situations may not be. Thus, even some types of economic strikes may be prohibited by statute or by contract.[38] Obviously, statutory prohibitions hinder solidarity actions and limit the ability of unions to respond to the new global world.[39] In the United States, at least, this is not surprising. U.S. courts and the NLRB have already made it difficult for unions to deal with multiunit and multiple-location firms and, especially, conglomerates.[40] In Canada, statutes have not altered the common law's hostility to sympathetic or secondary actions, even when the target is not other workers but consumer choices to shop elsewhere or to boycott particular products. And Japan, like some European countries, confines protected strikes to the specific workplace in which the dispute occurred. Thus, domestic legal restrictions provide serious obstacles to transnational labor activity, although unlawful action will, nevertheless, occur. The practical effect of such legislation, in Kenneth Wedderburn's words, "is to fragment and inhibit trade union action while the power of internationalized capital is constitutionally guaranteed the maximum flexibility."[41]

Secondary action is critical for labor to respond to contractors who bid against others in order to secure orders, for instance, from design houses or sneaker brand firms. Let me offer a domestic example of a problem that could easily be described in global terms. Hundreds of janitors in Los Angeles and other large cities work for contractor firms that bid for maintenance and cleaning work from office building owners. Wages and benefits, as they have been historically, are the cost items most under the contractors' control, and they are therefore kept low. To organize the contractors will be unhelpful as there will be non-union firms that can underbid them for cleaning work. Yet the building owners are usually deemed neutral employers, and pressure against them is often considered unlawful.[42] This parallels the international contracting system where, for instance, Nike, Levi Strauss, and many other brand names deal with production.

Concededly, the right to strike is not explicitly set out in any international labor organization convention or recommendation, yet the right is assumed to be critical. In addition, the Committee on Freedom of Association considers the right to strike to be a "basic right," even though the right is not explicitly expressed in the body's constitution or important labor conventions such as Conventions 87 and 98. The ILO's Committee of Experts as well as the Committee on Freedom of Association have created a considerable body of law on the right to strike by implication from a number of articles in Convention 87, considering the right to be "one of the essential means available to workers and their organization for the promotion of their social and economic interests."[43]

As I have noted elsewhere,[44] it is becoming more likely that worker interests will be affected by disputes in other countries. Nevertheless, several countries, including Canada and the United States, prohibit solidarity efforts on the grounds that sympathy or secondary strikes affect those employers not in a position to satisfy their workers' demands or because the goal of the pressure does not involve narrow collective bargaining concerns. Yet a number of European nations protect solidarity strikes if the workers can demonstrate a sufficient community of interest with the strikers, although the definition of "interest" may vary and may be tested objectively or subjectively. Spain, Ireland, Italy, and France protect solidarity actions so long as workers are acting in defense of what they perceive to be their interest in the primary dispute. Other nations have explicitly recognized the legitimacy of solidarity actions to protect or respect employees elsewhere or to respond to disputes in other countries.[45]

Nevertheless, although the state of U.S. labor law might suggest the value of international labor law, the standards have had little salience in normal domestic legal practice or discussion in the United States. As mentioned earlier, not only has the United States failed to ratify most of the ILO conventions, but it is also safe to say that most American lawyers do not know about international labor law. And if they were aware, it is not at all clear that they would attempt to use those standards. In part this is because American labor lawyers, given their pragmatism, will not rely on documents that they perceive will have little impact on American courts or agencies. Moreover, international law is seen as "soft" law, or law that cannot be enforced. Lawyers seek to advance client interests, that is, they aspire rather than inspire.

Conclusion

It is true that there are numerous scholarly texts in the United States demonstrating that the NLRA is not effectively enforced and that the statute has been whimsically or narrowly defined. Nevertheless, the notion is strong in the United States that international law is simply not useful to affect outcomes in domestic cases. Thus, it is not at all clear that the argument that labor rights are human rights will have positive effects in the United States. If the argument is asserted, some will adopt human rights as simply a useful lever to try to advance labor rights in the United States.

It is clear, however, that for labor law to change in the United States, there must in fact be a change in the way labor is perceived. As I have argued elsewhere, many believe it is time to alter not only the legal rules themselves but also the ideas and values embedded in those rules to alter the way workers in enterprise are regarded: "If this does not occur, legal conflicts will still involve the rights of workers perceived to have limited abilities and thus limited rights to involve them in the workplace, challenging what is thought to be the greater wisdom and the 'property' rights of employers. The goal should be to develop a vocabulary that treats workers as a valuable, organic part of the enterprise, as long-term participants with the valuable investment and citizenship stake in the operation."[46]

It is possible that international labor rights, if seen as relevant in the United States, will aid the necessary re-envisioning of worker rights. Yet, focusing on the United States, I would certainly not argue that a change in ideas, no matter how important, will come about simply by argument or by academic scholarship. The most effective stimulus for labor law reform, I believe, is a vibrant, assertive labor movement. I understand that this may seem ironic in a period where organized labor seems weak and far from militant. Yet, from the vantage point of American history, the Wagner Act of 1935 remains the only federal statute that is directly supportive of collective action. Its passage, given the more common response of the courts, legislature, and executive labor issues during most of American history, suggests that "it is only when unions are perceived to be a force to be reckoned with that the legal system responds in favorable ways. Although the legal system acts repressively, there will be little possibility of a positive response unless unions are perceived to be vital and troublesome economic actors."[47]

As Virginia Leary has noted, there is a clear connection between the notion of human rights and social justice, upon which most labor principles are based. She has noted, "We use the terminology of 'human rights' rather than 'social justice,' but human rights cannot exist without social justice. The rights of workers must be seen as essential to issues of social justice, human rights, and democracy and must be promoted as such."[48]

Chapter 9
Deconstructing Barriers
The Promise of Socioeconomic Rights for People with Disabilities in Canada

Sarah Armstrong, Mindy Noble, and Pauline Rosenbaum

Canada acceded to the International Covenant on Economic, Social and Cultural Rights (ICESCR) in 1976. Now, thirty years later, it is time to appraise our thinking, actions, and socioeconomic policies concerning people with disabilities in Canada to see how well we are living up to these commitments.

The government of Canada's voluminous reports and judicial decisions on disability issues indicate a shift in disability policy from a "worthy poor" approach to a human rights approach. This model may hold promise for disability equality. Indeed, the reports and the policies enacted pursuant to them suggest some willingness on the part of provincial and federal governments to design programs to fulfill the social and economic rights of people with disabilities. Unfortunately, it is not clear that these responses have had a meaningful impact.

People with disabilities remain a substantially disadvantaged minority in Canada. They are often unable to access a meaningful education. They are overrepresented among the poor, the unemployed, and social assistance recipients. Low socioeconomic status exacerbates disability as individuals must focus on obtaining the necessities of life and are unable to manage their health properly.

Current programs appear insufficient to meet the needs of people with disabilities and Canada's obligations under the ICESCR. It appears that, for all levels of government in Canada, social and economic rights continue to be viewed as "policy objectives" rather than fundamental human rights. Consequently, for many people with disabilities in Canada, the rights in the ICESCR are empty.

In this chapter, we first examine models of disability and how they reflect our understanding of disability rights. We then outline existing policies and jurisprudence affecting the socioeconomic rights of people with disabilities in Canada, with a particular focus on education, employment, and income maintenance. Finally, drawing on specific provisions of the ICESCR, we examine the impact of these policies and judicial decisions on the lives of Canadians with disabilities.

Models of Disability

The 1982 Canadian Charter of Rights and Freedoms (our fundamental constitutional guarantee of rights) (hereafter the Charter), provincial human rights legislation, and other laws about accessibility and barrier removal have all helped improve the lives of people with disabilities to a certain extent. However, much more can be done to recognize and enhance the values of participation, accommodation, and respect for difference.

In any given population, variations in physical and intellectual capabilities are natural occurrences. Several models have developed as ways to categorize these variations. Although the models differ in focus, each seeks to deal with the implications of disability for individuals and society. Each model has generated a group of so-called experts, a discourse and vocabulary, and a representative image of people with disabilities.[1] Each also points to different normative bases on which to ground social obligations. International standards to describe and measure health and disability have shifted from measuring disability according to mortality rates to evaluating how people live with their health status and how conditions can be improved for each person to achieve productivity and individual fulfillment.[2] We now canvas three standard models of disability (the biomedical, economic, and sociopolitical/human rights models) to introduce the frameworks and underlying theories that have informed much of Canadian disability policy in the twentieth century.

Biomedical Model

The biomedical model relies on what some view as a commonsense approach to disability, in that there is nearly always a biomedical condition underlying an individual's experience of disabling phenomena in society. Typically, people who experience "disablement" have a "significant level of physical, sensory or mental incapacity which affects their daily life in some way."[3] This model sees disability as an "individual pathology" related to the physiological, biological, or cognitive impairment of a particular person.[4] The person with a disability might be seen as sick, injured, or having an illness arising from birth, accident, or chronic causes. As Lepofsky points out, illness and disability may be intertwined: "Illness can cause a disability. A disability can make a person susceptible in some circumstances to illness. A pre-existing disability can compound some conditions caused by the disability including circumstances of pain."[5]

Under the biomedical model, social policy centers on medical and health intervention, focusing on prevention, cure, containment of disease, pain management, rehabilitation, and palliative care.[6] Accordingly, our measure of accommodating disability also comes from the medical field. This model is sometimes criticized as being insensitive to the social character of disability and to the impact of disability on the socioeconomic dimensions of the lives of people with disabilities and their families.

Historically, the biomedical paradigm has informed Canadian disability policy. As Rioux and Prince argue, Canada's welfare state traces its roots to the English Poor Laws, "which established a distinction between the worthy and the unworthy poor."[7] People who were physically and mentally able but who appeared unwilling to work were considered unworthy of state aid, whereas the "worthy poor" (people with disabilities, seniors, and other infirm people) were entitled to some form of assistance. The state used distinctions based on individual impairment (and the "special needs" created thereby) to establish legal and social paradigms differentiating the worthy from the unworthy.[8]

Economic Model

The economic model sees disability in terms of the various *disabling effects* of an impairment on a person's capabilities, and in particular on labor and employment capabilities. According to this model, disability is a function of the limitations on a person's productivity, capacity, and skills. Economic analysis of disability balances the value of the labor capacity of the person with a disability against the societal cost of assisting people with disabilities to participate in the labor market and daily life. The person with a disability "embodies an economic cost that must be factored into society-wide economic policy decisions."[9] Disability equality claims are explicitly subject to cost-benefit analyses, which are often a product of a short-term outlook about the economic impact of providing a service or benefit to a class of people rather than long-term estimations of the potential contributions of people with disabilities to the labor market or to the purchasing market in general.

When the view is short term, people with disabilities face a double bind: it is seen as too costly to accommodate and integrate them into the workplace, so they cannot gain a livelihood through the labor market, and their purchasing power and ability to contribute to the economy is thereby removed. The economic model would not be inappropriate if its cost-benefit analysis were properly calibrated, without inappropriate and stereotypical assumptions about alleged exorbitant up-front costs of accommodation.

Sociopolitical/Human Rights Model

The sociopolitical approach to disability, reflecting ideas about how social systems create handicapping conditions, draws from emancipatory civil rights discourse.[10] This movement owes much of its framework to British sociologist Michael Oliver, who developed the idea of disability as a *social* construction based on *physical* difference.[11] The sociopolitical approach seeks to reveal the many "societal factors which interplay with personal experiences and together create, reinforce and potentially perpetuate the subordination of people with disabilities."[12] The social model shifts focus from the so-called impaired individual to the disabling effects of the social environment. Disability is seen as a social injustice attributed to stigmatizing attitudes and discriminatory practices within society. Because society's structures and customs are not necessarily fixed and inflexible, the sociopolitical model posits that barriers preventing full access and participation are socially constructed. Therefore, the agenda for reform under this model seeks to remove handicapping phenomena.

Barriers can be removed under this model by framing arguments that consciously adopt rights language. This strategy can work well in Canada because disability is a prohibited ground of discrimination in constitutional and human rights legislation. Advocates can seize upon the strategies of so-called minority group politics, which work to increase the opportunities and social benefits available to various constituencies, to seek political power and recognition and to validate and celebrate their group identity by creating a sense of solidarity.[13] This model can also encourage self-organization, capitalizing on the notion that people with disabilities—not politicians, health care professionals, or economists— are the experts on living with disability and should form networks and focus their energies on the needs and goals that they themselves identify.

However, there is ambivalence about whether to embrace a "minority rights" model as an appropriate representation of people with disabilities.[14] Identity politics requires that clear eligibility requirements define membership in a particular group, but this can be problematic with disability because of the difficulty in collecting and interpreting disability statistics, and because of the tendency to reinforce elements of the biomedical/epidemiological conception of disability by relying on empirical data to establish the incidence of disability.[15] Emphasizing the physical dimension of disability in order to utilize a minority rights strategy risks reinforcing the social separateness of people with disabilities and perpetuating their ghettoization.[16]

Within the sociopolitical framework lies another human rights model that may hold promise for disability equality: universalism. Sociologist Irving Zola argued that, in the long run, a coherent approach to disability must comprise "more universal policies that recognize that the entire population is 'at risk' for the concomitants of chronic illness and disability."[17] Disability is a non-discriminating condition that crosses the lines of race, sex, ethnicity, and the like, and it is linked to increased age. In this view, mobility, ability, intellect, and chemical-emotional makeup are all on a continuum, wherein everyone is in some ways "challenged" and in other ways "able." If we accept the promise of equal human dignity, and we consider that ability is on a continuum, the corollary is the proposition that human dignity attaches to each point on the continuum. This fundamental principle is a basis for all modern human rights: it underlies the grandest statements of universality, most notably in the Universal Declaration of Human Rights, which states that "recognition of the inherent dignity and of the equal and inalienable rights of all members of the human family is the foundation of freedom, justice and peace in the world."[18] The universalist model underscores the principle of equal dignity and fundamental human rights as it attaches human dignity to all points along the fluid, continuous, contextual conception of disability. As Bickenbach argues, universalist disablement policy "begins by demystifying the 'specialness' of disability."[19]

Disability Policy Relating to Social and Economic Rights in Canada

In this section, we outline existing Canadian public policy and judicial decisions affecting the socioeconomic rights of people with disabilities. We begin with an overview of Canada's federal structure and how this structure influences disability policy. We then examine how the entrenchment of the Charter has affected disability policy and the work of disability groups. Finally, we explore a selection of governmental policies designed to enhance the socioeconomic rights of people with disabilities in Canada in the areas of education, employment, and income security. Where appropriate, we also briefly mention judicial decisions.

Canada does not have a national disability law, such as the 1990 Americans with Disabilities Act (ADA) in the United States.[20] We are aware that the ADA is open to criticism on several fronts, which we do not intend to detail here, but we note the ADA's presence to highlight the fact that no Canadian jurisdiction has analogous comprehensive legislation. The province of Ontario does have a weak Ontarians with Disabilities Act, but in its current form it carries little weight.[21] Therefore, government social programs and court decisions have primacy in Canadian disability policy.

Canada's Federal Regime and Disability Policy

The framework for Canada's federal system of governance was set out in the British North America Act of 1867 and was supplemented by the Constitution Act, 1982. Together these documents are the supreme law of the land. Accordingly, all legislation and policies, emanating from all levels of government, must comply with their provisions. A basic understanding of the areas of federal and provincial responsibility is essential to this exploration of programs and policies affecting the economic and social rights of persons with disabilities in Canada.[22] Article 28 of the ICESCR states that the Covenant's provisions "shall extend to all parts of federal States without any limitations or exceptions." Thus, the federal and provincial governments are each bound by the ICESCR insofar as the obligations in the Covenant are within their areas of responsibility.

In general, jurisdiction over areas affecting the well-being of the entire country falls to the federal government. The federal government has responsibility for several income security and employment training programs. Provinces have jurisdiction over health- and welfare-related issues, with specific provisions granting them power over areas such as hospitals, municipal institutions, and property and civil rights.

In addition, the overlapping jurisdiction of these two levels of government complicates planning and delivery in several areas, including income security, health, education, welfare, and social services. Therefore, although health and social services are generally seen as areas of provincial jurisdiction, the federal government is heavily involved. With respect to disability policy, the federal government is involved in health and social services in three major ways. First, through the federal income tax system, it provides tax relief to people with disabilities for the costs of disability-related goods and services. Second, it delivers health and social services to Inuit and Aboriginal Canadians living on reserves. Finally, it transfers funds to the provinces for investment in health, education, welfare, and social services through the Canada Health and

Social Transfer (CHST). Disability advocates are increasingly focusing their attention on the federal minister of finance, because the minister is seen as a "major driver" of government policy, especially in areas of health and social services.[23]

There are frequent and ongoing conflicts over areas of overlapping jurisdiction and the amount of money transferred to the provinces for service delivery in areas such as health care and social services. Tjorman calls these conflicts a "major concern" for people with disabilities: "[T]he federal-provincial struggle and the rethinking of federalism in Canada have become the major concern of the disability community. There are two reasons for the marrying of these issues. Disability is on the federal agenda because Ottawa is trying to forge a new set of working relationships with the provinces. It has identified disability as a major focus for this work. . . . At the same time, federalism is on the agenda of the disability community which has long advocated for the need for a strong federal role to protect its issues and advocate its interests."[24]

The efforts of the federal and provincial governments on disability issues are well documented in several voluminous, well-intentioned task force reports.[25] Taken together, these reports illustrate a willingness to create and enhance programs and services for people with disabilities. They also show that Canadian governments increasingly view disability issues from a human rights perspective rather than from the "worthy poor" perspective, described earlier, which characterized much of the government's earlier disability policy. The reports also suggest that governments are becoming more open to providing opportunities to people with disabilities to influence the direction of the policies affecting them. What remains to be seen is whether there is adequate political will at both levels of government to inject the good intentions and human rights rhetoric found in these reports with adequate resources. Most importantly, as we discuss later, it does not yet appear that the ideas set out in the numerous reports have translated into enhanced socioeconomic rights for Canadians with disabilities.

The Prohibition of Disability Discrimination in the Charter

The Constitution Act, 1982, introduced a constitutionally entrenched Charter of Rights and Freedoms enshrining the democratic, mobility, legal, equality, and minority language rights of all Canadians. Of particular importance to people with disabilities, Section 15, on equality rights, specifically prohibits discrimination on the basis of physical or mental disability.[26] This provision in the Charter made Canada's constitution the first in the world to guarantee a right to equality for persons with disabilities.[27]

The inclusion of mental and physical disability in Section 15 of the Charter was the result of significant efforts by disability advocates.[28] When Section 15 was first presented to Parliament, it did not include such protection for people with disabilities. In fact, the federal government actively resisted disability groups, saying it was concerned that terms like "physical and mental disability" were too vague and that statutory human rights codes provided a better guarantee of equality for this group. It argued that it would be too expensive to fund new services potentially required by such a provision. However, at no point did the government set out the costs argument or present statistical support for this claim.[29]

Disability advocates actively resisted all of these claims. They forwarded several suggested definitions of disability and argued that terms such as "physical and mental disability" were no more difficult to define than other terms in the constitution, such as "religion." They refuted the cost argument, saying that there was no proof that disability equality would be more costly in the long term and that disability was the only ground of discrimination to which this cost-benefit analysis was being applied. Furthermore, disability advocates argued that existing statutory human rights codes could not provide universal protection.[30]

The disability community was assisted by the fact that the constitutional debate took place during the United Nations International Year of Disabled Persons (UNIYDP). One author described this timing as "fortuitous," arguing that it was "difficult for the government to ignore the demands of people with disabilities to have their rights enshrined in Canada's new Constitution."[31] This argument was reinforced by the fact that Canada had signed the 1975 Declaration of the Rights of Disabled Persons.[32] Both federal opposition parties had also made it clear that they supported the addition of disability to the Constitution Act.

The justice minister eventually decided to add "mental and physical disability" to the list of specifically protected grounds in Section 15 of the Charter. Constitutional recognition of their equality rights provided a significant boost for people with disabilities. As Peters commented, "to provide people with disabilities with constitutional recognition of their rights has certainly meant that people with disabilities have come a long way from being considered sick and in need of medical care."[33] Constitutional recognition of the rights of Canadians with disabilities provided a focal point for disability advocates and encouraged them to express their interests in rights-based language. Moreover, it prompted a dedicated network of disability advocates to enforce disability rights through the courts. These groups use the Charter in legal and political arenas to fight for the removal of barriers to the full participation of people with disabilities in all aspects of Canadian society and to prevent new barriers being erected.[34]

Disability Policies and Judicial Decisions

This section examines education, employment, and income mainte-nance/socioeconomic status to provide an overview of the policies of the federal and provincial governments in each area. Given the impor-tant role played by Charter jurisprudence in shaping Canadian social policy, this section also comments on judicial decisions touching on each area.

Education

The federal government recognized in its report *Advancing the Inclusion of Persons with Disabilities* that education is essential to the future for all people, particularly those with disabilities, and even more so for Aborigi-nal people with disabilities.[35] The report notes that education improves the chance of finding employment for all Canadians.[36] Government has a key role to play in ensuring that students with disabilities have equal access to education. The Supreme Court of Canada has stated that gov-ernments have an obligation to take positive steps to ensure that mem-bers of disadvantaged groups can equally access those benefits and services that the government provides to the general population.[37]

However, the provinces are responsible for providing education to most people living in Canada,[38] through schools, school boards, educa-tors, and specialized professionals. Approaches and policies relating to education for people with disabilities thus vary by province and, indeed, by individual school. Therefore, this section attempts to provide only a general overview of the approach that Canadian governments and courts have taken on the issue of equal access to education for children with disabilities in Canada.

For most of the twentieth century, educational policies regarding chil-dren with disabilities in Canadian provinces centered around institu-tionalization, segregation, and residential schooling.[39] By the 1920s, when most provincial legislation mandated compulsory public educa-tion, children with disabilities were excluded from public education or placed in special classes,[40] on the theory that including children with disabilities in regular classrooms would detract from the ability of other children to learn. At the end of the 1970s, there was still inadequate pro-vision for children with disabilities in the public school system—these children were typically sent to expensive private institutions or were home-schooled.[41] Parents and disability advocates lobbied governments to enact legislation to integrate students with disabilities into regular classrooms.

The equality rights provision of the Charter, which came into force in 1985, provided a new resource for parents and advocates. Integration was brought before the Supreme Court of Canada in *Eaton v. Brant County Board of Education*.[42] The case involved a claim by the parents of Emily Eaton, a twelve-year-old girl with cerebral palsy, alleging that the board violated her right to equality by moving her from her integrated classroom to a "special needs" class.

The Supreme Court decided that the board had not violated Section 15(1) of the Charter when it placed Emily in a special education class. While the Court acknowledged that integration should be a norm of general application, it did not apply this norm to Emily. Instead, the Court made the observation that the board had acted in Emily's best interest and then proceeded to ask Emily's parents to prove the disadvantages of a special education classroom. Disability advocates who wanted a presumption of integration applied in all cases saw this decision as a tremendous disappointment. Debate continues today over how best to provide education services to students with disabilities, but it is clear that governments must ensure that these students have equal access to education, whether in an integrated or a special education environment.

Employment

In 1996, the Federal Task Force on Disability Issues reported that employment was among the top concerns of Canadians with disabilities. The report said that work "is important for the dignity of individuals. People told us about the dignity of work, the sense of accomplishment it brings them, its value to the community and to society, and the way it contributes a sense of belonging. The tangible benefits of income, learning, and participating in the goals of an enterprise give us a sense of control over our destiny. Work is fundamental to one's sense of well-being and to citizenship."[43] Yet, in that same year, the federal census found that persons with disabilities were only half as likely to be employed as those without disabilities.[44] The likelihood of employment for women and Aboriginal Canadians with disabilities was even lower. Moreover, there was a huge gap between the earnings of people with disabilities and those for people without.[45]

Recognizing this, the federal and provincial/territorial governments set out five employment objectives for people with disabilities in their 1998 report *In Unison*. They sought to reduce reliance on income support programs, promote access to training programs available to all Canadians, increase the availability of work-related supports, encourage employers to make appropriate job/workplace accommodation, and promote work and volunteer opportunities for persons with disabilities. Both the 1998 *In Unison* report and the *In Unison 2000* report discuss opportunities for employment as a necessary element of full citizenship. They also emphasize the need for employers to take a proactive approach to recruiting and maintaining persons with disabilities as part of their workforce. Finally, they note the important role played by community organizations in facilitating workplace accommodation.

The rhetoric of citizenship, human rights, and dismantling barriers in these reports is crucial. It illustrates a shift away from previous policy approaches where people with disabilities were seen as unemployable objects of charity toward recognition that persons with disabilities have much to contribute to the workforce. In these reports, the government appears to adopt a perspective highlighting the human rights of people with disabilities and recognizing that disability often results from systemic barriers and socially constructed ideas about disability.

Two key programs run by Human Resources Development Canada, Employment Assistance for People with Disabilities (EAPD) and the Opportunities Fund for Persons with Disabilities (OF), attempt to put into action the objectives set out in the previously mentioned reports. EAPD is a joint federal-provincial/territorial program through which the government of Canada contributes funding for provincial programs and services designed to help working-age adults with disabilities prepare for, obtain, and retain employment. The programs and services delivered through EAPD vary among the provinces and tend to reflect local priorities and circumstances. The OF assists people with disabilities who do not qualify for benefits under Canada's Employment Insurance (EI) to prepare for, find, and maintain employment. Those who benefit from this program include social assistance recipients, those who have never worked, or those who have worked but have been unemployed for a prescribed length of time.[46]

Statutory federal and provincial human rights codes include physical and mental disability as prohibited grounds of discrimination. Under these codes, employers must not discriminate against people with disabilities and must accommodate them to the point of "undue hardship." The federal government has also introduced employment policies to improve the numbers of persons with disabilities working in the public and private sectors through the Employment Equity Act and the Federal Contractors Program.[47]

Income Maintenance/Socioeconomic Status

Three major types of social insurance are available to Canadians who meet the respective eligibility requirements. The first is the Canada/ Quebec Pension Plan.[48] The federal government and the provincial/territorial governments share responsibility for the Canada Pension Plan (CPP), which protects workers and their families from long-term or permanent interruption of earnings stemming from retirement, severe and prolonged disability, or death. The federal government administers the CPP disability program, a special income security program for Canadians with disabilities. Through this program, individuals who contributed to the CPP who can no longer work regularly, and their dependent children, are eligible to receive replacement earnings based on the amount and duration of their contributions to CPP while they were working.

The second type of social insurance available to Canadians is workers' compensation. The costs of this program, which replaces between 75 and 90 percent of lost insured earnings after occupational injury, disability, or disease, are covered entirely by employers. Workers' compensation programs exist in each jurisdiction in Canada.

The third type of social insurance is the aforementioned EI, a program administered by the federal government and designed to provide income protection from temporary work absences due to unemployment, illness, disability, or birth of a child. EI does not provide assistance to individuals who are out of work for a prolonged period of time. These individuals must seek assistance through CPP, discussed earlier, or through social assistance or "welfare," which is only available to Canadians who have exhausted all other avenues of support. In the area of housing, the federal government operates a program called Residential Rehabilitation Assistance Program for Persons with Disabilities (RRAP-D), through which they offer financial help to homeowners and landlords for eligible modifications that improve the accessibility of dwellings occupied by low-income persons with disabilities.[49]

Tjorman describes the current system of disability income support as a "patchwork of uncoordinated programs" composed of categorical systems that compensate for the effects of injuries from specific causes or events, social insurance, private insurance, and social assistance.[50] In part, this disjointed arrangement is a product of the division of responsibilities between the federal and provincial/territorial governments on these issues.

On a positive note, Rioux and Prince have commented that the shift in thinking and embracing of the human rights framework is also evident in the area of income assistance. They note: "Income assistance programs have been established that provide direct funding to people with disabilities to contract for their own choice of services, an alternative to traditional funding through service agencies. . . . All of these changes reflect a shift toward ensuring the social well-being of people with disabilities, their self-determination and participation in decisions that affect their person."[51]

Unfortunately, while the rhetoric in government reports and methods of program delivery appear to be moving to a human rights framework, governments across the country are cutting funding for social assistance and narrowing the eligibility criteria. These cuts directly conflict with Canada's obligations under the ICESCR and, it has been argued, the Charter.[52] For example, in *Masse v. Ontario*,[53] an Ontario court denied an equality challenge to a 21 percent cut to provincial social assistance rates. Although the court accepted evidence that the cuts would have an adverse impact on vulnerable groups, it rejected the claim on the grounds that economic and social rights were not justiciable and that such areas were far beyond its institutional competence.

While the Ontario Court of Appeal has recognized that receipt of social assistance is an analogous ground of prohibited discrimination under Section 15(1) of the Charter,[54] the Supreme Court of Canada has stopped short of saying that rights to equality and to security of the person impose positive obligations on governments to ensure an adequate level of income for Canadians when they are unable to provide for themselves. Specifically, in *Gosselin v. Quebec*,[55] the Supreme Court was asked to consider whether denying members of a disadvantaged group adequate financial assistance, resulting in homelessness and deprivation of other basic necessities, violates the Charter. The majority of the Court said that it did not. Notably, however, a dissenting judge unequivocally concluded that Section 7 of the Charter imposes a positive obligation on the state to offer basic protection for the life, liberty, and security of its citizens.

In short, several provincial and federal government programs provide income maintenance and social assistance to all Canadians, including Canadians with disabilities. Whether an individual with a disability is eligible for these programs and benefits often depends largely on the "cause of their disability—how and why the disability occurred—rather than on level of need."[56] Incongruity also exists among provinces, resulting in individuals with similar needs receiving very different levels of assistance depending on the cause of their disability and where they live in Canada.

The Current Status of People with Disabilities

Previously, we discussed policies and judicial decisions in the areas of education, employment, and income maintenance. Now we examine those areas to determine the impact of these policies and decisions on the lives of Canadians with disabilities. For each area, we consider our governments' goals in relation to the ICESCR and whether these policies and laws are achieving these goals, with a particular emphasis on the province of Ontario.

Education

While the right to education set out in Article 13 of the ICESCR is recognized in Canada, it is unclear whether people with disabilities are able to access this right in an appropriate and meaningful way. The Canadian Council on Social Development (CCSD), a nonprofit social policy and research organization, in 2001 released a report that indicated that approximately 30 percent of children under the age of eleven have a chronic condition or activity limitation.[57]

Another report by the Roehr Institute suggests that between 5 and 20 percent of families have children with disabilities, and that 15 percent of these children have a moderate or severe disability.[58] The notion that these children should receive equal access to education is not controversial. However, the definition of equal access is controversial. While some disability activists would like to see a presumption of integration into mainstream classrooms for all children with disabilities, others believe that the analysis should be more individualized or that a segregation model would be more beneficial.

Whether in a mainstream or integrated classroom, children with disabilities cannot enjoy the full benefit of their rights without proper supports. Educational assistants, therapists, adaptations, and other accommodations are necessary for children with disabilities to access an education that is "directed to the full development of the human personality and the sense of its dignity" as the ICESCR requires.

Parents of primary and secondary school-aged children with disabilities report that their children are sometimes unable to start school at the beginning of the school year, or are only able to attend part-time because supports and accommodations are not available.[59] In addition, those who can attend school find that their teachers are not provided with adequate training, information, or in-class support.[60] Without these supports, the quality of education for these children is compromised, and their right to education is not fully realized.

Many concerns have been raised regarding barriers to education for children with disabilities, including inappropriate responses to the behaviors linked to certain disabilities. In June 2000, the Ontario legislature passed the Safe Schools Act, 2000. This law applies to all publicly funded schools in Ontario and makes suspensions mandatory for specified infractions, such as uttering threats or swearing at teachers. Expulsions are mandatory for more serious offences, such as physical assaults. Although suspension or expulsion is not mandatory in circumstances where the student is unable to control his or her behavior, children with behavioral disabilities have been suspended or expelled for their disability-related behaviors.[61] This problem is exacerbated for children from immigrant or other minority groups, because language or cultural barriers may further impact their disadvantage.

Another area of concern is determining what constitutes proper accommodation for a particular child. In many cases, schools may have a different perception than parents, and some children lose significant portions of their school year because of disputes over appropriate accommodation. The Ontario Human Rights Commission has also received reports of private schools and vocational colleges refusing to permit students with disabilities to attend their schools or requiring students to waive their right to accommodation as a precondition to entrance.[62]

Children with disabilities who cannot properly access the education system are less likely to continue with higher education. The CCSD considered statistics from Statistics Canada's Survey of Labor and Income Dynamics[63] and found that, in 1998, only 36.4 percent of persons with disabilities between the ages of sixteen and sixty-four had graduated from a postsecondary program, as compared to 51.4 percent of persons without a disability. This is particularly problematic in light of the link between education and employment.

More than half (53.4 percent) of people with disabilities in the sixteen to thirty-four age group who did not have a high school diploma were unemployed, while only 14.7 percent of their non-disabled counterparts were unemployed. These numbers dropped to 39.4 percent and 6.8 percent, respectively, for those who had a high school diploma, and were even lower for people who had completed further schooling. Only 13 percent of people with disabilities with a postsecondary education reported that they were not in the labor force at all in 1998.[64] These statistics indicate the importance of accessing a meaningful and appropriate education for people with disabilities, and the impact of the inaccessibility of this right on the life of a person with a disability.

Employment

Despite the guarantee of the right to work in Article 6 of the ICESCR, Canadians with disabilities face many challenges in employment. For people with disabilities, the connection between employment and emotional well-being is especially strong. According to a CCSD report that analyzed Statistics Canada's National Population Health Survey 1998/99 (NPHS), individuals with disabilities who had been involved in the labor market in the previous year were more likely to report higher and more positive indicators of well-being than people with disabilities who had not been in the labor market. The difference between the two groups was not as pronounced for non-disabled individuals.[65] This research indicates that having a job has an even greater impact on measures of well-being for persons with disabilities than for non-disabled persons.

As noted earlier, the 1998 *In Unison* report listed five priorities with regard to employment for persons with disabilities. In this section we consider the impact of four of these goals. The issue of reliance on income support programs is discussed later in the chapter.

Promoting Access to Training Programs

Within the Canadian workforce, there is an increasing focus on education, training, and skills. It has become even more essential to ensure that persons with disabilities have access to the training programs available to non-disabled persons. The CCSD analyzed the data from Statistics Canada's 1999 Workplace and Employee Survey and found only small differences in percentages of people with and without disabilities who had no workplace training. The statistics indicated that 47.7 percent of men with disabilities reported having no training of any sort, compared with 46.9 percent of men without disabilities. For women, the statistics indicated that 45.1 percent of those with disabilities and 43.6 percent of those without disabilities had no training.[66]

However, significant differences existed between the groups of people with disabilities and those without with respect to the types of training that people had received. Persons without disabilities were more likely to have received classroom training (training related to one's job, with predetermined content), while persons with disabilities were more likely to have received on-the-job training (less formal learning during the course of employment). This may indicate that fewer resources are being allocated to training persons with disabilities.[67]

Increasing Work-Related Supports

As noted earlier, employment is an important factor in most people's sense of well-being, particularly for persons with disabilities. However, it is difficult to determine if having social supports facilitates paid work, or if paid work offers greater access to social supports. This effect likely goes both ways.

Encouraging Employers to Make Appropriate Accommodations.

Workers with disabilities report the highest level of job stress. They are twice as likely as non-disabled workers to report high stress and are more likely to report medium levels of job stress and to perceive that they will lose their job in the next year.[68]

For people with disabilities to be properly supported in the workplace, employers must develop a greater awareness of their employees' disabilities and further must work with these employees to ensure that their needs have been accommodated. Provincial human rights codes require private employers to make these accommodations. However, people with disabilities who make requests from their employers often face discriminatory attitudes, including the belief that the costs of accommodation are too high. Further education is required to ensure that employers develop a realistic knowledge of the costs associated with accommodation, as compared to the harm caused by refusing to accommodate and support employees with disabilities.

Promoting Work and Volunteer Opportunities

Promoting work and volunteer opportunities for people with disabilities is important, as long as it actually leads to employment. However, until people with disabilities are able to access a meaningful education, and employers are properly educated on how to appropriately accommodate their employees, it will be difficult to increase the percentage of people with disabilities who are employed full-time.

The impact of disability on an individual's ability to find and maintain consistent employment can be influenced by a number of disability-related factors, such as the type of disability, the severity of the disability, and the time of onset. Individuals with minor physical impairments or with a late onset of their disabilities may have had an opportunity to achieve high levels of education and may therefore have an easier time finding and keeping employment. However, individuals with more severe physical impairments, with earlier onset, or individuals with cognitive or emotional disabilities may face greater barriers in accessing education and employment. They may also find that the social response to their disabilities more negatively impacts their ability to find and maintain employment.

It is also essential to note the impact of combined disadvantage. Individuals with disabilities who face additional barriers because of their race, religion, sexual orientation, language, economic status, gender, or other characteristics may find that this combined disadvantage has an even greater impact on their ability to finding and keeping employment.

Income Maintenance/Socioeconomic Status

Despite Articles 9 and 11 of the ICESCR, persons with disabilities are more likely to be poor than those without disabilities and are often unable to access the necessities of life.[69] Women with disabilities have a particular disadvantage. In 1991, one-fourth of all adult women with disabilities were poor, while 18 percent of adult men with disabilities were poor. Poverty rates also vary with extent of disability. In 1991, the poverty rates were 17.7 percent for adults with mild disabilities, 23.7 percent for those with moderate disabilities, and 30.3 percent for those with severe disabilities.

In 1998, the Ontario provincial government introduced the Ontario Disability Support Program Act. This legislation was intended to provide financial supports for persons with disabilities and was touted as a new beginning in providing fair treatment to these individuals. However, as reported in *Denial by Design*, a 2003 publication of Toronto's Income Security Advocacy Centre, the reality was quite different.[70] Although the supports in the Ontario Disability Support Program (ODSP) were better than those in previous programs, the ODSP was problematic in many ways.

Denial by Design indicated that the ODSP application process is exceedingly complicated and lacking in supports. The nature of this system means that thousands of people who should be receiving ODSP are instead struggling on meager welfare benefits or no benefits at all. This jeopardizes their health, housing, and overall well-being.[71]

Denial by Design outlines difficulties in the initial application process that are likely to prevent many deserving individuals from accessing these supports and that are particularly problematic for individuals with mental disabilities, those who are homeless, and those who have cultural or language barriers that make it difficult for them to communicate or follow complex application procedures.[72] Even those who are successful in the initial application process are likely to be disappointed, because many recipients find the level of the benefits inadequate and the employment supports and client services poor.[73]

Those who are denied ODSP or who are awaiting a determination of their eligibility often rely on benefits under the Ontario Works (OW) general welfare program. These benefits are even lower than those received under the ODSP. In 2003 a single person received a maximum monthly allowance of CAN$520 under OW. This is only 56 percent of the $930 he or she would receive on ODSP. A family of four on OW received between $1,178 and $1,250 per month but could receive between $1,770 and $2,130 under ODSP.[74]

These low benefit rates can have a devastating impact on all aspects of the life of a person with a disability and his/her family, as they make it extremely difficult to provide the basic necessities of life. As noted in *Denial by Design,*

The receipt of lower benefits under OW often results in households resorting to inadequate and substandard housing (which may also not be properly accessible for a person with a disability). . . . The housing, while inadequate, will also likely be expensive as rents across Ontario have risen dramatically in recent years. People receiving OW are regularly forced to pay a huge proportion of their income on rent. It is not unusual for these households to devote over 70% of their income to rent. [D]isabled food bank users who were not in receipt of ODSP benefits had only about $18.30 per week per person to purchase *all* other basic necessities.[75]

People with disabilities are more likely than those without disabilities to experience what the CCSD calls "food insecurity." This means that they are more likely to go without food or to eat less than necessary because of lack of money. This is particularly true for persons with disabilities between the ages of fifteen and thirty-four. Statistics from the NPHS 1998/99 indicate that in this age group, 24.4 percent of women and 25 percent of men with disabilities experienced food insecurity, compared to 12 percent and 10.6 percent, respectively, of their non-disabled counterparts. Although food insecurity decreases with age, even people with disabilities in the higher age groups experience this problem at least three times more than people who do not have disabilities.[76]

Conclusion

Although governments have begun to acknowledge the economic barriers faced by people with disabilities, it is not clear that these responses have had a meaningful impact. Research indicates that children with disabilities are often unable to access a meaningful education. The public school system lacks the funding required to create full and appropriate accommodations. Without necessary services, children with disabilities cannot be properly integrated and do not receive the education that they are entitled to under the ICESCR.

As these children grow into adults, they cannot access the higher education that is often necessary for them to obtain employment. Barriers to education, combined with employers' reluctance to properly accommodate disability, place people with disabilities in a disadvantaged position in the workforce. Therefore many people with disabilities are unemployed or underemployed and must rely on government supports to provide the necessities of life.

The many people with disabilities who find themselves in this position run into a new barrier because these programs are very difficult to access. Individuals who are able to navigate these processes and receive benefits may find that the amounts are too low to cover their needs. This affects their ability to obtain adequate housing, food, and other necessities, including the medications required to manage their disability.

This discussion suggests that for many people, the rights set out in the ICESCR are empty rights. Many Canadians with disabilities are living in poverty, and this poverty has far-reaching consequences. Until the government creates more integrated systems to address the needs of people with disabilities in a meaningful way, these individuals will continue to be forced to the margins of society and will be unable to achieve their full potential. Society suffers from the loss of their contributions.

The government of Canada's voluminous reports on disability indicate a shift in policy from a "worthy poor" approach to a human rights approach. The reports suggest a willingness to create and enhance programs designed to fulfill the socioeconomic rights of people with disabilities. What is in doubt is whether the political will exists to put adequate funding behind these initiatives. Canada's federal structure also creates an imbalance in service delivery among provinces and a more difficult landscape in which to apply political pressure. Specifically, the disability community has argued that fragmentation of government services, both within and across government jurisdictions, is one of the most important obstacles preventing persons with disabilities from participating in society. At the same time, people with disabilities are especially vulnerable to the kinds of cuts that all levels of government have instituted to welfare and social assistance programs.

Since the entrenchment of the Charter, people with disabilities have also directed their energy toward the courts. Bickenbach notes that advocates of the sociopolitical model of disability "put their faith in the legal enforcement of rights, not because they believe that courts and judges are immune to the effects of handicapping attitudes, but because they feel that the law, at least potentially, can protect the inherent rights of people with disabilities more effectively than political institutions can."[77]

Although advocates for people with disabilities have seen some success under the Charter in fueling their cause both inside and outside of the courts, legal challenges to social assistance cuts and the narrowing of eligibility criteria have not yet been helpful. Rather, the trend in the courts has been to find that social and economic rights are not justiciable. Social and economic rights tend to be described by courts as "policy objectives" of governments rather than fundamental human rights.

Chapter 10
The Economic Rights of Migrant and Immigrant Workers in Canada and the United States

Vic Satzewich

Canada and the United States are widely recognized as "countries of immigration."[1] Compared to other countries that do not have the same histories of in-migration, both are seen to have relatively open immigration policies, treat immigrants relatively fairly, and provide comparatively easy access to citizenship. In addition, they do not put significant legal obstacles in the way of legal permanent residents who want to move up the socioeconomic ladder. Both also use immigration as part of their respective self-understandings and nation and population building strategies,[2] and both define immigrants as economic agents who can and should contribute certain skills, talents and/or resources to the economy and/or labor force. Furthermore, for many people around the world, having an opportunity to move to either Canada or the United States is akin to winning the lottery, insofar as it is perceived as a way of improving individual and household economic standing.[3] In short, Canada and the United States need and want immigrants for an interrelated set of nation-building, economic, and demographic reasons, and many individuals around the world see both countries as quite desirable locations to live and work.

In a context where the supply of and the demand for immigrants is robust, it may seem paradoxical to suggest that there is a "problem" associated with the economic rights of immigrants and migrant workers in these two countries. Canada and the United States may in fact constitute models for other countries to emulate in terms of the admission and absorption of immigrants. At the same time, the relatively welcoming attitude toward immigrants in both countries should not blind us to the fact that migrants and immigrants in these countries face serious problems associated with economic rights. Economic rights are broadly conceived within the United Nations International Covenant on Economic, Social and Cultural Rights (ICESCR) as having do with the right to work, the right to enjoy favorable conditions of work, the right to form trade unions, the right to social security, and the right to an adequate standard of living. Given the multiplicity of ways that economic considerations are relevant to immigration, it is worthwhile to reflect on the extent to which migrants and immigrants in these two countries face limits on their economic rights.[4] This chapter begins with some introductory comments on different categories of in-migration. It then discusses substantive issues associated with migrants' and immigrants' access to certain social benefits, followed by inquiry into the question of whether migrants and immigrants experience "just and favorable conditions of work." The next section discusses state efforts to control illegal immigration, particularly economic rights issues associated with employer sanctions. The chapter ends with a discussion of the role of courts, legislatures, and international agreements in protecting migrant and immigrant economic rights.

Migrants, Immigrants, and "Illegal" Immigrants

The characterization of Canada and the United States as "countries of immigration" is not inaccurate. However, this broad generalization tends to blur important differences among categories of foreign-born individuals who arrive in the two countries in order to live and work; the varying conditions of entry; and the different bundles of rights and obligations that are attached to each category. Very broadly, *immigrants* are individuals who are granted the right of permanent residence in a country and who face relatively few restrictions on their ability to circulate freely within respective national labor markets. In both countries there are four general mechanisms whereby individuals can become legal permanent residents:[5] (1) through family reunification and family sponsorship, (2) through the possession of certain skills, qualifications, and talents that are deemed to be in demand in the labor market, (3) through business immigration programs, and (4) through acceptance as a refugee. Of course, each country has specific criteria for admitting these categories, but they cannot be discussed in detail here.

Those who are granted the right of permanent residence can, following a probationary period, apply for citizenship. In both countries, critics have argued that the bar for acquiring citizenship is set too low.[6] In Canada, permanent residents need to be over the age of eighteen, live in Canada for at least three of the fours years before applying, be able to communicate in either French or English, and "know about Canada and the rights and responsibilities of citizenship." The last qualification is assessed through a multiple choice test. Individuals over sixty are not required to take the test.[7] Generally, in the United States, a permanent resident can apply for naturalization once they are eighteen years old and they have lived in the country continuously for five years. They must not have been arrested or convicted of a crime involving moral turpitude in the previous five-year period; must be able to read, write, and speak English; and must have a knowledge of the history and government of the United States. Part of the United States citizenship exam involves writing a simple sentence in English. There are, however, provisions for relaxing the English language proficiency requirements for certain categories of legal permanent residents who are over the age of fifty. As is the case in Canada, once permanent residents acquire United States citizenship, they enjoy the same rights, privileges, and obligations as the native-born residents.

Migrant workers are granted the right of temporary entry and face restrictions on their ability to circulate in the labor market. Traditionally, migrant workers have been understood as those who are recruited to do the "dirty work" of a society: that is, some jobs are difficult to fill because of poor pay and/or poor working conditions, and so migrant workers are often recruited to fill niches left open by permanent residents and citizens.[8] This view is accurate, but one-sided. In the context of globalization, migrant workers are occupationally diverse and can also include highly skilled professional and technical workers who enter a country for limited periods to work on specific projects.

A number of terms are used to describe what are variously called "illegal migrants" or "illegal aliens."[9] This category is the inevitable by-product of laws created to control migration.[10] Some individuals enter a country without going through established channels (called EWIs in the United States because they "enter without inspection"), others may enter a country legally but stay beyond the time allowed in their entry visa, while still others enter a country legally but subsequently violate their entry conditions.[11] The two countries have, on occasion, instituted amnesties for illegal aliens. Indeed, both are currently considering amnesties that would enable illegal aliens to acquire legal temporary resident status, and eventually a pathway to legal permanent residence.[12]

In 2001, Canada admitted 250,346 immigrants and refugees and the United States admitted 1,064,318. In Canada, 27 percent were family-class immigrants, 62 percent were economic immigrants (including skilled workers, business immigrants, and live-in caregivers), and 11 percent were refugees. There are proportionately more family-class immigrants in the United States: in 2001, family-class immigrants were nearly

63 percent of the total inflow. Seventeen percent were employment based, 10 percent were refugees, and 10 percent were "other," including 42,015 "diversity" immigrants.[13] Immigrants currently make up about 17 percent of the population of Canada and 10 percent of the population of the United States.

In 2002, the United States admitted nearly 200,000 "temporary workers,"[14] and in 1999 there were nearly 77,000 foreign workers in Canada who were legally entitled to work there temporarily.[15] There are an estimated 200,000 illegal immigrants in Canada; approximately 36,000 are failed refugee claimants who have been ordered deported, another 64,000 are visa overstayers, and the remaining 100,000 are assumed to be EWIs.[16] There are between 5 and 8 million illegal aliens in the United States, and that number is estimated to grow by between 300,000 and 450,000 per year.[17] In the case of the United States, most EWIs come from Mexico, while overstayers come from a variety of countries. In 1996, Canada was the fourth largest source of illegal immigrants in the United States.[18]

Public attention in both countries has tended to focus on those who enter, or try to enter, without going through legal channels (EWIs). Certainly both countries have seen heart-wrenching stories of human smuggling operations, some of which have gone horribly wrong and have resulted in the deaths of illegal entrants. Arguably, the focus of public debate on EWIs as opposed to visa overstayers and those who violate their conditions of entry is a reflection of the "neo-racism" that characterizes debates about immigration control in Canada and the United States.[19]

Immigration flows to Canada are currently being restructured in three ways. First, over the past fifteen years, immigration flows have shifted away from family-class to "economic" immigrants. In the mid-1980s, family-class immigrants made up nearly half of the yearly flow of immigrants, but they now make up less than 30 percent of the annual intake. This shift is due, in part, to a narrowing of the range of relatives who can be sponsored. This in turn has been driven by the perception, within a number of circles, that family-class immigrants provide fewer economic benefits for Canada and perform more poorly in the labor market than economic class immigrants, who are selected on the basis of a points system. This perception may not, however, be an accurate reflection of how family-class immigrants fare in the labor market over the long term. Although recent cohorts of family-class immigrants to Canada earn less than Canadians whose mothers arrived in the country a year before their children's birth, evidence shows that they catch up to the earnings levels of Canadian-born persons in about seven years.[20]

Some analysts have suggested that the American immigration program needs to also place less emphasis on family reunification and more emphasis on employment-based immigration.[21] In this context, American commentators sometimes make favorable references to the Canadian immigration program, which puts proportionately more emphasis on the qualifications that immigrants bring to the labor market.[22]

Second, there is arguably a shift within the Canadian immigration program toward admitting more migrant workers who fill short-term niches in the labor market as opposed to permanent residents who possess a fuller range of economic and political rights. According to some commentators, this is being done in order to create a more vulnerable and exploitable labor force for Canadian employers.[23]

Third, a process of restructuring has begun that involves efforts to harmonize Canadian and American immigration programs. Calls for harmonization began in the late 1990s, but events surrounding September 11, 2001 heightened the sense of urgency for the creation of a common North American approach to immigration.[24] Harmonization, or what is officially referred to as "the multiple borders strategy," has been likened to the creation of a "Fortress North America," which plays off the notion of "Fortress Europe." In theory, improved border control and security around a common North American perimeter will facilitate the movement of individuals and the flow of goods as it makes it more difficult to initially get inside.[25] The promise to collaborate through mechanisms such as the Canada-United States Smart Border Declaration, the Joint Statement on Border Security and Regional Migration Issues, and the Statement of Mutual Understanding on Information Sharing may involve the development of comparable immigrant databases, coordinated visa policies, integrated border enforcement teams, the use of common biometric identifiers in immigration documentation, and the sharing of information about individuals. It is unclear whether this will lead the two countries to develop common policies and criteria for the admission of immigrants, temporary workers, and refugees.[26]

Access to Social Benefits of Migrant and Immigrant Workers

To what extent do Canada and the United States differentiate between legal permanent residents (immigrants) and citizens in terms of employment-related rights and access to social benefits? Immigrants who are admitted as refugees and as "economic immigrants" have the same economic rights as Canadian citizens, although they do face some restrictions on certain kinds of public sector employment. They are eligible for the same range of social benefits as Canadian citizens. Immigrants who are admitted under the family class, however, face restrictions on access to certain social benefits. According to the 2001 Immigration and Refugee Protection Act,[27] Canadian citizens and permanent residents who are over the age of eighteen may sponsor close relatives or family members to become permanent residents. The list of relatives eligible to be sponsored includes spouses, common-law or conjugal partners, parents and grandparents, dependent children, and brothers, sisters, nephews, nieces, or grandchildren who are under eighteen years of age and not married or in a common-law relationship. Until the introduction of the 2001 act, access to the family-class category was limited to heterosexual couples who were legally married. In 2001, the rules were changed to allow common-law and same-sex couples to be included within the family class.[28]

If a sponsor has previously sponsored relatives or family members who have received social assistance, they may not be allowed to sponsor more relatives as immigrants. In order to sponsor a relative, the sponsor must sign an "undertaking," which is considered a legal contract with the minister of citizenship and immigration. Depending on the type of relationship, the sponsor must guarantee that he or she will provide financial support for the sponsored relative for between three and ten years so that the relative will not need to apply for social assistance. Individuals who are sponsored must also "promise to make every effort to become self-supporting."[29] Recent changes strengthen provisions for the collection of money through the garnishing of wages in cases where sponsors default on their obligations.

Like Canada, the United States also restricts access to social benefits for family-class immigrants. Within the U.S. Illegal Immigration Reform and Immigrant Responsibility Act of 1996, family-sponsored aliens may not be admitted to the country unless the sponsor agrees to support the applicant at an annual income that is not less than 125 percent of the federal poverty guidelines until the person becomes a United States citizen or until he or she has worked in the United States for ten years. These undertakings are legally enforceable against the sponsor by the sponsored alien, the federal government, state governments, or by other organizations that provide means tested public benefits.[30]

These kinds of sponsorship provisions have created difficulties for sponsored immigrants who are in abusive relationships with their sponsors.[31] Some sponsors have taken advantage of the economic dependence that is reinforced by the sponsorship provisions. In the past, provisions that limited sponsored immigrants' access to public benefits made it extraordinarily difficult for spouses and children to leave abusive relationships. Recent changes to immigration regulations in Canada, however, have partially addressed this issue, and sponsored immigrants who have been abused are now eligible for welfare and other forms of public assistance.[32] In the United States, alien spouses, children of United States citizens, or permanent residents who are abused by their sponsor are also eligible for means-tested public benefits.[33]

Unlike Canada, however, the United States has taken a number of steps to restrict access to social benefits not only for family-class immigrants but also for immigrants more generally. According to Fragomen, the 1996 Illegal Immigration Reform and Immigrant Responsibility Act, combined with the 1996 Personal Responsibility and Work Opportunity Reconciliation Act, "completely reinvents a welfare system that has been in place for more than six decades."[34] Qualified aliens (or legal permanent residents) who entered the United States on or after August 22, 1996, are not eligible for any federal means-tested public benefit for a period of five years. Further, qualified aliens are not eligible for supplemental security income and food stamps, although lawful permanent residents who have worked forty qualifying quarters may receive such benefits. In cases where aliens are eligible for federal means-tested benefits, the incomes of their spouses and/or sponsor will be factored into the calculation of the amount of benefit. The exception to this "deeming" provision is in cases where an alien, or his or her children, has been battered or subjected to extreme cruelty, and the battery or cruelty has a connection to the need for the benefits for which the alien has applied.[35] In addition, some states have imposed citizenship requirements for certain public sectors jobs such as teachers, police officers, and probation officers.[36]

Considerable academic, media, and public attention was devoted to Proposition 187 in California in 1994, where the intention was to prevent illegal immigrants, and the children of illegal immigrants, from accessing state-funded educational, health care, and social service programs.[37] Even though the proposition was struck down by the courts, recent federal legislation has arguably gone some way in addressing the concerns underlying the California proposition.[38] According to Kristen Hill Maher, the denial of social benefits, and of rights more generally, to illegal immigrants stems in part from a particular reading of liberal political thought. She suggests that in the United States "the liberal assumption of rational, autonomous action by all individuals, [means that] migrants who have 'chosen' to cross state borders without authorization are imagined to have consented to the conditions of 'rightslessness.' Their border crossing involves a 'knowing defiance' of American law, a 'calculated risk' . . . in which migrants exchange their right to rights for economic opportunity."[39] Put simply, illegal aliens in the

United States are not eligible for any federal, state, or local public bene-fit.[40] There are similar provisions in Canada.

Legally admitted migrant workers also face a wide range of restrictions on their access to state-funded social benefits. Canada and the United States both have special programs to admit agricultural workers on a migrant labor basis, and for the purpose of this discussion I will focus specifically on the rights implications of these two programs.

In addition to making use of Canadian-born workers and landed immigrants, agricultural employers in Canada have access to labor through the Caribbean/Mexican Seasonal Agricultural Workers Pro-gram. In 1999, about fifteen thousand seasonal agricultural workers were admitted to Canada, with roughly equal numbers coming from Mexico and from various Caribbean countries. In 1998, the United States admitted approximately thirty-five thousand agricultural workers under the H-2A program, and they augmented the approximately 2.5 million U.S. and foreign-born (both legal permanent residents and ille-gal aliens) workers who work in agriculture.[41]

In both countries, legal jurisdiction over migrant agricultural workers involves both federal and provincial/state law. For instance, in the United States, the federal government has jurisdiction over minimum employment standards legislation, occupational health and safety, and general Social Security issues, while states have jurisdiction over workers' compensation, unemployment benefits, and income security. As a result, the economic rights of migrant agricultural workers not only vary between countries but can also vary within a country.[42]

One of the elements common to both programs is that the workers who are admitted are unable to circulate freely in the labor market. Both groups of workers are employed under stringent conditions. If they quit or change jobs without permission of their employers and the respective government employment officials, they are subject to depor-tation at their own expense.[43] As a result of this inability to circulate in the labor market, Caribbean and Mexican migrant farm workers in Can-ada have been referred to as "unfree migrant labor."[44] Other temporary workers face similar restrictions over circulation in the respective national labor markets and, as a result, may also qualify as forms of unfree labor.[45]

Regarding other economically relevant rights in Canada, migrant agricultural workers pay into the Employment Insurance (EI) program, but are never able to collect this benefit because they are not allowed to be unemployed while in Canada. Offshore seasonal agricultural workers are also required to pay into the Canada Pension Plan (CPP), but they are able to collect benefits when they reach the age of sixty-five, even though they may not be residents of Canada. Access to health care and coverage under employment standards and occupational health and safety legislation varies by province.[46] Prior to December 2001, workers in agriculture in Ontario, including offshore seasonal agricultural workers, were excluded from the Ontario Labour Relations Act. This meant, in part, that workers in this sector did not have the right to strike or to form unions. However, the Supreme Court of Canada ruled that the exclusion from the act of agricultural workers violated the freedom of association provisions of the Canadian Charter of Rights and Freedoms. As a result, it suspended the portion of the act excluding agricultural workers, and gave the provincial government eighteen months to pass new legislation.[47]

In the United States, the H-2A program establishes a number of minimum employment standards. These include minimum rates of pay, notice to the employees of the contractual terms and conditions of employment, reimbursement for travel expenses, and guaranteed opportunity to work at least three-fourths of the contract period. Employers of H-2A workers are not subject to the Federal Unemployment Tax Act, and so unlike the case of Canada, workers are not required to financially contribute to a program from which they can never derive a benefit. Employers have to provide H-2A workers with workers' compensation coverage or equivalent insurance that is similar to what agricultural workers are entitled to in each jurisdiction. Workers under this program are excluded from Medicare and Medicaid coverage. H-2A workers, as well as illegal aliens and unauthorized immigrants, are excluded from federal Social Security programs.[48]

Just and Favorable Conditions of Work: Equal Pay for Work of Equal Value

In the ICESCR, individuals are entitled to "just and favorable conditions of work." The Covenant elaborates on this right in the following terms: "fair wages and equal remuneration for work of equal value without distinction of any kind, in particular women being guaranteed conditions of work not inferior to those by enjoyed men, with equal pay for equal work."[49] One dimension to the problem of economic rights is therefore the extent to which immigrants have equal access to jobs, and the extent to which, once they are in those jobs, they receive financial returns that are consistent with those of similarly qualified native-born workers. Two specific issues relevant to the just and favorable conditions of work aspect of the Convention are considered here: the devaluation of educational credentials of immigrants and earnings differences between immigrants and the native-born.

There is evidence that certain foreign educational credentials are undervalued in both labor markets. That is, some immigrants with high levels of education and extensive job qualifications have difficultly translating these into positions in North America that reflect their skills, training, and talent. The issue of devaluation of credentials is complex. In Canada, some researchers suggest that the devaluation of immigrant credentials is a form of neo-racism,[50] insofar as visible minority immigrants appear to face the biggest hurdles to having their credentials acknowledged. It is worth noting, however, that while some of the problem of the devaluation of credentials in Canada can be linked to the issue of "race," other evidence suggests that it also happens to "white" immigrants who come from eastern Europe.[51]

Part of the issue in Canada is that professional licensing bodies are autonomous and have only weak ties to the immigration bureaucracy. These bodies are interested in both quality control and protecting their members from competition. Without doubt, there are differences in the quality of education that professionals receive in different educational institutions around the world. As a result, there can be little argument about the legitimacy of licensing bodies who want to maintain professional standards and ensure that practitioners are suitably qualified. However, the tendency of some professional licensing bodies to make it difficult for highly trained immigrants who have the skills to practice their profession in Canada may, to some extent, also reflect an interest in reducing potential market competition. As a result, organizational efforts to maintain market closure are becoming a source of tension with the Canadian federal government.

A second area about which there is considerable research is how the earnings of immigrants compare with those of native-born workers. In Canada, a common technique to examine wage discrimination is to compare gross and net earnings of different ethnic, racial, immigrant and nativity groups. Gross earnings refer to actual earnings, whereas net earnings refer to earnings that take into account differences in human capital and other variables. Generally, what research in Canada shows is that while immigrants as a whole appear to be doing better than native-born individuals when gross earnings are compared, immigrants do less well when their human capital and skills are considered. Research also suggests that "race" plays a role in the shaping of earnings of both immigrants and the native-born. For instance, one study of large Canadian cities compared net earnings of four groups: visible minority[52] immigrants, white immigrants, native-born visible minorities, and native-born whites. That study introduced statistical controls on variations in earnings due to human capital variables (such as education, occupational training, language abilities, and experience) and structural variables (such as industrial sector of employment, number of weeks worked, and region of residence). The analysis found that, after variations in earnings due to human capital and structural variables are controlled for, male visible minority immigrants earn $6,300 per year less than white immigrant men, $12,000 per year less than white native-born men, and $7,000 per year less than visible minority native-born men.[53] (Figures are in Canadian dollars.)

According to Waters and Eschbach, there is not a clear-cut pattern of earnings inequality along "racial" lines among post-1965 immigrants in the United States.[54] Asians, for instance, have relatively high education and gross earnings, whereas Mexicans have relatively low levels of education and gross earnings. However, as in Canada, some have suggested that the returns to education may be lower for Asian Americans than for whites, which means that Asian men and women need more education to receive the same income as whites.[55]

Some argue that the differences in net earnings between groups can be explained by other unobserved differences in human capital or labor market conditions, while others argue that the net differences in earnings are a reflection of discrimination in the labor market where immigrants, particularly visible minority immigrant men, are treated unequally.[56] According to Peter Li, "In the case of migrants in the Canadian labor market, how well they perform relative to the native-born population is not only a function of immigrants' human capital, but also a function of how prepared Canadian society is to reward them in the same manner as native-born Canadians, irrespective of superficial differences in gender, race, and nativity."[57]

According to Reitz and Breton's review of data from the United States and Canada, there are reasonable grounds to conclude that "racial discrimination may indeed account in part, in both countries, for these disadvantages."[58] In sum, evidence from both countries suggests that the economic rewards that individuals receive in the labor market are structured by immigration status and having a skin color that is perceived to be "non-white."

Negative Sanctions on Employers

So far, much of the discussion in this chapter has focused on individuals who are legally entitled to live and work in Canada and in the United States. However, issues of economic rights are also relevant to illegal aliens. As noted earlier, illegal aliens consist of visa overstayers, those who violate their initial conditions of entry, and those who knowingly enter a country illegally in order to work. Illegal aliens are in precarious positions and are vulnerable to exploitation and unequal treatment because they are living and working contrary to the laws of the land and because they usually have less attractive economic options in the countries from which they migrated. The employment of illegal aliens can be lucrative for employers in certain economic sectors, particularly those whose profit margins are tight and where there are pressures to keep labor costs down. According to Gimpel and Edwards, "The practice of employing low-wage workers in squalid sweatshop conditions is surprisingly common in certain low-profit-margin businesses. The illegitimate employers routinely dodge wage and labor laws because they know the illegal workers they employ will not go to the authorities out of fear of being discovered and deported."[59] As the recent case of Wal-Mart in the United States shows, the employment of illegal aliens is not confined to traditionally understood "sweatshops." In 2002, Wal-Mart is reported to have earned profits of US$8 billion, and its CEO received US$18 million in total compensation.[60]

In Canada, illegal aliens are subject to some of the provisions of the Charter of Rights and Freedoms, and in the United States, they are subject to some of the provisions of civil rights legislation, which protect them from discrimination. Generally, illegal aliens in the two countries do not have the right to work there legally, but they nevertheless possess certain civil rights. In Canada, non-citizens, including illegal immigrants, are protected against discrimination on the grounds of race, national or ethnic origin, color, religion, sex, age, or mental or physical disability, as are citizens and legal permanent residents. At the same time, the Supreme Court of Canada has ruled that governments may condition access to social benefits based on residency within their respective jurisdictions.

In the United States, under the Fifth and Fourteenth Amendments of the U.S. Constitution, all persons, including undocumented aliens, have equal rights of access to the courts and to sue in order to enforce contracts and redress civil wrongs. For instance, 9 of the 300 illegal immigrant janitors who were caught in the October 2003 sweep of Wal-Mart by the Immigration and Naturalization Service (INS) are now suing the company for having cheated them out of overtime wages.[61]

The central statute that prohibits employment discrimination is Title VII of the Civil Rights Act of 1964. Title VII prohibits employment discrimination on the basis of "race, color, religion, sex or national origin." There is disagreement within the United States about whether unauthorized workers are protected under Title VII. The Equal Employment Opportunity Commission (EEOC) does, however, accept complaints from unauthorized workers and in the past has sued employers on behalf of illegal aliens.[62] However, the 2002 decision of the U.S. Supreme Court, in *Hoffman Plastic Compounds, Inc. v. National Labor Relations Board*, limits the ability of undocumented workers to receive back pay as a remedy for having been fired for engaging in union activities. That is, although back pay is a recognized remedy for workers who are fired for engaging in union activity, the Supreme Court ruled that this remedy is not available for illegal aliens, in part, on the grounds that doing so "not only trivializes the immigration laws, it also condones future violations."[63]

Some countries have tried to control the flow of illegal aliens through restrictions on access to public services and through measures that punish employers. As noted earlier, under the Illegal Immigration Reform and Immigrant Responsibility Act of 1996, illegal immigrants are ineligible for Social Security benefits, and subsidized housing is denied to families in which all members are illegal aliens. In cases where some family members are legal and some are illegal (for instance, when a child whose parents are both illegal is born in the United States, the child is an American citizen), the financial benefit is adjusted to the percentage of legally present family members in the household. The act also created an exception to the 1996 welfare reform law to allow illegal aliens who are victims of domestic violence to receive public benefits. In such cases, battered women and children had to be in the same household as the perpetrator, and the domestic violence and the need for public assistance had to be linked.[64]

In the 1986 Immigration Reform and Control Act, the United States joined the company of a number of western European states that had imposed sanctions on employers for hiring illegal aliens.[65] Sanctions were further refined by the passage of the Illegal Immigration Reform and Immigrant Responsibility Act of 1996. The 1986 legislation made it illegal for employers to knowingly hire unauthorized workers, and specified a number of penalties for employers who did so. Sanctions ranged from first-offense fines of between $250 and $2,000 for each illegal alien involved. Fines increased to $3,000–$10,000 per worker for third offenses. Terms of imprisonment for up to six months were provided for pattern or practice violations.[66] Under the 1986 legislation, employers are required to complete an employment eligibility verification form, and new employees can use any of seventeen different documents to establish their eligibility to work. The law took effect on December 6, 1986, but because of effective lobbying, agricultural employers were able to win a two-year delay in the implementation of the law.[67]

In Canada, individuals who employ illegal aliens commit an offense under the Immigration Act.[68] If it is determined that the employer did not carry out due diligence in determining whether the individual was legally entitled to work in Canada, they are subject to a maximum fine of $50,000, or two years' imprisonment, or both. Workers who are discovered to be working illegally in Canada are also subject to deportation, provided that they do not claim refugee status. If they do claim refugee status, then they must receive a hearing before the disposition of their case.

Miller identifies a number of limitations to the effectiveness of sanctions against employers in the United States. He notes that some employer groups who traditionally make use of illegal aliens have effectively lobbied to undermine the intent of the legislation. For example, employers in agriculture must be notified in advance that an inspection of the workplace is to take place. He also argues that under-funding of the INS hampers enforcement of sanctions, as does the lack of experience of INS employees in workplace inspections.[69] During the 1990s, the average number of completed INS employer inspections was 6,100 per year, whereas between 2000 and 2003 the average number of yearly inspections fell to 1,900.[70] In the aftermath of the terrorist attacks in New York and Washington, D.C., on September 11, 2001, federal immigration officials in the United States have focused their "immigration arrests on facilities, like airports, that might be terrorist targets,"[71] rather than on employers in less economically and politically sensitive sectors.

One indication of the relative ineffectiveness of employer sanctions in the United States is that between 1994 and 1996, only 3,765 of the more than 15,000 employers charged with knowingly hiring illegal aliens received fines. Further, even though the fines totaled $34 million, only $14 million was collected. According to Koslowski, employers simply consider the fines to be a relatively small cost of doing business.[72]

One of the concerns raised about employer sanctions is whether they have an adverse effect on the economic rights of citizens and immigrants who are of the same background as the perceived majority of illegal aliens. Because a large proportion of illegal aliens in the United States are, or are perceived to be, individuals from Mexico and Latin America, legally resident individuals from Mexico and Latin America, and American-born Mexican Americans and Latinos, may experience discrimination because employers do not want to risk being fined for hiring an illegal alien.

Empirical evidence supports the conclusion that legally resident Mexicans and Latinos have experienced adverse effects, in the form of reduced job opportunities and lower wages, because of employers' fear of sanctions for hiring undocumented workers. According to a survey of employers conducted by the U.S. Government Accounting Office (GAO), "an estimated 227,000 employers reported that they began a practice, as a result of IRCA [Immigration Reform and Control Act], not to hire applicants whose foreign appearance or accent led them to suspect that they might be unauthorized aliens. Also, contrary to IRCA, an estimated 346,000 employers said that they applied IRCA's verification system only to persons who had a 'foreign' appearance or accent. Some employers began both practices."[73]

Another study conducted by the GAO involved sending pairs of "auditors," one Hispanic and one non-Hispanic white, to employers in San Diego and Chicago. That study found that "foreign appearing, foreign-sounding" Hispanic members of the matched pairs were three times more likely to encounter unfavorable treatment than the non-Hispanic, non-foreign appearing members of the pairs. Further "the Anglo members received 52 percent more job offers than the Hispanics. These results, taken together with the survey responses, show a serious problem of national origin discrimination that GAO believes IRCA has exacerbated."[74]

Protecting Economic Rights of Migrant Workers

Christian Joppke argues that, in many Western countries, immigrant rights theoretically derive either from behind the "closed doors of ministries or [from] . . . courtrooms."[75] He argues, though, that on balance the courts have been the main force pushing for the expansion of migrant and immigrant rights and that government legislation tends to be the main force leading to the narrowing of rights. In his view, "courts are uniquely shielded from the populist pressures that democratically accountable governments face, and in the past half century they have emerged more generally as champions of individual rights against a growing state machinery." In his case studies of the United States, Germany, and the European Union he finds that independent courts have clashed with restriction-minded state executives, and rights expansion for immigrants "had to be achieved against rather than with the latter."[76]

Joppke also argues that, within liberal democracies, the main sources of immigrant rights tend to be domestic in nature. While not discounting the role of international human rights norms, regimes, and conventions, Joppke argues that in states with a "robust liberal infrastructure and tradition, there is no need to resort to international norms." In contrast, he suggests that international human rights norms matter mostly in "illiberal or newly liberalizing states."[77] Two examples may provide at least some support for Joppke's observation. For instance, the UN Convention on the Protection of the Rights of Migrant Workers, which came into force in July 2003,[78] appears to have generated more interest in "liberalizing states" than in the "developed world." The thirty-two states that adopted the Convention as of January 1, 2004, include Azerbaijan, Bangladesh, Belize, Bolivia, Bosnia and Herzegovina, Burkina Faso, Cape Verde, Chile, Colombia, Comoros, Ecuador, Egypt, El Salvador,

Ghana, Guatemala, Guinea-Bissau, Kyrgyzstan, Mali, Mexico, Morocco, Paraguay, Philippines, Sao Tome and Principe, Senegal, Seychelles, Sierra Leone, Sri Lanka, Tajikistan, Togo, Turkey, Uganda, and Uruguay.[79] Clearly, another common denominator to this list is that it is made up of immigrant-sending countries. There are a number of reasons why advanced, industrialized immigrant-receiving countries have not signed this Convention.[80] In Joppke's terms, there may not be a "need." However, for immigrant-receiving countries the Convention may also be seen as a nuisance, in that signing would force them to address issues of migrant and immigrant economic rights.[81]

Further, Joppke's observation may also be relevant to the situation of migrant agricultural workers in Canada, the United States, and Mexico. One of the by-products of the North American Free Trade Agreement (NAFTA) was the creation of the North American Agreement on Labour Cooperation (NAALC). The latter agreement focuses specifically on the rights of migrant agricultural workers, because they are often the most vulnerable members of a society, receive low pay, and are subject to changing demands for their labor power. The NAALC sets out a number of objectives and obligations for the three countries, including an obligation to promote to the maximum extent possible eleven basic labor principles, including "providing migrant workers in a Party's territory with the same legal protection as the party's nationals in respect of working conditions." While the agreement does not provide for the creation of common laws or standards for working conditions, it does stipulate that the three member countries agree to "open themselves up to reviews and consultations on matters that are relevant to the agreement."[82]

In 1998, three separate complaints were filed under the NAALC, alleging that Mexican migrant workers in the United States were experiencing discrimination and that the United States government was failing to protect Mexican migrant workers against a variety of labor law violations. Following consultations with ministers of labor in Canada, the United States and Mexico, the Secretariat of the Commission for Labor Cooperation was directed to produce a trilingual guide "describing law and procedures covering labor rights and protections granted to migrant workers in the United States, Mexico and Canada which was to be made available to workers, individuals, businesses and organizations."[83] There is no question that the guide contains a wealth of information in both English and Spanish about labor rights in the three countries, along with telephone numbers and other contact information for unions and other organizations that deal with various rights-related issues. It seems, however, to be a rather half-hearted attempt to solve rights violations of migrant agricultural workers in the three countries.

Conclusion

David Weissbrodt, in his "General Comment on the Rights of Non-Citizens," prepared for the United Nations Sub-Commission on the Promotion and Protection of Human Rights, argues that "in general, international human rights law requires the equal treatment of citizens and non-citizens. Exceptions to this principle may be made only if they are to serve a legitimate State objective and are proportional to the achievement of that objective."[84] Clearly, Canada and the United States have much to be proud of when it comes to matters relating to immigration and citizenship. Every year, the two countries accept relatively large numbers of immigrants both for humanitarian reasons and for reasons of economic self-interest, and both make it relatively easy for legally admitted permanent residents to become citizens. At the same time, as this chapter has shown, migrants and immigrants in the two countries do face various restrictions on their economic rights. It is hard to see how the limits on economic rights noted in this chapter—such as the denial of the right of migrant workers to organize unions in some sectors of the economy; the denial of social benefits to migrants and immigrants; paying immigrants less than what their skills, qualifications and experience suggest they should be paid; and the denial of employment opportunities to individuals who may look like stereotypical illegal immigrants—serve legitimate state objectives. Further, the seeming reluctance of immigrant-receiving countries to sign the UN Convention on the Protection of the Rights of Migrant Workers serves as a telling reminder that it is easier for well-off capitalist countries to point to where other countries are "going wrong" in the area of rights violations than it is for them to deal with economic rights violations within their own borders.

Part IV
A European Comparison

Chapter 11
The Netherlands
A Walhalla of Economic and Social Rights?

Peter R. Baehr

This chapter deals with the role of economic and social rights in the Netherlands, a small[1] state in Western Europe with a strong human rights tradition, in its domestic as well as its foreign policy.[2] It is a relatively wealthy nation, ranking fifth on the United Nations Development Program's (UNDP's) Human Development Index.[3] The Netherlands is a prosperous and open economy, depending heavily on foreign trade. Its economy is noted for stable industrial relations, moderate unemployment and inflation, a sizable current account surplus, and an important role as a European transportation hub. Industrial activity is predominantly in food processing, chemicals, petroleum refining, and electrical machinery. A highly mechanized agricultural sector employs no more than 4 percent of the labor force but provides large surpluses for the food-processing industry and for exports.[4] It is a party to all major global as well as regional human rights treaties and reports periodically to the major UN human rights expert committees. Yet, several of these expert committees as well as domestic nongovernmental organizations (NGOs) have criticized it for shortcomings in the implementation of its human rights obligations. Indeed, Fried van Hoof wrote: "Evidently, the Netherlands is social-economically, a kind of Walhalla compared to most, if not all, other states in the world. This comparative conclusion implies at the same time the danger that a decline in an absolute sense is being disguised.[5]

The chapter examines economic and social aspects of recent national reports by the Netherlands under the following treaties: the International Covenant on Economic, Social and Cultural Rights (ICESCR),[6] the Convention on the Elimination of All Forms of Discrimination against Women (CEDAW), the International Convention on the Elimination of All Forms of Racial Discrimination (CERD), and the Convention on the Rights of the Child (CRC).[7] These UN conventions were chosen for the following reasons: (1) they cover a broad range of economic and social rights, (2) all of them provide for supervisory committees that examine the periodic reports of the States Parties and provide specific comments with regard to them, (3) the members of the supervisory committees are independent experts (i.e., not in the service of their governments) who are not supposed to have axes to grind with regard to any of the States Parties, and (4) the Netherlands is a party to all of them. This chapter looks respectively at the most recent of the Netherlands government's reports, the criticisms raised by domestic NGOs, the questions raised by (members of) the various supervisory committees, and their comments.

The Netherlands and Economic, Social, and Cultural Rights (ESC Rights)

The Netherlands has on various occasions officially expressed its commitment to economic, social, and cultural rights next to, and on an equal basis with, civil and political rights.[8] An often cited government memorandum, published in 1979, expressed its view as follows: "The Government subscribes to the view that the classic and the social human rights are of equal importance, in the sense that an existence worthy of human dignity is only possible if both categories of rights are enjoyed."[9] In 2001, this view was reiterated: "[T]he time is now ripe for acknowledging the close links that exist between civil and political rights and economic, social and cultural rights."[10]

However, academic experts as well as human rights organizations have repeatedly stated that actual policy has been insufficiently in line with these solemn pronouncements. For instance, Van Hoof has written: "But also in the developed and flourishing economy of the Netherlands there are 657,000 households living under the minimum existence level, while 11 percent of all households find themselves in a situation of uncertainty of existence. . . . The climate of a strongly improved promotion and protection of economic, social and cultural rights, appears not to be very positive."[11] Referring to a project by two researchers at Leiden University dealing with the effect of basic social rights that were incorporated in the constitution in 1983, he noted that their conclusions were "little less than devastating."[12] Apart from a few exceptions, he did not know of any Dutch court decision concerning a violation of an economic, social, or cultural right.[13]

In an advisory report, the official Advisory Council on International Affairs called it "unfortunate" that economic, social, and cultural rights had received "such scant attention" in the government memorandum.[14] It regretted especially that the government continued to resist the idea of a draft optional protocol for an individual right of complaint in this area, though it had supported the appointment by the UN Commission on Human Rights of an independent expert on the question of such a draft optional protocol.[15] It should be added that other governments share the Netherlands' reluctance in this field.[16]

On the whole, the Netherlands government's commitment to ESC rights is often questioned: "In most [Dutch] ministries, the view seems to persist that the ICESCR is still but a 'poor relation' of its sibling Covenant, the International Covenant on Civil and Political Rights."[17] The Dutch human rights expert Fried van Hoof, after noting that the Netherlands, unlike the United States, is a party to the ICESCR, expressed his skepticism on the Netherlands' performance on economic, social, and cultural rights as follows: "When it comes to an effective implementation of the rights contained therein, the Netherlands government has adopted a rather minimalist position."[18] The legal philosopher Paul Cliteur goes even further. He writes that ESC rights, though they are *named* rights, do not *function* as such and should therefore not be seen as human rights. He prefers the term "directive principles of state policy."[19] He thus comes close to prevailing opinion among United States policy makers.

In spite of the noted criticisms on the part of advisory bodies, academics, and NGOs, on the whole, the Netherlands seems to have met most of its human rights obligations in the field of ESC rights.[20] The UN Committee on Economic, Social and Cultural Rights supported this conclusion: "The Committee notes that the Netherlands has to a considerable extent met its obligations with regard to the protection of the rights set out in the Covenant."[21] Most of the problems relate to specific categories of persons. The Dutch section of the International Commission of Jurists (Nederlands Juristen Comité voor de Mensenrechten [NJCM]) has noted this, for instance, with regard to the issue of health care: "Over the years, a number of reports have been produced concerning disparities in the Dutch health care system in terms of accessibility, availability, and the quality of care. . . . According to these reports groups such as *women, the elderly,* and *members of ethnic minorities* experience, on an average, considerably more problems in obtaining the care they need than other groups."[22] The following sections of this chapter are devoted to these categories as well as to the position of children and students.

Women

A celebrated case occurred in 1987, when the UN Human Rights Committee found the Netherlands in violation of Article 26 of the International Covenant on Civil and Political Rights,[23] because the Dutch unemployment act stipulated the position of "breadwinner" as a condition for receiving social security benefits. The Human Rights Committee considered this condition, which was applicable only to married women and not to married men, discriminatory against women.[24] The committee reasoned that equal protection of the law "prohibits discrimination in law or in practice in any field regulated and protected by public authorities." While differentiation based on reasonable and objective criteria should not be considered discriminatory, in these particular cases the committee considered that the gender-specific distinction at issue in unemployment was not reasonable and amounted to discrimination.[25] As this decision had considerable repercussions of a financial nature, it was briefly considered by the Netherlands to denounce the Covenant and then ratify it again with a reservation regarding Article 26. This idea raised an uproar among human rights activists in the Netherlands and was not pursued.[26] The law was subsequently amended, thus losing its discriminatory nature. However, three years later, the ESC Committee expressed its concern about continuing discrimination against women at work: "Their higher rate of unemployment, their lower position on the wage scale, and their disproportionate representation in part-time work reveal that the principle of equality established by the law is not effectively enforced."[27]

The CEDAW Committee, in commenting on the second and third periodic reports of the Netherlands, expressed concern that the burden of unpaid care still fell mainly upon women. Women who work outside the home devote twice as much time as men to unpaid work, and there were still insufficient child care facilities.[28] It recommended that greater efforts be devoted to the development of additional programs and policies to encourage men to share family and caring responsibilities and that the government ensure the availability of sufficient child care facilities and an uninterrupted school day so as to prevent mothers from continuously having to go back and forth to the school to pick up their children and bring them back again.[29] "Noting the positive contributions of the Netherlands to the process of elaboration of the Optional Protocol," the committee urged it to ratify that instrument as soon as possible.[30] This the Netherlands did on August 22, 2002. Most of the other recommendations dealt with immigrant, refugee, and minority women, to which we will return later in this chapter.

Under Dutch law, women in paid employment have the right to stop work four to six weeks before the birth of their child. Women may take a maximum of twelve weeks' leave after the birth, at 100 percent of their salary. The costs are covered by the Exceptional Medical Expenses Act.[31] A constitutional amendment introduced by the government, to grant maternity leave to members of Parliament and to members of provincial and municipal councils, was not adopted by the First Chamber of Parliament in 1995. NGOs called attention to this issue, suggesting that such a right to maternity leave would have encouraged more women to be candidates for such organs; it would have removed a barrier to (younger) women to participate in such political functions and thus would have been in line with the obligations under Article 7 of CEDAW.[32] No change has occurred since then. In 2003, the parliamentary leader of the Green Left Party (Groen Links) announced that, though pregnant, she was not to receive maternity leave and would have to finance a replacement from her personal or party's funds.

Furthermore, the CEDAW Committee expressed concern over continuing discrimination in employment and business enterprises. It recommended efforts to improve the conditions for workingwomen so as to enable them to choose full-time rather than part-time employment.

Children and Education

During the meeting of the ESC Committee with the Netherlands delegation, ESC member Mr. Ahmed noted that, according to NJCM, 240,000 households, or almost 1 million persons, were living on an income below the social minimum, and some 250,000 children belonging to poor families participated very rarely in recreational and cultural activities. He expressed surprise that a country as wealthy as the Netherlands was unable to solve those problems.[33] The representative of the Netherlands firmly rejected these suggestions: "There seemed to be no basis for the allegation that 250,000 children were unable to exercise the rights provided in the Covenant."[34] According to the Children's Collective, there were, in 1999, 338,000 children in the Netherlands living in a family that earned the minimum income (or just earlier).[35] The committee appeared satisfied; the item was not mentioned in its concluding observations.

NJCM appeared more successful with its observations about educational policy. It claimed that, over the last ten years, the financial situation of students had been characterized by a reduction of the basic study grant, increasing loans from commercial banks, the abolition of indexing of basic grants, and increases of university fees: "These developments can only lead to the conclusion that there is a serious risk that accessible higher education is no longer available for all income and social groups in society."[36] It criticized especially the so-called voluntary tuition fee in primary and secondary schools: if this tuition fee was not paid, schools could refuse to permit pupils to take part in extracurricular activities financed mainly by these voluntary fees.[37]

During the meeting of the ESC Committee with the State Party, the representative of the Netherlands reacted to suggestions that his government should endeavor to make secondary education free of charge by saying that, in his view, a government's first responsibility was to ensure that secondary education was provided for all those who qualified and that no one was forced out of education for financial reasons. On the question of free education, the views of Parliament and of society at large had to be taken into account: "It could be argued that beyond the school-leaving age, which in the Netherlands was sixteen years, the nature of government responsibility changed and the decision concerning further education should be left to the parents and children."[38] Committee member Mr. Thalapia asked how the Netherlands' educational policy complied with the principle of free education: "Did the policy of accessibility to higher education not constitute a retrogressive step in relation to the standards of the Covenant?"[39] The Netherlands representative argued that education for those older than sixteen was not dependent on the financial status of the parents; contrary to the system in many other countries, grants were available to all—the cost of living in the Netherlands was lower than in many of the surrounding countries. "Generally speaking, the comprehensive system of student grants and bursaries opened up the possibility for each and every person in the Netherlands to pursue all forms of higher education."[40] In its concluding observations, the ESC Committee did not take up the issue of free education in principle, but expressed its concern about the consequences of the Tuition Fees Act, which had led to a constant increase in the cost of education: "Such increases are contrary to the principle of equality of opportunities between the children of rich families and children of poor families." It limited itself to asking the Netherlands government to take appropriate steps to alleviate or eliminate the adverse effects of the Tuition Fees Act.[41]

The Committee on the Rights of the Child "noted with concern" the reservations to Articles 26, 37 and 40 of the CRC.[42] These reservations entail inter alia that the provisions of Article 26[43] shall not imply an independent entitlement of children to social security, including social insurance. The committee "encouraged" the government of the Netherlands to withdraw all of its reservations.[44]

More particularly, the Committee on the Rights of the Child was concerned about the lack of information regarding the implementation of Article 4 of the Convention[45] and the use to the "maximum extent" of available resources to implement the economic, social, and cultural rights of children. The committee urged the Netherlands "to develop ways to establish a systematic assessment of the impact of budgetary allocations and macroeconomic policies on the implementation of children's rights and to collect and disseminate information in this regard."[46]

The Elderly and the Disabled

In its report to the ESC Committee, the Netherlands expressed the view that it would like to see the rate of employment among older persons rise.[47] This was quite a change from earlier policy, when older persons were encouraged to retire early so as to free places for the younger persons—obviously a result of changed market conditions. In his oral response, the representative of the Netherlands, replying to questions on age limits, discrimination on the grounds of handicap, and measures to combat age discrimination, said that the Netherlands had only recently started to rethink its attitude toward formerly widely accepted age limits; there was now a growing consensus that age limits were acceptable only under certain conditions, "such as necessity," and that any distinction on the ground of age without sufficient justification was discriminatory.[48]

NJCM called attention to the lack of employment opportunities for older and disabled persons. It requested in particular clarification as to the responsibility of the government for the disproportionate unemployment of disabled persons and the status of possible measures with a view to improving employment of the disabled.[49] It criticized the Dutch government for not mentioning in its report protective measures against discrimination of disabled persons, a phenomenon that was increasing, partly as a result of the privatization of social security services. In its concluding observations, the ESC Committee did not explicitly mention handicapped persons, but limited itself to expressing concern that the reform of the social security system might have certain adverse consequences for "the most underprivileged sectors of society." It did mention persons fifty-five to sixty-five years of age who suffered from discrimination in the labor market and whose unemployment rate was over 50 percent. It "encouraged" the Netherlands government to adopt measures to promote the access of those persons to the labor market.[50]

NJCM called attention to the position of elderly women in relation to health care. It criticized the Netherlands government for not dealing with this issue in its report, in particular referring to longer waiting lists for special care in hospitals; difficulties in obtaining home care when required as a result of problems related to the financing of care; increasing financial contributions to health care and higher health care insurance premiums; the shortage of general practitioners, especially in the larger cities; and longer waiting lists for institutionalized care for the elderly.[51] The issue was taken up by the CEDAW Committee, which "expressed concern" that elderly women might be marginalized within, as well as insufficiently covered by, the health insurance and pension system and urged the Netherlands government to pay special attention to the needs of elderly women.[52]

Migrants, Ethnic Minorities, and Asylum Seekers

In the course of recent years, the position of aliens, ethnic and racial minorities, and asylum seekers in the Netherlands has come under increasing pressure. Of a total population of 16.2 million inhabitants, the Netherlands has now 1.6 million persons of non-Western origin (*allochtonen*).[53] These are persons of whom at least one parent was born in a non-western country, meaning Turkey, Africa (mainly Morocco), Latin America, or Asia (except Indonesia and Japan). According to Central Bureau of Statistics estimates, this number will increase to almost 2 million by the year 2010. The annual number of asylum seekers has decreased from more than 45,000 in 1998 to 18,667 in 2002.[54] The socio-economic position of people of non-Western origin is, on the whole weaker, than that of the native Dutch. The rate of unemployment especially among young persons of Turkish and Moroccan origin as well as from the Netherlands Antilles and Suriname is relatively high. In 2002, the rate of unemployment among *allochtonen* was four to five times as high as among autochthonous Dutchmen (see Table 1).

Among young people the difference was even greater (see Table 2).

The Netherlands government, in its report to the ESC Committee, made reference to the Fair Employment of Ethnic Minorities Act, adopted by Parliament in 1994, which obliges employers to produce public annual reports on the composition of their workforce.[55] However, NJCM called attention to the tension between this legislation, which is meant to promote employment participation of ethnic minorities, and the protection of the right to privacy, "because it contained a system in which many personal data had to be registered by employers and submitted to government agencies." Another example was the discussion on measures to prevent ethnic segregation in the school system ("black schools"). This affects both public and private (religious) schools, depending on the neighborhoods in which autochthonous and "allochtonous" parents happen to live. Some of the proposed measures were seen as an unjustified interference with the freedom of school choice of the parents.[56] Three years later, the government pointed out that, "within the requisite quality criteria," pupils were able to attend the schools of their parents' choice: "In that sense, the choice lay with parents and pupils rather than with the Government."[57] However, in its concluding observations, the CERD Committee expressed concern at de

TABLE 1.   Rate of unemployment in the Netherlands according to ethnic origin, as a percentage of total professional population, 2002

Turks	Moroccans	Surinamese	Antilleans	Native Dutch
14	14	10	12	3

Socio-Cultural Planning Agency (SCP), *Rapportage Minderheden 2003* (Reporting on minorities 2003), p. 214. I thank Han Entzinger for this reference.

TABLE 2.   Rate of unemployment in the Netherlands among young people (ages 15–24) according to ethnic origin, as a percentage of the total professional young population, 2002

Turks	Moroccans	Surinamese	Antilleans	Native Dutch
18	17	30	27	7

SCP, *Rapportage Minderheden 2003* (Reporting on minorities 2003), p. 214

facto school segregation in a number of localities and recommended that the Government undertake further measures to reduce de facto segregation and to promote a multicultural educational system.[58]

The government made reference to a government-sponsored assessment of the general Association of Employment Agencies' code of conduct aimed at preventing racial discrimination in employment agencies.[59] But NJCM pointed out that the government neglected to report that this assessment resulted in the conclusion that the code was insufficiently effective: "Moreover, it remained unclear to what extent the Government accepted responsibility for racial discrimination on the labor market."[60] Furthermore, NJCM noted that there was nothing in the government report about the limitations of access to the labor market for non-citizens among ethnic minorities. It also criticized the absence of specific information on the policy of the government to tackle the problems of dropping out of school and criminal activities by young people from ethnic minorities.[61] Also not mentioned in the government report was the so-called Matching Bill (Koppelingswet); this bill excludes illegal immigrants from, among other programs, socialized medical care. Although the government did mention that "in principle" everybody had access to trained personnel for the treatment of common diseases and injuries,[62] NJCM pointed to the financial barrier that in practice obstructed this access for illegal immigrants. Illegally residing immigrants had to pay out of pocket for these medical expenses. It worried, therefore, that the health of illegal immigrants in the Netherlands would suffer from these new regulations: "Hospitals fear that they will not receive payment for medical care supplied to undocumented migrants, since this is only granted to them when they can prove that they are structurally burdened by undocumented immigrants who cannot pay the bill."[63] NJCM suggested that the Netherlands was thus in violation of Article 12 of the ICESCR and Article 12 of the Convention on the Elimination of All Forms of Discrimination against Women.[64]

NJCM was further concerned that participation in primary, secondary, and higher education of girls and women from ethnic minorities was lagging behind the educational participation of girls and women with a Dutch background: "[G]irls from ethnic minorities face a double educational back-log: as members of a minority who have no Dutch background, and as being girls."[65]

The CEDAW Committee took up this matter in its concluding observations. It expressed concern at the continuing discrimination against refugee and minority women who suffered from multiple discrimination, based both on their sex and on their ethnic background, particularly with regard to education, employment, and violence against women. It also expressed concern about manifestations of racism and xenophobia in the Netherlands. It urged the government to take effective measures to eliminate discrimination against immigrant, refugee and minority women, both in society at large and within their communities.[66]

The CRC Committee paid attention to the fate of unaccompanied asylum-seeking minors. It recommended that the government strengthen measures so as to provide immediate counseling and full access to education and other services for refugee and asylum-seeking children. It stated that the government should also take effective measures for the integration of these children into society.[67] It expressed concern about the sexual exploitation of children, often victims of trafficking, "including the disappearance of unaccompanied minor asylum-seekers from reception centers." It urged the Netherlands government to give prompt and serious attention to the need to ensure that asylum-seeking procedures effectively protect children from involvement in trafficking for sexual exploitation.[68] It noted the poorer educational performance of children from ethnic minorities and urged the Netherlands government to provide assistance to families from ethnic minorities with socioeconomic problems, thus addressing the root causes of poor educational performance.[69]

The CERD Committee noted that the Netherlands was one of the few countries to refer to minorities without making a distinction between nationals and non-nationals. Yet, the unemployment rate among such minority groups remained four times as high as among the native Dutch population, and the committee expressed concern about insufficient protection against discrimination in the labor market.[70] It asked the government, in its next report, to provide information about the further implementation of the Employment of Minorities (Promotion) Act, among others.[71]

Conclusion

As was mentioned at the outset of this chapter, the Netherlands has received extensive criticism in its pursuit of ESC rights from academics as well as NGOs. From a recent study, it appears that the economic and social rights of undocumented migrants in Belgium appear to be little better than in the Netherlands.[72] The authors conclude that undocumented migrants are de facto excluded from participating in the Belgian social security system.[73]

The Belgian situation, with regard to undocumented migrants, may not be unrepresentative for the rest of Europe. Certainly, the situation in the Netherlands seems to be rather similar. It would cause little surprise if the implementation of the full range of economic, social, and cultural rights for the population as a whole would also show similar characteristics for the remainder of Western Europe.[74] That remains, however, a matter of speculation. The conclusions of this chapter are based on the situation in the Netherlands only.

This chapter has made repeated reference to reports of one particular NGO: the Netherlands section of the International Commission of Jurists (NJCM).[75] Does this mean that the views of this organization are always more in line with the truth than that of the government? Not necessarily. NJCM provides the only independent and systematic comment on all the periodic reports by the Netherlands to the UN treaty committees. That does not make these reports necessarily more truthful or more factual than those submitted by the government itself. They do provide, however, challenges to the latter reports and raise issues that may be left out or ignored by the government. That makes these "shadow reports" highly useful to the treaty committees. As the French saying goes, "Du choc des opinions jaillit la vérité."[76]

The same is true, mutatis mutandis, for the findings of the treaty committees. They do not have a monopoly on wisdom, either. But they consist (mainly) of independent international experts, who may raise matters and ask questions that a government may preferably avoid. That makes the confrontation between these committees and the reporting government both interesting and useful. Moreover, all of the committees have now made it their habit to publish concluding observations after the discussion with the government in question has ended. These observations usually contain an evaluation of the state report and of the dialogue with representatives of the state party; they refer to positive developments, bottlenecks, and matters of concern to the committee and end with a number of suggestions and recommendations. These recommendations may serve as point of departure when the next periodic report of the state party is being considered. The committees seem on the whole to have become more daring in their pronouncements on the state party's record.[77]

Under the ICESCR, state parties are under the obligation to achieve progressively the full realization of the rights that are mentioned in the Covenant.[78] It is therefore only logical that the ESC Committee pays particular attention to possible developments of a *retrogressive* nature that are forbidden by the Covenant. The committee has declared that States Parties have a minimum core obligation to ensure the satisfaction of, at the very least, minimum essential levels of each of the rights.[79] The CEDAW and CERD committees naturally are concerned about all developments that are in fact or potentially discriminatory in their particular fields of attention, whereas the CRC committee looks at the ESC rights of children as mentioned in Article 4 of the Convention on the Rights of the Child.

In the legal order of the Netherlands, the ICESCR has a somewhat weak status, as it cannot be appealed to before the courts: it has no direct effect. Should the Netherlands nevertheless be considered a Walhalla of economic, social, and cultural rights? If compared to most of the states in the world, as listed in the UNDP's Human Rights Development Index, the response is bound to be "yes." But that is only the easy part of the problem, which applies of course to all developed countries. The response must, however, be far more qualified if we look at particular groups within Dutch society.

The chapter has shown aspects of discrimination against women at work. One may not necessarily agree with the CEDAW Committee, which seems to consider part-time work activities as inferior to full-time work. Yet one's judgment on this question will be determined by the extent to which the choice of part-time work is a free one or one forced upon women by prevailing circumstances. Neither the government reports nor the NJCM shadow reports nor the concluding observations of the committee offer a definitive answer. Be that as it may, the fact remains that, on average, women still are not paid equal salaries for equal work.[80] It is also true that the majority of the top positions in corporate and academic life are still occupied by men rather than women.[81] One of the reasons for this situation may be the problem of insufficient or prohibitively expensive child care facilities. Although in principle it could be the father as often as the mother who takes care of the children,[82] in actual practice it is usually the mother who carries the brunt of these responsibilities. That often leaves little time and opportunity for developing a professional career pattern. This still leaves open the question of why more women without children have not managed to break through the "glass ceiling" that prevents most women from reaching the top. I consider myself insufficiently qualified to deal with this question, though I tend to reject the classical feminist notion that men do not want to accept women in high positions. On the contrary, it seems that appointment committees often find it very hard to locate sufficiently qualified women for top positions.

The lack of paid maternity leave for members of representative bodies may be seen as a curious aberration in what otherwise seems to be an overall situation of genuine attempts to provide equal rights for men and women, in accordance with the relevant international human rights obligations.

The obligation to pay tuition for students in schools for secondary and higher education has drawn international attention. It comes close to a violation of the right to free tuition and at least falls short of the obligation mentioned in Article 13 of the ICESCR of the "progressive introduction of free education," no matter how generous the available scholarships and bursaries may be. It seems to be a curious phenomenon that this deficiency, though noted by human rights organizations, has drawn comparatively little attention from parliamentarians, political parties, and general public opinion. It may be called "curious" in view of the generally held conviction in the Netherlands that the country should and does in fact observe international human rights obligations. Could this be a matter of the exception that proves the rule?

The reservation by the Netherlands to the CRC, denying children a right to social security, is another limitation of children's ESC rights. It appears that other Western European states do not share the Netherlands' fears in this respect. However, the Netherlands' government recognizes the need for more employment of elderly persons. Until a few years ago, official policy was to encourage early retirement—as early as the middle fifties—in order to create jobs for younger persons. Nowadays, the view prevails that society is in need of the contributions of the elderly. Yet—unlike, for instance the United States—overall compulsory retirement at the age of sixty-five remains the rule.

The main problems in the field of ESC rights relate to the categories of (il)legal migrants, ethnic minorities, and asylum seekers. De facto school segregation ("black schools") is on the rise in the major cities.[83] This is partly a consequence of the fact that the members of ethnic minorities who belong to the lower socioeconomic strata, are forced, if only for financial reasons, to live in the same areas of the city. The quality of these schools is on the whole perceived as lower than that of "white" areas of the city. Nevertheless, the percentage of university students with an ethnic minority origin is rising, though the percentage that continues for a doctoral degree is not.[84] The CERD Committee has noted racial discrimination in employment, and there is limited access to the labor market for non-autochthon members of minority ethnic communities. As far as educational opportunities are concerned, as NJCM has noted, the situation is worst for girls, who suffer both for lacking a Dutch background and for being females.

The most pressing, though hardly documented, problem, however, is that of illegal residents. These vary from persons who are brought to the Netherlands by traffickers, mainly for economic reasons, to asylum seekers whose claim for asylum has been rejected (*uitgeprocedeerd*), but who for various—including humanitarian—reasons are not deported. They find it difficult to obtain employment, housing, health services, or social benefits. Estimates vary from one hundred thousand to two hundred thousand or more, but the precise size of this population is virtually unknown. I submit that here lies the main deficiency of the Netherlands in the area of economic, social, and cultural rights, which according to the ICESCR, supposedly apply to "everyone."

It has been the contention of this chapter that the Netherlands is not a Walhalla of economic, social, and cultural rights. Some readers may be left with the impression that, in spite of all, the situation of ESC rights in the Netherlands is still far better than in many other parts of the world—perhaps even including the United States and Canada, and I won't belabor that point.

Appendix 1
International Covenant on Economic, Social and Cultural Rights

Preamble

The States Parties to the present Covenant,

Considering that, in accordance with the principles proclaimed in the Charter of the United Nations, recognition of the inherent dignity and of the equal and inalienable rights of all members of the human family is the foundation of freedom, justice and peace in the world,

Recognizing that these rights derive from the inherent dignity of the human person,

Recognizing that, in accordance with the Universal Declaration of Human Rights, the ideal of free human beings enjoying freedom from fear and want can only be achieved if conditions are created whereby everyone may enjoy his economic, social and cultural rights, as well as his civil and political rights,

Considering the obligation of States under the Charter of the United Nations to promote universal respect for, and observance of, human rights and freedoms,

Realizing that the individual, having duties to other individuals and to the community to which he belongs, is under a responsibility to strive for the promotion and observance of the rights recognized in the present Covenant,

Agree upon the following articles:

Part I

Article 1

1. All peoples have the right of self-determination. By virtue of that right they freely determine their political status and freely pursue their economic, social and cultural development.
2. All peoples may, for their own ends, freely dispose of their natural wealth and resources without prejudice to any obligations arising out of international economic co-operation, based upon the principle of mutual benefit, and international law. In no case may a people be deprived of its own means of subsistence.
3. The States Parties to the present Covenant, including those having responsibility for the administration of Non-Self-Governing and Trust Territories, shall promote the realization of the right of self-determination, and shall respect that right, in conformity with the provisions of the Charter of the United Nations.

Part II

Article 2

1. Each State Party to the present Covenant undertakes to take steps, individually and through international assistance and co-operation, especially economic and technical, to the maximum of its available resources, with a view to achieving progressively the full realization of the rights recognized in the present Covenant by all appropriate means, including particularly the adoption of legislative measures.
2. The States Parties to the present Covenant undertake to guarantee that the rights enunciated in the present Covenant will be exercised without discrimination of any kind as to race, colour, sex, language, religion, political or other opinion, national or social origin, property, birth or other status.
3. Developing countries, with due regard to human rights and their national economy, may determine to what extent they would guarantee the economic rights recognized in the present Covenant to non-nationals.

Article 3

The States Parties to the present Covenant undertake to ensure the equal right of men and women to the enjoyment of all economic, social and cultural rights set forth in the present Covenant.

Article 4

The States Parties to the present Covenant recognize that, in the enjoyment of those rights provided by the State in conformity with the present Covenant, the State may subject such rights only to such limitations as are determined by law only in so far as this may be compatible with the nature of these rights and solely for the purpose of promoting the general welfare in a democratic society.

Article 5

1. Nothing in the present Covenant may be interpreted as implying for any State, group or person any right to engage in any activity or to perform any act aimed at the destruction of any of the rights or freedoms recognized herein, or at their limitation to a greater extent than is provided for in the present Covenant.
2. No restriction upon or derogation from any of the fundamental human rights recognized or existing in any country in virtue of law, conventions, regulations or custom shall be admitted on the pretext that the present Covenant does not recognize such rights or that it recognizes them to a lesser extent.

Part III

Article 6

1. The States Parties to the present Covenant recognize the right to work, which includes the right of everyone to the opportunity to gain his living by work which he freely chooses or accepts, and will take appropriate steps to safeguard this right.
2. The steps to be taken by a State Party to the present Covenant to achieve the full realization of this right shall include technical and vocational guidance and training programmes, policies and techniques to achieve steady economic, social and cultural development and full and productive employment under conditions safeguarding fundamental political and economic freedoms to the individual.

Article 7

The States Parties to the present Covenant recognize the right of everyone to the enjoyment of just and favorable conditions of work which ensure, in particular:

(a) Remuneration which provides all workers, as a minimum, with:
  (i) Fair wages and equal remuneration for work of equal value without distinction of any kind, in particular women being guaranteed conditions of work not inferior to those enjoyed by men, with equal pay for equal work;
  (ii) A decent living for themselves and their families in accordance with the provisions of the present Covenant;
(b) Safe and healthy working conditions;
(c) Equal opportunity for everyone to be promoted in his employment to an appropriate higher level, subject to no considerations other than those of seniority and competence;
(d) Rest, leisure and reasonable limitation of working hours and periodic holidays with pay, as well as remuneration for public holidays

Article 8

1. The States Parties to the present Covenant undertake to ensure:
  (a) The right of everyone to form trade unions and join the trade union of his choice, subject only to the rules of the organization concerned, for the promotion and protection of his economic and social interests. No restrictions may be placed on the exercise of this right other than those prescribed by law and which are necessary in a democratic society in the interests of national security or public order or for the protection of the rights and freedoms of others;
  (b) The right of trade unions to establish national federations or confederations and the right of the latter to form or join international trade-union organizations;
  (c) The right of trade unions to function freely subject to no limitations other than those prescribed by law and which are necessary in a democratic society in the interests of national security or public order or for the protection of the rights and freedoms of others;
  (d) The right to strike, provided that it is exercised in conformity with the laws of the particular country.
2. This article shall not prevent the imposition of lawful restrictions on the exercise of these rights by members of the armed forces or of the police or of the administration of the State.
3. Nothing in this article shall authorize States Parties to the International Labour Organization Convention of 1948 concerning Freedom of Association and Protection of the Right to Organize to take legislative measures which would prejudice, or apply the law in

such a manner as would prejudice, the guarantees provided for in that Convention.

Article 9

The States Parties to the present Covenant recognize the right of everyone to social security, including social insurance.

Article 10

The States Parties to the present Covenant recognize that:

1. The widest possible protection and assistance should be accorded to the family, which is the natural and fundamental group unit of society, particularly for its establishment and while it is responsible for the care and education of dependent children. Marriage must be entered into with the free consent of the intending spouses.
2. Special protection should be accorded to mothers during a reasonable period before and after childbirth. During such period working mothers should be accorded paid leave or leave with adequate social security benefits.
3. Special measures of protection and assistance should be taken on behalf of all children and young persons without any discrimination for reasons of parentage or other conditions. Children and young persons should be protected from economic and social exploitation. Their employment in work harmful to their morals or health or dangerous to life or likely to hamper their normal development should be punishable by law. States should also set age limits below which the paid employment of child labour should be prohibited and punishable by law.

Article 11

1. The States Parties to the present Covenant recognize the right of everyone to an adequate standard of living for himself and his family, including adequate food, clothing and housing, and to the continuous improvement of living conditions. The States Parties will take appropriate steps to ensure the realization of this right, recognizing to this effect the essential importance of international co-operation based on free consent.
2. The States Parties to the present Covenant, recognizing the fundamental right of everyone to be free from hunger, shall take, indi-

vidually and through international co-operation, the measures, including specific programmes, which are needed:

(a)   To improve methods of production, conservation and distribution of food by making full use of technical and scientific knowledge, by disseminating knowledge of the principles of nutrition and by developing or reforming agrarian systems in such a way as to achieve the most efficient development and utilization of natural resources;

(b)   Taking into account the problems of both food-importing and food-exporting countries, to ensure an equitable distribution of world food supplies in relation to need.

Article 12

1. The States Parties to the present Covenant recognize the right of everyone to the enjoyment of the highest attainable standard of physical and mental health.

2. The steps to be taken by the States Parties to the present Covenant to achieve the full realization of this right shall include those necessary for:

(a)   The provision for the reduction of the stillbirth-rate and of infant mortality and for the healthy development of the child;

(b)   The improvement of all aspects of environmental and industrial hygiene;

(c)   The prevention, treatment and control of epidemic, endemic, occupational and other diseases;

(d)   The creation of conditions which would assure to all medical service and medical attention in the event of sickness.

Article 13

1. The States Parties to the present Covenant recognize the right of everyone to education. They agree that education shall be directed to the full development of the human personality and the sense of its dignity, and shall strengthen the respect for human rights and fundamental freedoms. They further agree that education shall enable all persons to participate effectively in a free society, promote understanding, tolerance and friendship among all nations and all racial, ethnic or religious groups, and further the activities of the United Nations for the maintenance of peace.

2. The States Parties to the present Covenant recognize that, with a view to achieving the full realization of this right:

(a) Primary education shall be compulsory and available free to all;

(b) Secondary education in its different forms, including technical and vocational secondary education, shall be made generally available and accessible to all by every appropriate means, and in particular by the progressive introduction of free education;

(c) Higher education shall be made equally accessible to all, on the basis of capacity, by every appropriate means, and in particular by the progressive introduction of free education;

(d) Fundamental education shall be encouraged or intensified as far as possible for those persons who have not received or completed the whole period of their primary education;

(e) The development of a system of schools at all levels shall be actively pursued, an adequate fellowship system shall be established, and the material conditions of teaching staff shall be continuously improved.

3. The States Parties to the present Covenant undertake to have respect for the liberty of parents and, when applicable, legal guardians to choose for their children schools, other than those established by the public authorities, which conform to such minimum educational standards as may be laid down or approved by the State and to ensure the religious and moral education of their children in conformity with their own convictions.

4. No part of this article shall be construed so as to interfere with the liberty of individuals and bodies to establish and direct educational institutions, subject always to the observance of the principles set forth in paragraph I of this article and to the requirement that the education given in such institutions shall conform to such minimum standards as may be laid down by the State.

Article 14

Each State Party to the present Covenant which, at the time of becoming a Party, has not been able to secure in its metropolitan territory or other territories under its jurisdiction compulsory primary education, free of charge, undertakes, within two years, to work out and adopt a detailed plan of action for the progressive implementation, within a reasonable number of years, to be fixed in the plan, of the principle of compulsory education free of charge for all.

Appendix 2
Excerpts from President Franklin Delano Roosevelt's State of the Union Address, January 6, 1941

In the future days which we seek to make secure, we look forward to a world founded upon four essential human freedoms.

The first is freedom of speech and expression—everywhere in the world.

The second is freedom of every person to worship God in his own way—everywhere in the world.

The third is freedom from want, which, translated into world terms, means economic understandings which will secure to every nation a healthy peacetime life for its inhabitants—everywhere in the world.

The fourth is freedom from fear, which, translated into world terms, means a world-wide reduction of armaments to such a point and in such a thorough fashion that no nation will be in a position to commit an act of physical aggression against any neighbor—anywhere in the world.

Appendix 3
Excerpts from President Franklin Delano Roosevelt's State of the Union Address, January 11, 1944

It is our duty now to begin to lay the plans and determine the strategy for the winning of a lasting peace and the establishment of an American standard of living higher than ever before known. We cannot be content, no matter how high that general standard of living may be, if some fraction of our people—whether it be one-third or one-fifth or one-tenth—is ill-fed, ill-clothed, ill housed, and insecure.

This Republic had its beginning, and grew to its present strength, under the protection of certain inalienable political rights—among them the right of free speech, free press, free worship, trial by jury, freedom from unreasonable searches and seizures. They were our rights to life and liberty.

As our Nation has grown in size and stature, however—as our industrial economy expanded—these political rights proved inadequate to assure us equality in the pursuit of happiness.

We have come to a clear realization of the fact that true individual freedom cannot exist without economic security and independence. "Necessitous men are not free men." People who are hungry and out of a job are the stuff of which dictatorships are made.

In our day these economic truths have become accepted as self-evident. We have accepted, so to speak, a second Bill of Rights under which a new basis of security and prosperity can be established for all regardless of station, race, or creed.

Among these are:

The right to a useful and remunerative job in the industries or shops or farms or mines of the Nation;

The right to earn enough to provide adequate food and clothing and recreation;

The right of every farmer to raise and sell his products at a return which will give him and his family a decent living;

The right of every businessman, large and small, to trade in an atmosphere of freedom from unfair competition and domination by monopolies at home or abroad;

The right of every family to a decent home;

The right to adequate medical care and the opportunity to achieve and enjoy good health;

The right to adequate protection from the economic fears of old age, sickness, accident, and unemployment;

The right to a good education.

Abbreviations

AAAS	American Association for the Advancement of Science
ADA	Americans with Disabilities Act
ADC	Aid to Dependent Children
AFDC	Aid to Families with Dependent Children
AI	Amnesty International
CCF	Co-operative Commonwealth Federation
CCSD	Canadian Council on Social Development
CEDAW	Convention on the Elimination of All Forms of Discrimination against Women
CERD	International Convention on the Elimination of All Forms of Racial Discrimination
CHST	Canada Health and Social Transfer
CPP	Canada Pension Plan
CRC	Convention on the Rights of the Child
EAPD	Employment Assistance for People with Disabilities
ECOSOC	Economic and Social Council
EEOC	Equal Employment and Opportunity Commission
EI	Employment Insurance
ESC	Economic, social, and cultural
EWI	enter without inspection
GAO	Government Accounting Office
GDP	gross domestic product
HMO	health maintenance organizations
HRW	Human Rights Watch
HUD	Housing and Urban Development
ICCPR	International Covenant on Civil and Political Rights
ICESCR	International Covenant on Economic, Social and Cultural Rights
ILO	International Labor Organization
INS	Immigration and Naturalization Service
IRCA	Immigration Reform and Control Act
KWRU	Kensington Welfare Rights Union

MDG	Millennium Development Goals
NAALC	North American Agreement on Labour Cooperation
NASW-PA	Pennsylvania Chapter of the National Association of Social Workers
NDP	New Democratic Party
NGO	nongovernmental organizations
NJCM	Netherlands section of the International Commission of Jurists
NLRA	National Labor Relations Act
ODSP	Ontario Disability Support Program
OECD	Organisation for Economic Co-operation and Development
OF	Opportunities Fund
OW	Ontario Works
PPEHRC	Poor People's Economic Human Rights Campaign
PRWORA	Personal Responsibility and Work Opportunity Reconciliation Act
RRAP-D	Residential Rehabilitation Assistance Program for Persons with Disabilities
SCPI	Supporting Communities Program Initiatives
TANF	Temporary Assistance to Needy Families
TRJI	Transnational Racial Justice Initiative
UDHR	Universal Declaration of Human Rights
UN	United Nations
UNDP	United Nations Development Program
UNESCO	United Nations Educational, Scientific and Cultural Organization
UNIYDP	United Nations International Year of Disabled Persons

Notes

Introduction

1. Anatole France, *The Red Lily* (Le lys rouge), trans. Winifred Stephens (New York: John Lane, 1910), p. 95.

2. Karl Marx, "Critique of the Gotha Program," in Lewis S. Feuer, ed., *Marx and Engels: Basic Writings on Politics and Philosophy* (Garden City, N.Y.: Anchor Books, 1959), p. 119.

3. Friedrich Engels, "The Anti-Duhring" [1878], in Micheline R. Ishay, ed., *The Human Rights Reader: Major Political Essays, Speeches and Documents from the Bible to the Present* (New York: Routledge, 1997), p. 217.

4. Both figures from CIA (Central Intelligence Agency), *World Factbook 2003*, http://www.cia.gov/cia/publications/factbook/geos/us.html and http://www.cia.gov/cia/publications/factbook/geos/ca.html.

5. Calculated from figures in World Bank, *2004 World Development Indicators* (Washington, D.C.: World Bank, 2004). See ibid., Table 2.7, "Distribution of Income or Consumption," pp. 60 and 62.

6. Figures from Andrew Hacker, "The Underworld of Work," *New York Review of Books* 51, no. 2 (February 12, 2004): 38.

7. Steven Greenhouse, "Workers Assail Night Lock-Ins by Wal-Mart," *New York Times*, January 18, 2004, pp. 1 and 23; and Steven Greenhouse, "Wal-Mart: A Nation unto Itself," *New York Times*, April 17, 2004.

8. Barbara Ehrenreich, *Nickel and Dimed: On (Not) Getting By in America* (New York: Henry Holt, 2001).

9. David K. Shipler, "A Poor Cousin of the Middle Class," *New York Times Magazine*, January 18, 2004, pp. 22–27.

10. We recognize that the American terminology is "Native Americans," whereas Canadians tend to refer to "Aboriginals," or "indigenous peoples."

11. Frank Chalk and Kurt Jonassohn, *The History and Sociology of Genocide: Analyses and Case Studies* (New Haven, Conn.: Yale University Press, 1990), pp. 173–203.

12. Geoffrey York, *The Dispossessed: Life and Death in Native Canada* (Toronto: Lester and Orpen Dennys, 1989), pp. 246 ff.

13. Canadian Council on Social Development, "Poverty Rates for Selected Non-elderly Family Types, 1980–1995," http://www.ccsd.ca/fs_pov95.htm.

14. Campaign 2000, "Child Poverty in Ontario: Report Card 2000," p. 10, http://www.campaign2000.ca.

15. Walter Korpi and Joakim Palme, "New Politics and Class Politics in the Context of Austerity and Globalization: Welfare State Regress in 18 Countries, 1975–95," *American Political Science Review* 97, no. 3 (August 2003): 435.

16. Frances Fox Piven, "Retrospective Comments," *Perspectives on Politics* 1, no. 4 (December 2003): 707–10.

17. For further information, see Jacob Riis, *How the Other Half Lives: Studies among the Tenements of New York* [1890], ed. Sam Bass Warner, Jr. (Cambridge, Mass.: Belknap Press of Harvard University Press, 1970); Marilyn Fischer, *On Addams* (Toronto: Thomson, 2004); Maurice Isserman, *The Other American: The Life of Michael Harrington* (New York: Public Affairs, 2000).

18. William Julius Wilson, *The Truly Disadvantaged: The Inner City, the Underclass, and Public Policy* (Chicago: University of Chicago Press, 1987).

19. Robert Justin Goldstein, "The United States," in Jack Donnelly and Rhoda E. Howard, eds., *International Handbook of Human Rights* (New York: Greenwood Press, 1987), pp. 432–33.

20. Louis Henkin, "Rights: Here and There," *Columbia Law Review* 81, no. 8 (December 1981): 1588–90.

21. Abdullahi A. An-Na'im, "Promises We Should All Keep in Common Cause," in Susan Moller Okin (with Respondents), *Is Multiculturalism Bad for Women?* (Princeton, N.J.: Princeton University Press, 1999), pp. 61–62.

22. Vienna Declaration and Programme of Action: World Conference on Human Rights, Vienna, June14–25, 1993 (UN Doc. A/Conf. 157/23, par. 5). This statement echoed earlier affirmations of the indivisible nature of human rights. Witness, e.g., the Universal Declaration of Human Rights, General Assembly Resolution 217 A (III), adopted December 10, 1948, and the 1968 Proclamation of Teheran, which commented, "Since human rights and fundamental freedoms are indivisible, the full realization of civil and political rights is impossible." UN Doc. A/Conf. 32/41, par. 13.

23. Henry Shue, *Basic Rights: Subsistence, Affluence, and United States Foreign Policy* (Princeton, N.J.: Princeton University Press, 1980), pp. 13–74.

24. Michael Ignatieff, *Human Rights as Politics and Idolatry* (Princeton, N.J.: Princeton University Press, 2001), p. 90.

25. Ibid., 95.

26. Carter also signed the two International Covenants and the Inter-American Convention on Human Rights. The Senate gave its formal "advice and consent" to the International Covenant on Civil and Political Rights in 1992, but has taken no action on the American Convention. As Stark emphasizes, the United States is the only major industrialized democracy that has yet to ratify the ICESCR. Barbara Stark, "U.S. Ratification of the Other Half of the International Bill of Rights," in David P. Forsythe, ed., *The United States and Human Rights: Looking Inward and Outward* (Lincoln: University of Nebraska Press, 2000), pp. 75–93.

27. On health care, see Nick Eberstadt, *The Poverty of Communism* (New Brunswick, N.J.: Transaction Publishers, 1990).

28. Office of the High Commissioner for Human Rights, "Introduction to the Human Rights Committee," http://www.unhchr.ch/html/menu2/6/a/intro hrc.htm (accessed May 27, 2004).

29. Philip Alston, "The Committee on Economic, Social and Cultural Rights," in Alston, ed., *The United Nations and Human Rights: A Critical Appraisal* (Oxford: Clarendon Press, 1992), p. 475.

30. "The Limburg Principles on the Implementation of the International Covenant on Economic, Social and Cultural Rights," *Human Rights Quarterly* 9, no. 2 (May 1987): 122–35; and "The Maastricht Guidelines on Violations of Economic, Social and Cultural Rights," *Human Rights Quarterly* 20, no. 3 (August 1998): 691–704.

31. For a highly informed commentary from a participant-critic, see Morton E. Winston, "Assessing the Effectiveness of International Human Rights NGOs: Amnesty International," in Claude E. Welch, Jr., ed., *NGOs and Human Rights: Promise and Performance* (Philadelphia: University of Pennsylvania Press, 2001), pp. 25–54.

32. Human Rights Watch, *World Report 2002: Events of 2001* (New York: Human Rights Watch 2002). Human Rights Watch organizes its reports in terms of its five geographical divisions plus the United States; it also reports on its programs, including armaments, children's rights and women's human rights, as well as a variety of special issues and campaigns. For information on Canada and the United States, see respectively http://www.hrw.org/americas/canada.php, and http://www.hrw.org/us/usdom.php. See also Kenneth Roth, "Defending Economic, Social and Cultural Rights: Practical Issues Faced by an International Human Rights Organization," *Human Rights Quarterly* 26, no. 1 (February 2004): 63–73.

33. UN Development Program, Human Development Reports, "Questions about the Human Development Index (HDI)," http://www.undp.org/hdr 2003/faq.html (accessed May 27, 2004).

34. For an early assessment of these reports, see Judith Innes de Neufville, "Human Rights Reporting as a Policy Tool: An Examination of the State Department Country Reports," *Human Rights Quarterly* 8, no. 4 (November 1986): 681–99.

35. "China Assails Human Rights Record of United States," *New York Times*, March 5, 1997. For China's 2003 report, see Information Office of the State Council of the People's Republic of China, "The Human Rights Record of the United States in 2003," March 1, 2004, http://www.china-embassy.org/eng/ xw/t69901.htm.

36. E.g., David L. Cingranelli and David L. Richards, "Measuring the Impact of Human Rights Organizations," in Welch, ed., *NGOs and Human Rights*, pp. 225–37.

37. Isfahan Merali and Valerie Oosterveld, eds., *Giving Meaning to Economic, Social, and Cultural Rights* (Philadelphia: University of Pennsylvania Press, 2001).

38. Seymour Martin Lipset, *Continental Divide: The Values and Institutions of the United States and Canada* (New York: Routledge for C. D. Howe Institute [Canada] and National Planning Association [USA], 1990), p. 2.

39. Robert Mills, *Health Insurance Coverage in the United States: 2002*, Current Population Reports P60–223, United States Census Bureau (September 2003), quoted in Center on Budget and Policy Priorities, "Number of Americans without Health Insurance Rose in 2002" (Washington, D.C., October 8, 2003): p. 1.

40. A. J. Hobbins, "Eleanor Roosevelt, John Humphrey, and Canadian Opposition to the Universal Declaration of Human Rights," *International Journal* 53, no. 2 (spring 1998): 325–42.

41. Anne Bayefsky, "The Human Rights Committee and the Case of Sandra Lovelace," *Canadian Yearbook of International Law* 20 (1982): 244–66.

42. Percentages calculated from theft and homicide figures for Canada, from Statistics Canada, "Crime Statistics," *The Daily*, July 17, 2002, http://www .statcan.ca/Daily/English/020717/d020717b.htm; and theft and homicide figures for the United States, from Rothstein Catalog on Disaster Recovery, "United States Crime Rates 1960–2000," http://www.disastecenter.com/ crime/uscrime.htm (accessed July 2, 2003).

43. Richard Block, "Firearms in Canada and Eight Other Western Countries:

Selected Findings of the 1996 International Crime (Victim) Survey: Working Document," Department of Justice Canada, WD1997–4e, December 1997, http://www.tamerlane.ca/library/research/firearms_block.pdf. For an explanation of the differences in gun ownership and gun control laws, see Leslie A. Pal, "Between the Sights: Gun Control in Canada and the United States," in David M. Thomas, ed., *Canada and the United States: Differences That Count*, 2nd ed. (Peterborough, ON: Broadview Press, 2000), pp. 68–93.

44. All figures in earlier paragraph from L. Kenworthy, "Do Social-Welfare Policies Reduce Poverty? A Cross-National Assessment," Working Paper No. 188, Luxembourg Income Study, 1998; figures cited in Robert M. Solow, "Welfare: The Cheapest Country," *New York Review of Books* 47, no. 5 (March 2000): 21.

45. Figures from David Perry, "What Price Canadian? Taxation and Debt Compared," in Thomas, ed., *Canada and the United States*, Table 4, p. 57, and Table 6, p. 61.

46. Figures from an unpublished table, "International Trade Union Membership Data," accessed July 2, 2003, via Cornell University, School of Industrial and Labor Relations, Catherwood Library, Reference: FAQ (frequently asked questions), http://www.ilr.cornell.edu/library/reference/faq/faq_display.html?faq ID = 46.

47. Lorne and Caroline Brown, *An Unauthorized History of the RCMP* (Toronto: James Lewis and Samuel, 1973), p. 44.

48. Robert Bothwell and J. L. Granatstein, eds., Introduction, *The Gouzenko Transcripts* (Ottawa: Deneau Publishers, 1982), pp. 3–22.

49. G. Horowitz, "Conservatism, Liberalism and Socialism in Canada: an Interpretation," *Canadian Journal of Economics and Political Science* 32, no. 2 (May 1966): 143–70. The French in Quebec were conquered by the English in 1759. *Seigneuries* were large landholdings.

50. On the Canadian West, see Seymour Martin Lipset, *Agrarian Socialism: The Cooperative Commonwealth Federation in Saskatchewan: A Study in Political Sociology* (Garden City, N.Y.: Doubleday, 1968).

51. Ibid., p. 1.

52. Ibid., pp. 10–11.

53. Ibid., p. 37.

54. Doug Baer, Edward Grabb, and William A. Johnston, "The Values of Canadians and Americans: A Critical Analysis and Reassessment," *Social Forces* 68, no. 3 (March 1990): 693–713; and Mebs Kanji and Neil Nevitte, "Who Are the Most Deferential—Canadians or Americans?" in Thomas, ed., *Canada and the United States*, pp. 121–40.

55. Lynn McIntyre et al., "Do Low-Income Mothers Compromise Their Nutrition to Feed their Children?" *Canadian Medical Association Journal* (hereafter *CMAJ*) 168, no. 6 (March 18, 2003), http://www.cmaj.ca/cgi/content/full/ 168/6/686.

56. 1996 figure from Canadian Council on Social Development, "Poverty Statistics," based on data from Statistics Canada, Cat. 13–569-XPB, http://www .ccsd.ca/factsheets/fscphis2.htm (accessed July 2, 2003).

57. Christa Freiler, Laurel Rothman, and Pedro Barata, "Pathways to Progress: Structural Solutions to Address Child Poverty: Summary," *Campaign 2000 Policy Perspectives* (May 2004): 3

58. Lynn McIntyre, Sarah K. Connor, and James Warren, "Child Hunger in Canada: Results of the 1994 National Longitudinal Survey of Children and Youth," *CMAJ* 163, no. 8 (October 17, 2000), http://www.cmaj.ca/cgi/con tent/full/163/8/961.

59. Economic Research Service, United States Department of Agriculture, "Household Food Security in the United States, 2002" (October 30, 2003)), http://www.ers.usda.gov/publications/fanrr35 (accessed May 28, 2004).

60. Angus McLaren, *Our Own Master Race: Eugenics in Canada, 1885–1945* (Toronto: McClelland and Stewart, 1990).

61. Stephen Jay Gould, *The Mismeasure of Man* (New York: W.W. Norton, 1981).

62. Percentages calculated from Statistics Canada, *2001 Census*, "Visible Minority Population by Age," http://www.statcan.ca/english/Pgdb/demo41/htm, and "Population by Aboriginal Group, Provinces and Territories," http://www.statcan.ca/english/Pgdb/demo39a.htm. "Visible minority" is the Canadian term for people who are neither of white (European) genetic ancestry nor Aboriginal.

63. Derek Hum and Wayne Simpson, "Wage Opportunities for Visible Minorities in Canada," *Canadian Public Policy* 25, no. 3 (September 1999): 390.

64. Adam Jones, "Of Rights and Men: Toward a Minoritarian Framing of Male Experience," *Journal of Human Rights* 1, no. 3 (September 2002): 387–403.

65. Margaret E. Keck and Kathryn Sikkink, *Activists beyond Borders: Advocacy Networks in International Politics* (Ithaca, N.Y.: Cornell University Press, 1998), 1–38.

66. Rhoda E. Howard-Hassmann, *Compassionate Canadians: Civic Leaders Discuss Human Rights* (Toronto: University of Toronto Press, 2003), 178–99.

67. Denis Stairs, "Myths, Morals and Reality in Canadian Foreign Policy," *International Journal* 58, no. 2 (spring 2003): 239–56.

68. China Society for Human Rights Studies, Information Office of the State Council of the People's Republic of China, "United States Human Rights Record in 2000" (February 27, 2000), http://www.humanrights-china.org/whitepapers/white_u04.htm.

69. Christopher Howard, "Is the American Welfare State Unusually Small?" *Political Science and Politics* 36, no. 3 (July 2003): 414.

70. Centers for Disease Control and Prevention, "Cases of HIV Infection and AIDS in the United States, 2002," *HIV/AIDS Surveillance Report* 14 (2002), p. 14, http://www.cD.C..gov/hiv/stats/hasr1402.htm, accessed July 20, 2004.

71. Division of Vital Statistics, National Center for Health Statistics, Mortality Tables, "LCWK1. Deaths, Percent of Total Deaths, and Death Rates for the 15 Leading Causes of Death in 5-year Age Groups, by Race and Sex: United States, 2001," http://www.cD.C..gov/nchs/datawh/statab/unpubd/mortabs.htm (accessed July 20, 2004).

72. Korpi and Palme, "New Politics and Class Politics," p. 435.

Chapter 1. Justifying Socioeconomic Rights

1. See David Weissbrodt's Chapter 2 for more information in this regard.

2. Brian Orend, *Human Rights: Concept and Context* (Peterborough, ON: Broadview Press, 2002).

3. An argument probably made first by John Stuart Mill, in his 1859 work *On Liberty* (Indianapolis, Ind.: Hackett, 1978). This is to say, e.g., that we may forcefully resist and punish human rights violators.

4. John Rawls, *A Theory of Justice* (Cambridge, Mass.: Harvard University Press, 1971).

5. Michael Walzer, *Thick and Thin: Moral Argument at Home and Abroad* (Notre Dame, Ind.: Notre Dame University Press, 1994).

6. James Nickel, *Making Sense of Human Rights* (Berkeley: University of California Press, 1987), pp. 51–52.

7. David Wiggins, *Needs, Values and Truth* (Oxford: Basil Blackwell, 1986).

8. Judith Thomson, "A Defence of Abortion," *Philosophy and Public Affairs* (1976): 47–66.

9. Mill, *On Liberty*.

10. Indeed, many of the fine essays in this volume cast a critical eye regarding human rights realization in America and Canada. We are good, but not as good as we would wish, or as some politicians would have us believe.

11. For more on this flexible model, and strategies to avoid human rights inflation, see Orend, *Human Rights*, pp. 120–25.

12. Whether this is true globally is, empirically, more problematic. I have a hunch it might still be so, but in any event, the costs of realizing genuinely global socioeconomic human rights are beyond the ambit of this chapter, which remains focused on North America. I do take up the question in Orend, *Human Rights*, pp. 129–55. See also Rhoda E. Howard-Hassmann, "Moral Integrity and Reparations for Africa," in John Torpey, ed., *Politics and the Past* (Lanham, Md.: Rowman and Littlefield, 2003), pp. 193–215.

13. One of the great strengths of many of this volume's chapters is the detailed descriptions of the extremely difficult lives of some of these people. Note especially the papers on those with disabilities and the homeless. I sense that if accurate descriptions of their conditions were more generally known, the policy environment toward them would improve.

14. Milton Friedman, "The Case for the Negative Income Tax," *National Review* (1967): 8–28. See also http://www.canadiansocialresearch.net/GAI paper.pdf.

15. But I don't think we can actually cut off anyone who genuinely cannot provide subsistence for themselves. We can threaten to do so as an incentive, but in the end they remain human beings, and we must therefore provide for their needs.

16. Maurice Cranston, *What Are Human Rights?* (New York: Basic Books, 1973). Jan Narveson, more recently, asks whether starving people have the right to be fed. His answer is that it's good—charitable—if they get fed, but that it's wrong to coerce everyone through the taxation system to provide the money needed to feed them. That, he says, is theft, a violation of taxpayers' liberty. Indeed, such a policy makes us all "slaves to the badly off." This is a persistent theme in North American libertarianism, and I view it rooted in conceptual linkages called into question in the following text. Jan Narveson, *Moral Matters*, 2nd ed. (Peterborough, ON: Broadview Press, 1999), pp. 143–57, with quote at 156.

17. Henry Shue, *Basic Rights*, 2nd ed. (Princeton, N.J.: Princeton University Press, 1996); and Nickel, *Making Sense of Human Rights*, pp. 147–70.

18. Shue, *Basic Rights*, 2nd ed., pp. 3–65.

19. Ibid., Afterword.

20. Amartya Sen, *Development as Freedom* (New York: Anchor, 2000).

Chapter 2. International Law of Economic, Social, and Cultural Rights

The author is grateful for the assistance of Clay Collins, who helped research and write portions of this manuscript related to the Bush administration's views of economic, social and cultural rights. The author is also grateful for assistance and comments received from Richard Elliott and Mary Rumsey.

1. David Weissbrodt and Teresa O'Toole, "The Development of International Human Rights Law," in Beth Andrus and Sonia A. Rosen, eds., *The Universal Declaration of Human Rights 1948–1988* (New York: Amnesty International USA Legal Support Network, 1988).

2. See Franklin D. Roosevelt, "'Four Freedoms' Speech," *Congressional Record* 87 (1941). See Appendix 2.

3. See Appendix 3.

4. United Nations, Charter, June 26, 1945, 59 *Stat.* 1031, *T.S.* 993, 3 *Bevans* 1153, entered into force October 24, 1945, Art. 55.

5. Ibid., Art. 56.

6. John R. Humphrey, *On the Edge of Greatness: The Diaries of John Humphrey, First Director of the United Nations Division of Human Rights 1948–1949*, ed. A. J. Hobbins (Montreal: McGill-Queen's University Press, 1994), vol. 1; John R. Humphrey, *Human Rights and the United Nations: A Great Adventure* (Dobbs Ferry, N.Y.: Transnational Publishers, 1984).

7. United Nations, Universal Declaration of Human Rights, G.A. res. 217A (III), UN Doc. A/810 at 71 (1948).

8. See Appendix 1.

9. United Nations, International Covenant on Civil and Political Rights, G.A. res. 2200A (XXI), 21 UN GAOR Supp. (No. 16) at 52, UN Doc. A/6316 (1966), 999 *UNT.S.* 171, entered into force March 23, 1976. Art. 2.

10. See Appendix 1.

11. United Nations, Committee on Economic, Social and Cultural Rights (1990) General Comment 3, The Nature of States Parties Obligations (Art. 2, par. 1 of the Covenant), in *Compilation of General Comments and General Recommendations adopted by Human Rights Treaty Bodies*, UN Doc. HRIGENRev.1 (1994), p. 45.

12. Matthew C. R. Craven, *The International Covenant on Economic, Social, and Cultural Rights: A Perspective on Its Development* (Oxford: Oxford University Press, 1995).

13. United Nations, *Compilation of General Comments and General Recommendations*.

14. Ibid.

15. United Nations, Committee on Economic, Social and Cultural Rights. (1997). General Comment 9, The Domestic Application of the Covenant, UN Doc. E/C.12/1998/24 (1998).

16. Amnesty International, *Rights for All* (New York: Amnesty International Publications, 1995), p. 132.

17. A renewed interest in states rights began in 1995 with the Supreme Court decision in *United States v. Lopez*, 514 U.S. 549 (1995). That decision was the first time in sixty years that the Supreme Court struck down a federal statute as exceeding Congress's powers under the Commerce Clause of the United States Constitution.

18. David Weissbrodt, "United States Ratification of the Human Rights Covenants," *Minnesota Law Review* 63, no. 1 (1978): 38–39 n. 45.

19. David Weissbrodt, "Human Rights Legislation and U.S. Foreign Policy," *Georgia Journal of International Comparative Law* 73, supplement (1977): 236 n. 26.

20. The 1951 Convention Relating to the Status of Refugees and its 1967 Protocol provide that refugees should be entitled to treatment at least as favorable

as that accorded to citizens with respect to protection of intellectual property, elementary education, public relief and assistance, labor legislation, and social security. United Nations, Convention Relating to the Status of Refugees, G.A. res. 429 (V), 5 UN GAOR Supp. (No. 20) at 48, UN Doc. A/1775 (1950), *189 UNT.S. 150*, entered into force April 22, 1954; United Nations, Protocol Relating to the Status of Refugees, G.A. res. 2198 (XXI), 21 UN GAOR Supp. (No. 15) at 48, UN Doc. A/6316 (1966) *606 UNT.S. 267*, entered into force October 4, 1967 (applying the Convention without temporal or geographical limitations). The Convention and Protocol also require that States Parties accord to refugees treatment no less favorable than that accorded to non-citizens generally with respect to acquisition of property, trade unions, wage-earning employment, self-employment, professions, housing, and post-elementary education.

21. Jimmy Carter, "President's Human Rights Treaty Message to the Senate," *Weekly Compilation of Presidential Documents* 14 (February 23, 1978): 395–96.

22. Cyrus Vance, "Human Rights and Foreign Policy," *Georgia Journal of International Comparative Law* 73 supplement (1977): 223–24.

23. United Nations General Assembly, *Declaration on the Right to Development*, G.A. res. 41/128, annex, 41 UN GAOR Supp. (No. 53) at 186, UN Doc. A/41/53 (New York: United Nations, 1986).

24. Warren Christopher, *Democracy and Human Rights: Where America Stands* (Washington, D.C.: U.S. Department of State Bureau of Public Affairs, 1993), http://dosfan.lib.uic.edu/ERC/briefing/dossec/1993/9306/930614dossec .html (accessed November 18, 2003).

25. Article 5(e) of the International Convention on the Elimination of All Forms of Racial Discrimination, 660 UNT.S. 195, entered into force January 4, 1969, forbids racial discrimination in regard to such economic, social, and cultural rights as "(i) The rights to work, to free choice of employment, to just and favorable conditions of work, to protection against unemployment, to equal pay for equal work, to just and favorable remuneration; (ii) The right to form and join trade unions; (iii) The right to housing; (iv) The right to public health, medical care, social security and social services; (v) The right to education and training; (vi) The right to equal participation in cultural activities."

26. Betty King, *USUN Press Release #175* (New York: United States Mission to the UN, 1998), http://www.un.int/usa/98_175.htm (accessed November 18, 2003).

27. Betty King, *USUN Press Release #165* (New York: United States Mission to the UN, 1998), http://www.un.int/usa/98_165.htm (accessed November 18, 2003).

28. Kathleen L. Roberts, "The United States and the World: Changing Approaches to Human Rights Diplomacy under the Bush Administration," *Berkeley Journal of International Law* 21, no. 3 (2003); see, e.g., *National Security Strategy of the United States of America* (2002), http://www.whitehouse.gov/nsc/ nss.pdf (accessed November 18, 2003); George W. Bush, "Proclamation 7404— National African American History Month," *Weekly Compilation of Presidential Documents* 37, no. 5 (2001); George W. Bush, "Address Before a Joint Session of the Congress on the State of the Union," *Weekly Compilation of Presidential Documents* 38, no. 5 (2002); George W. Bush, *President Bush Discusses Freedom in Iraq and Middle East* (United States Office of the Press Secretary, 2003), http://www .whitehouse.gov/news/release/2003/11/print/20031106–2.html (accessed November 18, 2003); George W. Bush, "Address to the UN General Assembly in New York City," *Weekly Compilation of Presidential Documents* 39, no. 39 (2003);

George W. Bush, *President's Remarks on Iraq from the Rose Garden* (United States Office of the Press Secretary, 2003), http://www.whitehouse.gov/news/releases/2003/04/print/20030416–3.html (accessed November 18, 2003).

29. Harold Hongju Koh, "A United States Human Rights Policy for the 21st Century," *St. Louis University Law Journal* 46 (2002): 309–10.

30. U.S. Mission to the UN Food and Agriculture Organization, "Annex II: Explanatory Notes/Reservation," in *Report of the World Food Summit: Five Years Later* (Rome: UN Food and Agriculture Organization, 2002), http://www.fao.org/DOCREP/MEETING/005/Y7106E/Y7106E03.htm (accessed November 18, 2003). The United States has not been entirely consistent in viewing the right to adequate food as only an aspect of the right to an adequate standard of living. E.g., in November 2002, the Third Committee of the General Assembly was considering a resolution on the right to adequate food. The U.S. delegation to the Third Committee proposed an amendment to the resolution that would have had the Assembly encourage "all States to take steps with a view to achieving the progressive realization of the right to adequate food, including steps to promote the conditions for everyone to be free from hunger and, as soon as possible, to enjoy fully the right to food, and to elaborate and adopt national plans to combat hunger." United Nations, Draft Resolution: The Right to Food. UN Doc. A/C.3/57/L.68 (November 13, 2002). Although the proposed U.S. amendment was not successful, it showed that the United States can consider the right to adequate food as a separate right. See United Nations, Press Release, "Approves 12 Other Draft Resolutions on Human Rights, Refugee Issues, Including Texts on Cambodia, Sudan, Right to Food, Children's Rights," November 20, 2002.

31. Jackie Sanders, *Jackie Sanders: Statement at the UNICEF Executive Board—Second Regular Session 200—on the UNICEF Medium Term Strategic Plan, December 10, 2001* (U.S. Mission to the UN, 2001), http://www.un.int/usa/01_185.htm (accessed November 18, 2003).

32. See Richard Wall, *Statements and Press Releases: April 7, 2003: Item 10* (The United States Government Delegation to the 59th Session of the UN Commission on Human Rights, 2003), http://www.humanrights-usa.net/statements/0407Item10.htm (accessed November 18, 2003).

33. Joel Daniels, *April 25, 2003: Right to Development, EOV* (The United States Government Delegation to the 59th Session of the UN Commission on Human Rights, 2003), http://www.humanrights-usa.net/statements/0425RtoD.htm (accessed November 18, 2003).

34. George W. Bush, "Remarks to the World Affairs Councils of America Conference," *Weekly Compilation of Presidential Documents* 38, no. 3 (2002): 78.

35. George W. Bush, "Remarks at the Summit of the Americas Working Session," *Weekly Compilation of Presidential Documents* 37, no. 17 (2001): 641.

36. Ibid.

37. See *National Security Strategy*.

38. See *President Bush Discusses Freedom in Iraq and Middle East*.

39. Laura Altieri, "NAFTA and the FTAA: Regional Alternatives to Multilateralism," *Berkeley Journal of International Law* 23, no. 3 (2003).

40. See *National Security Strategy*.

41. Altieri, "NAFTA and the FTAA," p. 849.

42. Ibid., p. 863.

43. Mari Alkatiri, "Address by Mr. Mari Alkatiri, Prime Minister of the Democratic Republic of Timor-Leste," in *Official Records of the Fifty-Eighth Session of the UN General Assembly* (New York: United Nations, 2003).

44. Altieri, "NAFTA and the FTAA."
45. Elisabeth Bumiller, "Bush Says He Will Ask Congress to Extend Africa Trade Benefits," *New York Times*, January 16, 2003.
46. Bhekh Bahadur Thapa, "Address by Mr. Bhekh Bahadur Thapa, Chairman of the Delegation of the Kingdom of Nepal," in *Official Records of the Fifty-Eighth Session of the UN General Assembly* (New York: United Nations, 2003).
47. U.S. Const., art. IV, § 2.
48. These cases reflect a long-standing rule of statutory construction first enunciated by Chief Justice Marshall: "an act of Congress ought never to be construed to violate the law of nations, if any other possible construction remains." [*Murray v. Schooner*] *Charming Betsy*, 6 U.S. (2 Cranch) 34 (1804), quoted in *Lauritzen v. Larsen*, 345 U.S. 571, 578 (1953); see also "we generally construe Congressional legislation to avoid violating international law." *Ma v. Reno*, 208 F.3d 815 (9th Cir. 2000) [citing *Weinberger v. Rossi*, 456 U.S. 25 (1982)], affirmed sub nom. *Zadvydas v. Davis*, 533 U.S. 678 (2001).
49. *The Paquete Habana*, 175 U.S. 677 (1900), quoted most recently in *Sosa v. Alvarez-Machain*, 124 S.Ct. 2759, 2764 (2004).
50. Ibid., p. 700.
51. Harry A. Blackmun, "The Supreme Court and the Law of Nations: Owing a Decent Respect to the Opinions of Mankind," *American Society of International Law Newsletter* 1 (March–May 1994): 6–9. While this section of the chapter focuses principally upon the role of courts in implementing economic, social, and cultural rights, there are nonjudicial mechanisms—such as administrative agencies, ombudsmen, legislative mechanisms, and education—for implementing those rights. See Barbara von Tigerstrom, "Implementing Economic, Social and Cultural Rights: The Role of National Human Rights Institutions," in Isfahan Merali and Valerie Oosterveld, eds., *Giving Meaning to Economic, Social and Cultural Rights* (Philadelphia: University of Pennsylvania Press, 2001), pp. 139–52.
52. See, e.g., *Lawrence v. Texas*, 123 S.Ct. 2472 (2003); *Atkins v. Virginia*, 536 U.S. 304 (2002); *Thompson v. Oklahoma*, 487 U.S. 815 (1988).
53. See, e.g., *United States v. Alvarez-Machain*, 504 U.S. 655 (1992); *Stanford v. Kentucky*, 492 U.S. 361 (1989); *Bowers v. Hardwick*, 478 U.S. 186 (1986).
54. *Pauley v. Kelly*, 255 S.E.2d 859 (W. Va. 1979).
55. Other state courts, however, have found that education is not a fundamental right. These courts relied on a Supreme Court case holding that education is not a fundamental right protected by the Constitution, *San Antonio Ind. School Dist. v. Rodriguez*, 411 U.S. 1 (1973), rather than international standards. See Connie de la Vega, "The Right to Equal Education: Merely a Guiding Principle or Customary International Legal Right," *Harvard BlackLetter Law Journal* 11 (1994): 37–60.
56. *Moore v. Ganim*, 233 Conn. 557, 660 A.2d 742 (1995).
57. Ibid., pp. 771–72.
58. Ibid.
59. Ibid., pp. 780–82 (footnotes and some citations omitted).
60. Ibid., pp. 783–85 (footnotes omitted).
61. *Boehm v. Superior Court*, 178 Cal.App.3d 494, 223 Cal.Rptr. 716 (1986).
62. *Lipscomb v. Simmons*, 884 F.2d 1242 (9th Cir. 1989).
63. 22 U.S.C. §§ 2304(b); see, e.g., U.S. Department of State, *Country Reports for Human Rights Practices for 2002* (2002), http://www.state.gov/g/drl/rls/hrrpt/2002/ (accessed January 9, 2004).

64. 22 U.S.C. §§ 262(d), 2151n, 2304.

65. Neither Canada nor the United States has ratified the American Convention on Human Rights or accepted the jurisdiction of the Inter-American Court of Human Rights.

66. See generally William A. Schabas, *International Human Rights Law and the Canadian Charter*, 2nd ed. (Toronto: Carswell, 1996). The Canadian courts have had several opportunities to incorporate the Covenant on Economic, Social and Cultural Rights into protections for poor people in Canada. See, e.g., *Charter Committee on Poverty Issues* (n.d.), http://www.equalityrights.org/ccpi/cases/ (accessed January 9, 2004). In *Gosselin v. Quebec*, 2002 SCC 84 (2002), the Supreme Court of Canada rejected a claim by welfare recipients under the age of thirty that the social assistance program subjected them to age-based discrimination under Sections 7 (right to life, liberty, and security of the person) and 15(1) (equal protection) of the Canadian Charter of Rights and Freedoms by requiring them to participate in work and training programs. The Supreme Court of Canada refused to interpret Section 7 to establish a positive state obligation to guarantee adequate living standards. Having subjected itself to monitoring under the Covenant on Economic, Social and Cultural Rights, Canada has been found to have failed to pay sufficient attention to the adverse consequences of some of its policies for the enjoyment of economic, social, and cultural rights by certain vulnerable groups. United Nations, Committee on Economic, Social and Cultural Rights, *Consideration of Reports Submitted by States Parties under Article 16 and 17 of the Covenant, Canada*. UN Doc. E/C.12/1/Add.31 (1998), http://www1.umn.edu/humanrts/esc/canada1998.html (accessed January 9, 2004).

Chapter 3. On the Margins of the Human Rights Discourse

1. We do not address labor and education rights, although they are found in the Universal Declaration and ICESCR. Sometimes called social rights, they can also be viewed as civil rights. More importantly, they comprise a different category from welfare rights, being more broadly endorsed by states. E.g., American opposition to the ICESCR does not hinge on labor rights or rights to education in principle but to welfare rights more narrowly defined. The current name of the human rights bureau in the State Department is the Bureau of Democracy, Human Rights, and Labor, indicating ideological acceptance of labor rights. The annual State Department human rights reports also cover labor rights (but not welfare rights). We do not wish to engage on the theoretical point of the dividing line between the various categories of rights. We believe those categories are a useful shorthand, but without definitive boundaries. Labor rights are traditionally seen as social or civil rights, they may be essential for economic welfare for some, and they can have political significance on occasion.

2. See, e.g., A. Glenn Mower, Jr., *International Cooperation for Social Justice: Global and Regional Protection of Economic/Social Rights* (Westport, Conn.: Greenwood, 1985); Paul Hunt, *Reclaiming Social Rights: International and Comparative Perspectives* (Aldershot, UK: Dartmouth, 1996); Theo C. van Boven et al., eds., *The Maastricht Guidelines on Violations of Economic, Social and Cultural Rights* (Utrecht: SIM Special No. 20, 1998); Audrey Chapman and Sage Russell, eds., *Core Obligations: Building a Framework For Economic, Social and Cultural Rights* (Antwerp: Intersentia, 2002); Asbjorn Eide, Cararina Krause, and Allan Rosas, eds.,

Economic, Social and Cultural Rights: A Textbook (Dordrecht: Nijhoff, 1995); Allan McChesney, *Promoting and Defending Economic, Social and Cultural Rights: A Handbook* (Washington, D.C.: American Association for the Advancement of Science, 2000); and Merali and Oosterveld, eds., *Giving Meaning to Economic, Social, and Cultural Rights.*

3. See, e.g., among Western authors, Henry Shue, *Basic Rights: Subsistence, Affluence, and U.S. Foreign Policy,* 2nd ed. (Princeton, N.J.: Princeton University Press, 1996); A. Belden Fields, *Rethinking Human Rights for the New Millennium* (New York: Palgrave, 2003); David Beetham, "What Future for Economic and Social Rights?" *Political Studies* 43 (1995): 41–60; William Felice, *The Global New Deal: Economic and Social Human Rights in World Politics* (Lanham, Md: Rowman and Littlefield, 2003). But this is not a new development. Thomas Paine included economic rights among his "rights of man" in the eighteenth century.

4. See further David Marcus, "Famine Crimes in International Law," *American Journal of International Law* 97, no. 2 (2003): 245–81.

5. Chapter 17 in Charlotte Ku and Paul F. Diehl, eds., *International Law: Classic and Contemporary Readings* (Boulder, Colo.: Lynn Rienner, 1998), p. 358.

6. See Monique C. Castermans-Holleman, "The Protection of Economic, Social, and Cultural Rights within the UN Framework," *Netherlands International Law Review* 42 (1995): 353–73.

7. Stark, "U.S. Ratification," pp. 75–93.

8. See further James T. Patterson, *Grand Expectations: The United States, 1945–1974,* vol. 10 of *Oxford History of the United States* (Oxford: Oxford University Press, 1996); and Alonzo Hamby, *Man of the People: A Life of Harry S Truman* (New York: Oxford University Press, 1995).

9. See especially Garry Wills, *Reagan's America: Innocents at Home* (New York: Penguin, 1985), particularly on how Reagan's life in America reflected anything but rugged individual competition. In fact, Reagan and his family benefited from considerable governmental policies of a socioeconomic nature, not to mention Reagan's being "carried" by big corporations such as General Electric rather than rising to the top through economic competition.

10. Alain Noel and Jean-Phillippe Therien, "From Domestic to International Justice," *International Organization* 49, no. 3 (1995): 523–53.

11. Rhoda Howard, *Human Rights and the Search for Community* (Boulder, Colo.: Westview, 1995).

12. Human Rights Research and Education Centre, University of Ottawa, http://www.uottawa.ca/hrrec/publicat/bull35.html (accessed July 21, 2004).

13. Raynell Andreychuk, "Human Rights and Canadian Foreign Policy," *University of New Brunswick Law Journal* 45 (1996): 311–17.

14. For an optimistic account, see Costas Melakopides, *Pragmatic Idealism: Canadian Foreign Policy, 1945–1995* (Montreal: McGill-Queen's University Press, 1998). For a more critical account, see Cranford Pratt, "The Limited Place of Human Rights in Canadian Foreign Policy," in Irving Brecher, ed., *Human Rights, Development and Foreign Policy: Canadian Perspectives* (Halifax: Institute for Research on Foreign Policy, 1989). In general see the various views presented in Brecher, *Human Rights, Development and Foreign Policy.*

15. Robert O. Matthews and Cranford Pratt, eds., *Human Rights in Canadian Foreign Policy* (Montreal: McGill-Queen's University Press, 1988), pp. 295–96; Robert Matthews and Cranford Pratt, "Human Rights and Foreign Policy: Principles and Canadian Practice," *Human Rights Quarterly* 7, no. 2 (1985): 159–88.

16. Mark W. Charlton, *The Making of Canadian Food Aid Policy* (Montreal: McGill-Queen's University Press, 1992).

17. Peter Baehr, Monique Castermans-Holleman, and Fred Grunfeld, *Human Rights in the Foreign Policy of the Netherlands* (Antwerp: Intersentia, 2002), pp. 219–20. References omitted.

18. Quoted in Asbjorn Eide, "Linking Human Rights and Development: Aspects of the Norwegian Debate," in Brecher, ed., *Human Rights, Development and Foreign Policy*, p. 15.

19. Elena Fierro, *The EU's Approach to Human Rights Conditionality in Practice* (The Hague: Martinus Nijhoff, 2003). EU policy on human rights conditionality of course results from the interplay of state foreign policy with EU organs such as the Commission, staffed by nonstate personnel. See also Karin Arts, *Integrating Human Rights into Development Cooperation: The Case of the Lomé Convention* (The Hague: Kluwer, 1998). More generally, see Philip Alston, ed., with Mara Bustelo and James Heenan, *The EU and Human Rights* (New York: Oxford University Press, 1999), especially sections F and G; and R. Youngs, *The European Union and the Promotion of Democracy* (New York: Oxford University Press, 2001). See further Henry J. Steiner and Philip Alston, *International Human Rights in Context: Law, Politics, Morals*, 2nd ed. (New York: Oxford University Press, 2000), p. 249.

20. See especially Silvana Sciarra, "From Strasbourg to Amsterdam: Prospects for the Convergence of European Social Rights Policy," in Alston, ed., *The EU and Human Rights*, pp. 473–505. Also see Youngs, *European Union*.

21. Makau Wa Mutua, "Politics and Human Rights: An Essential Symbiosis," in Michael Byers, ed., *The Role of Law in International Politics: Essays in International Relations and International Law* (New York: Oxford University Press, 2000), p. 153; and Kristen Sellars, *The Rise and Rise of Human Rights* (Stroud, UK: Sutton Publishing, 2002).

22. We are speaking of public statements by high officials. The State Department's annual human rights reports are generally balanced, recording criticisms even of allies.

23. See Andreychuk, "Human Rights," for example.

24. See further Peter R. Baehr, *The Role of Human Rights in Foreign Policy*, 2nd ed. (London: Macmillan, 1996).

25. Martin Wolf, "The Morality of the Market," *Foreign Policy* 138 (September/October 2003): 46–51.

26. Sen, *Development as Freedom*.

27. Thomas Risse, Stephen C. Ropp, and Kathryn Sikkink, eds., *The Power of Human Rights* (Cambridge: Cambridge University Press, 1999).

28. Lawyers Committee, *In the National Interest 2001* (New York: Lawyers Committee, 2001).

29. Amnesty International Annual Report, 2001, http://web.amnesty.org/web/ar2001.nsf (accessed July 21, 2004). The executive director of AI-USA is personally in favor of welfare rights, but stresses civil-political rights. When he addresses health issues in China, e.g., his argument is that the basic health problem is compounded by the lack of individual civil-political rights for Chinese citizens. See William F. Schulz, *In Our Own Best Interest: How Defending Human Rights Benefits Us All* (Boston: Beacon, 2001).

30. Human Rights Watch, e-mail from organization, September 12, 2003, in possession of the authors.

31. It is possible that we are seeing some change on this point, as various NGOs are active in the new World Social Forum that meets regularly to press for action on a broad agenda that includes international welfare rights. See, e.g., Berma Klein Goldewijk et al., eds., *Dignity and Human Rights: The Implementation*

of Economic, Social and Cultural Rights (Antwerp: Intersentia, with T.M.C. Asser Press, 2002).

32. One answer, mentioned briefly above, is that one uses the discourse on human rights to generate pressure on officials to see rights as entitlements that are trumps in the sense that entitlements must be met—there supposedly is no policy choice about the primacy of entitlements. See, e.g., United Nations Development Program, *Human Development Report 2000: Human Rights and Human Development* (New York: Oxford University Press, 2000), p. 21. But in the reality of foreign policy, often national security is treated as trump, not human rights.

33. Harold Hongju Koh, "On American Exceptionalism," *Stanford Law Review* 55 (May 2003): 1479–1528. Koh served in the Clinton administration and was clearly sympathetic to a broad range of human rights.

34. Compare Katarina Tomasevski, *Development Aid and Human Rights* (London: Pinter, 1989).

35. Mary Robinson, as UN High Commissioner for Human Rights, made emphasis on the ICESCR one of her priorities, but that is a subject for analysis elsewhere.

36. However, treaties on the rights of the child contain socioeconomic provisions, as does the treaty prohibiting discrimination against women, and so forth.

37. Edward Newman and Oliver P. Richmond, eds., *The United Nations and Human Security* (New York: Palgrave, 2002), pp. 17–18.

38. See further Edward Clay and Olav Stokke, *Food Aid and Human Security* (London: Frank Cass, 2000); and Allan Rosas and Monika Sandvik, "Armed Conflicts," in Eide et al., eds., *Economic, Social and Cultural Rights*, pp. 341–54.

39. Sadako Ogata and Johan Cels, "Human Security: Protecting and Empowering the People," *Global Governance* 9, no. 3 (July–September 2003): 273–82.

40. See further Thomas G. Weiss, David P. Forsythe, and Roger A. Coate, *The United Nations and Changing World Politics*, 4th ed. (Boulder, Colo.: Westview, forthcoming), part III.

41. John Gerard Ruggie, "The United Nations and Globalization: Patterns and Limits of Institutional Adaptation," *Global Governance* 9, no. 3 (July–September 2003): 301–22.

42. Weiss et al., *Changing World Politics*.

43. N. J. Udombana, "The Third World and the Right to Development: Agenda for the Next Millennium," *Human Rights Quarterly* 22, no. 3 (2000): 753–87.

44. James C. N. Paul, "International Development Agencies, Human Rights, and Humane Development Projects," in Brecher, ed., *Human Rights, Development and Foreign Policy*, p. 290.

45. On a large subject, see further Adam Przeworski, *Democracy and Development* (Cambridge: Cambridge University Press, 2000).

46. In the case of the UNDP, we see both programs on the ground and acceptance of the notion of welfare rights as human rights.

47. Section 596, Foreign Operations Appropriation Act, 2001. We are indebted to Mutuma Ruteere for bringing this to our attention.

48. We do think progress is being made in specifying standards of obligation for welfare rights; see note 2, *supra*.

49. At the same time, a strictly legal approach has its place, as in the attempt to sue corporations for complicity in violations of internationally recognized human rights through U.S. courts.

Chapter 4. Homelessness in Canada and the United States

The author wishes to acknowledge the research assistance of Andrew Banfield in the development of this chapter.

1. One hundred fifty-one states had ratified the Covenant, as of July 22, 2005. See UN Development Report, *Human Development Report 2002* (New York: Oxford University Press, 2002), pp. 243–47.

2. Canada, *Report of the Task Force on Housing and Urban Development*, a.k.a. "The Hellyer Report" (Ottawa: Queen's Printer, 1969), p. 22.

3. Kirk Makin, "High Court Supports Mentally-Ill Physicist," *Toronto Globe and Mail*, June 7, 2003, p. A7.

4. Paula W. Dail, "Introduction to the Symposium on Homelessness," *Policy Studies Journal* 28, no. 2 (2000): 331–37; and T. Peressini et al., *Estimating Homelessness: Toward a Methodology for Counting the Homeless in Canada* (Ottawa: CMHC, 1996).

5. Mark H. Maier, *The Data Game: Controversies in Social Science Statistics*, 2nd ed. (New York: M. E. Sharpe, 1995).

6. Jack Layton, *Homelessness: The Making and Unmaking of a Crisis* (Toronto: Penguin/McGill Institute, 2000).

7. "Core need" is defined as those paying more than 30 percent of their gross income for shelter and those living in substandard housing. Seventeen percent of Canadians are defined as experiencing core need.

8. United States Conference of Mayors, *A Status Report on Hunger and Homelessness in America's Cities: A 25-City Survey* (Washington, D.C.: UCSF, 2002).

9. See Canada Mortgage and Housing Corporation (hereafter CMHC), *Children and Youth in Homeless Families: Shelter Spaces and Services* (Ottawa: CMHC, 2001); and CMHC, *Inventory of Projects and Programs Addressing Homelessness* (Ottawa: CMHC, 1995).

10. John Engeland, *Homeless Individuals and Families Information System (HIFIS)* (Ottawa: CMHC, 2001).

11. Talmadge Wright, "Resisting Homelessness: Global, National and Local Solutions," *Contemporary Sociology* 29, no. 1 (2000): 27–43.

12. Barbara Wake Carroll, "The Political Economy of Housing Policy," in R. Loreto and T. Price, eds., *Urban Political Issues: A Reader* (Toronto: McClelland and Stewart, 1990).

13. John Kromer, "Special Needs Housing: The Unfinished Policy," *Journal of Housing and Community* 57, no. 3 (2000): 13–19; and William Harris Troutman, John D. Jackson, and Robert B. Ekelund, Jr., "Public Policy: Perverse Incentives and the Homeless Problem," *Public Choice* 98 (1999): 195–212.

14. Personal communication from Jeff Wingard of the Hamilton (Ontario) Social Planning and Research Council, who has done extensive research on homelessness, October 2003.

15. Joel Bakan and D. Schneiderman, "What's Wrong with Social Rights?" in Joel Bakan and D. Schneiderman, eds., *Social Justice and the Constitution: Perspectives on a Social Union for Canada* (Ottawa: Carleton University Press, 1992), p. 8.

16. Richard Harris, "Housing and Social Policy: An Historical Perspective on Canadian-American Differences—A Comment," *Urban Studies* 36, no. 7 (1999): 1169–75; Martin E. Wexler, "A Comparison of Canadian and American Housing Policies," *Urban Studies* 33, no. 10 (1996): 1909–21; and Martin E. Wexler, "Housing and Social Policy—A Historical Perspective on Canadian-American Differences—A Reply," *Urban Studies* 36, no. 7 (1999): 1177–80.

17. Carroll, "Political Economy of Housing Policy"; Martin Meyer, *The Builders* (New York: Norton and Company, 1978); and John C. Weicher, *Housing: Federal Policies and Programs* (Washington, D.C.: American Enterprise Institute, 1982).

18. Carroll, "Political Economy of Housing Policy"; and William G. Grigsby, "Housing Finance and Subsidies in the United States," *Urban Studies* 27, no. 6 (1990): 831–45.

19. Barbara Wake Carroll, "Housing Policy in the New Millennium: The Uncompassionate Landscape," in E. P. Fowler and D. Siegel, eds., *Urban Policy Issues: Canadian Perspectives* (Toronto: Oxford University Press, 2002), p. 92.

20. United States Conference of Mayors, *Status Report.*

21. Edward G. Goetz, "Potential Effects of Federal Policy Devolution on Local Housing Expenditures," *Publius* 25, no. 3 (1995): 99–116.

22. National Alliance to End Homelessness, *Ending Homelessness: From Ideas to Action, Policy Papers* (Washington, D.C.: NAEH, 2002).

23. Barbara Wake Carroll and Ruth J. E. Jones, "Road to Innovation, Convergence or Inertia: Devolution in Housing Policy in Canada," *Canadian Public Policy* 26, no. 3 (2000): 277–93.

24. Carroll, "Housing Policy in the New Millennium."

25. George Fallis, "Housing Finance and Housing Subsidies in Canada," *Urban Studies* 27, no. 6 (1990): 877–903.

26. Jeanne M. Wolfe, "Canadian Housing Policies in the Nineties," *Housing Studies* 13, no. 1 (1998): 121–33.

27. The SCPI program has been identified as a best practice by the UN Habitat Dubai International Awards, but this simply underlines the functionary-driven nature of the program. Everyone interviewed for this chapter cited excessive paperwork, uncertain criteria, vague deadlines, and a general "crapshoot" about the program.

28. Lois M. Baron, "When a Roof Isn't Enough," *Journal of Housing and Community Development* 60, no. 1 (2003): 21–24; Gordon J. Campbell and Elizabeth McCarthy, "Conveying Mission through Outcome Measurement: Services to the Homeless in New York City," *Policy Studies Journal* 28, no. 2 (2000): 338–52; Kristen M. Novotny, "Experts in Their Own Lives: Emphasizing Client-Centeredness in a Homeless Program," *Policy Studies Journal* 28, no. 2 (2000): 382–401; and Karin Ringheim, "Investigating the Structural Determinants of Homelessness: The Case of Houston," *Urban Affairs Quarterly* 28, no. 4 (1993): 617–40.

29. Rosanna Hemakom, "New Directions," *Journal of Housing and Community Development* 59, no. 5 (2002): 32–40.

30. CMHC, *Inventory of Projects and Programs* and *Children and Homeless Families*; and Deborah Kraus and Paul Dowling, *Family Homelessness: Causes and Solutions, Final Report* (Ottawa: CMHC, 2003).

31. Alberta Ministry of Community Development, *Moving Forward . . . Homelessness Policy Framework: Implementation Strategy* (Edmonton: Alberta Community Development, Communications Branch, 2000); and Luba Serge, *Documentation of Best Practices Addressing Homelessness* (Ottawa: CMHC, 1999).

32. Social Data Research Ltd., *Applicability of a Continuum of Care Model to Address Homelessness: Final Report* (Ottawa: CMHC, 2002).

33. Jim Ward and Associates, *Involving Homeless and Formerly Homeless Clients in Projects and Programs to Address Homelessness: Final Report* (Ottawa: CMHC, 2001).

34. Merrill Cooper, *Housing Affordability: A Children's Issue* (Ottawa: Canadian Policy Research Networks, 2000); and Mignon Senders, "Women and the Right

to Adequate Housing," *Netherlands Quarterly of Human Rights* 16, no. 2 (1998): 175–200.

35. Deborah Kraus et al., *Environmental Scan on Youth Homelessness* (Ottawa: CMHC, 2001); Sylvia Novacs et al., *No Room of Her Own: A Literature Review on Women and Homelessness* (Ottawa: CMHC, 1996); and Sylvia Novacs et al., *Women on the Rough Edge: A Decade of Change for Long-Term Homeless Women* (Ottawa: CMHC, 1999).

36. Robert L. Fischer, "Toward Self-Sufficiency: Evaluating a Transitional Housing Program for Homeless Families," *Policy Studies Journal* 28, no. 2 (2000): 402–20; and Lance Freeman, "America's Affordable Housing Crisis: A Contract Unfulfilled," *American Journal of Public Health* 92, no. 5 (2002): 709–12.

37. Novacs et al., *Women on the Rough Edge.*

38. Ralph S. Hambrick, Jr., and Debra J. Rog, "The Pursuit of Coordination: The Organizational Dimension in the Response to Homelessness," *Policy Studies Journal* 28, no. 2 (2000): 353–64; and Kromer, "Special Needs Housing," pp. 13–19.

39. Thomas Huckin, "Textual Silence and the Discourse of Homelessness," *Discourse and Society* 13, no. 3 (2002): 347–72.

40. Keith Dowding and Desmond King, "Rooflessness in London," *Policy Studies Journal* 28, no. 2 (2000): 365–81.

41. The material in this section is largely based on Steiner and Alston, *International Human Rights in Context.*

42. Canada, "Hellyer Report," p. 22.

43. . See Appendix 3.

44. ICESCR, 1991, as cited in Steiner and Alston, *International Human Rights,* pp. 318–19.

45. Senders, "Women and the Right to Adequate Housing."

46. Larry Bourne, *The Geography of Housing* (London: Edward Arnold, 1981).

47. William Duncombe and Jeffrey D. Straussman, "Judicial Intervention and Local Spending: The Case of Local Jails," *Policy Studies Journal* 22, no. 4 (1994): 604–16; and Correctional Services of Canada, *Our Story: Organizational Renewal in Federal Corrections* (Ottawa: Canadian Centre for Management Development, 1991).

48. Barbara Wake Carroll, "Program Drift: The Rational Road to Policy Perversity," *Canadian Journal of Urban Research* 3, no. 1 (1995): 21–42.

49. G. Vierdag, "The Legal Nature of the Rights Granted by the ECESCR," *Netherlands Yearbook of International Law* 69, no. 103 (1978).

50. Miloon Kothari, "The Right to Adequate Housing Is a Human Right," *United Nations Chronicle* 38, no. 1 (2001): 36–38.

51. Bakan and Schneiderman, "What's Wrong with Social Rights?"

52. Joel Bakan, Introduction, in Bakan and Schneiderman, eds., *Social Justice and the Constitution.*

53. F. L. Morton and Leslie Pal, "The Impact of the Charter of Rights on Public Administration: A Case Study of Sex Discrimination in the Unemployment Insurance Act," *Canadian Public Administration* 28, no. 2 (1985): 221–44.

54. Karen Selick, "Rights and Wrongs in the Canadian Charter," in Anthony A. Peacock, ed., *Rethinking the Constitution: Perspectives on Canadian Constitutional Reform, Interpretation and Theory* (Toronto: Oxford University Press, 1996), p. 108.

55. Bret Thiele, "The Human Right to Adequate Housing: A Tool for Prompting and Protecting Individual and Community Health," *American Journal of Public Health* 92, no. 5 (2002): 712–15.

56. Carroll, "Program Drift."

57. Barbara Wake Carroll and Terrence Carroll, "Civic Networks, Legitimacy and the Policy-Process," *Governance* 12, no. 1 (1999): 1–28.

58. Kothari, "Right to Adequate Housing"; and S. Leckie, "The UN Committee on Economic, Social and Cultural Rights and the Right to Adequate Housing: Toward an Appropriate Approach," *Human Rights Quarterly* 11, no. 4 (1989): 522–60.

59. T. S. Nesslein, "Housing: The Market versus the Welfare State," *Urban Studies* 25 (1988): 95–108.

60. Bo Bengdesston, "Housing as a Social Right: Implications for Welfare State Theory," *Scandinavian Political Studies* 24, no. 4 (2001): 255–75. Quotation on p. 257, emphasis in original.

61. R. C. Ellickson, "The Untenable Case for an Unconditional Right to Shelter," *Harvard Journal of Law and Public Policy* 15, no. 1 (1992): 17–34.

62. See *San Antonio Independent School District v. Rodriguez* (1973). For a discussion of these distinctions and the case law, see David M. O'Brien, *Constitutional Law and Politics*, Volume II: *Civil Rights and Civil Liberties*, 4th ed. (New York: W.W. Norton, 2000), pp. 1282–84.

63. See *Bernard v. Dartmouth Housing Authority* (1989).

64. See *Eldrigde v. British Columbia (Attorney General)* (1997).

65. Makin, "High Court Supports Mentally-Ill Physicist."

66. Duncombe and Straussman, "Judicial Intervention and Local Spending."

67. Correctional Services of Canada, *Our Story*, p. 6.

68. Andrew I. Batavia and Kay Schriner, "The Americans with Disabilities Act as Engine of Social Change: Models of Disability and the Potential of a Civil Rights Approach," *Policy Studies Journal* 29, no. 4 (2001): 690–702.

69. Bradley R. Haywood, "Note: The Right to Shelter as a Fundamental Interest Under the New York State Constitution," *Columbia Human Rights Law Review* 157 (2002).

70. See *McCain v. Guiliani,* 676 NYS2d 151 App. Div. (1998).

71. Marcia H. Rioux, Cameron Crawford, and Jane Anweiler, "Undue Hardship and Reasonable Accommodation: The View from the Court," *Policy Studies Review* 29, no. 4 (2001): 621–29.

72. Nick Falvo, *Gimme Shelter! Homelessness and Canada's Social Housing Crisis* (Toronto: CSJ Foundation for Research and Education [mimeo], 2003).

73. Howard-Hassmann, *Compassionate Canadians*; Sidney Verba, Kay Lehman Schlozman, and Henry E. Brady, *Voice and Equality: Civic Volunteerism in American Politics* (Cambridge, Mass.: Harvard University Press, 1995).

74. John C. Courtney, "Parliament and Representation: The Unfinished Agenda of Electoral Redistributions," *Canadian Journal of Political Science* 31, no. 4 (1998): 675–90.

75. *Report of the Provincial Task Force on Homelessness* (Toronto: Ministry of Community and Social Services, 2000).

76. Matthew Cooper and Margaret Rodman, *New Neighbours: A Case Study of Cooperative Housing* (Toronto: University of Toronto Press, 1992).

77. Carroll, "Program Drift."

78. See *Finlay v. Canada (Minister of Finance)* (1993).

79. Selick, "Rights and Wrongs," p. 110.

Chapter 5. Welfare Racism and Human Rights

1. Timothy M. Smeeding, Lee Rainwater, and Gary Burtless, "United States Poverty in a Cross-National Context," in Sheldon H. Danziger and Robert H.

Haveman, eds., *Understanding Poverty* (New York and Cambridge, Mass.: Russell Sage Foundation and Harvard University Press, 2002), pp. 162–89.

2. Michael Katz, *The Price of Citizenship: Redefining the American Welfare State* (New York: Metropolitan Books, 2001); Edward N. Wolff and Richard C. Leone, *Top Heavy: The*
Increasing Inequality of Wealth in America and What Can Be Done about It, 2nd ed. (New York: Free Press, 2002).

3. U.S. Bureau of the Census, *Statistical Abstract of the United States: 2003* (Washington, D.C.: U.S. Government Printing Office, 2003), p. 459.

4. U.S. Bureau of the Census, *Poverty in the United States: 2002* (Washington, D.C.: U.S. Government Printing Office, 2003), p. 3.

5. Randy Albelda and Chris Tilly, *Glass Ceilings and Bottomless Pits: Women's Work, Women's Poverty* (Boston: South End Press, 1997); Holly Sklar, Laryssa Mykyta, and Susan Wefald, *Raise the Floor: Wages and Policies That Work for All of Us* (Boston: South End Press, 2002).

6. U.S. Bureau of the Census, *Poverty in the United States,* p. 7.

7. Ibid., p. 9.

8. Center on Budget and Policy Priorities, "Poverty Increases and Median Income Declines for Second Consecutive Year," press release (September 29, 2003), available at http://www.cbpp.org.

9. Samuel Rosenman, ed., *The Public Papers and Addresses of Franklin D. Roosevelt* (New York: Harper, 1950). See Appendix 3.

10. Anuradha Mittal and Peter Rosset, eds., *America Needs Human Rights* (Oakland, Calif.: Food First Books, 1999).

11. Ibid.

12. Howard, *Human Rights,* chap. 7.

13. Joseph Wronka, *Human Rights and Social Policy in the 21st* Century, rev. ed. (Lanham, Md: University Press of America, 1998); Robert Drinan, *The Mobilization of Shame* (New Haven, Conn.: Yale University Press, 2001).

14. Mittal and Rosset, *America Needs Human Rights.*

15. Gwendolyn Mink, *Welfare's End* (Ithaca, N.Y.: Cornell University Press, 2002).

16. Alan Weil and Kenneth Finegold, eds., *Welfare Reform: The Next Act* (Washington, D.C.: The Urban Institute, 2002).

17. U.S. Department of Health and Human Services, "HHS Releases Data Showing Continuing Decline in Number of People Receiving Temporary Assistance," news release (September 3, 2003), http://www.hhs.gov/news/press/2003pres/20030903.html.

18. Mimi Abramovitz, *Regulating the Lives of Women: Social Welfare Policy from Colonial Times to the Present,* rev. ed. (Boston: South End Press, 1996).

19. Everett Carll Ladd and Karlyn H. Bowman, *Attitudes toward Economic Inequality* (Washington, D.C.: AEI Press, 1998).

20. L. Richard Della Fave, "The Meek Shall Not Inherit the Earth: Self-Evaluation and the Legitimacy of Stratification," *American Sociological Review* 45 (1980): 955–71; L. Richard Della Fave, "Toward an Explication of the Legitimation Process," *Social Forces* 65 (1986): 476–500.

21. Frances Fox Piven and Richard A. Cloward, *Poor People's Movements: Why They Succeed, Why They Fail* (New York: Pantheon Books, 1977).

22. Goldstein, "The United States," pp. 429–56.

23. Theda Skocpol, *Social Policy in the United States: Future Possibilities in Historical Perspective* (Princeton, N.J.: Princeton University Press, 1995).

24. G. William Domhoff, *Who Rules America? Power and Politics*, 4th ed. (New York: McGraw-Hill, 2002).

25. Frances Fox Piven and Richard A. Cloward, *Regulating the Poor: The Functions of Public Welfare*, rev. ed. (New York: Vintage Books, 1993).

26. Abramovitz, *Regulating the Lives of Women*.

27. Kenneth J. Neubeck and Noel A. Cazenave, *Welfare Racism: Playing the Race Card against America's Poor* (New York: Routledge, 2001), p. 36.

28. Eduardo Bonilla-Silva, *White Supremacy and Racism in the Post-Civil Rights Era* (Boulder, Colo.: Lynne Rienner, 2001).

29. Stephen Steinberg, *Turning Back: The Retreat from Racial Justice in American Thought and Policy* (Boston: Beacon Press, 1995).

30. Joe R. Feagin, *Racist America: Roots, Current Realities, and Future Reparations* (New York: Routledge, 2001); Joe R. Feagin, Hernan Vera, and Pinar Batur, *White Racism: The Basics*, 2nd ed. (New York: Routledge, 2000).

31. Bonilla-Silva, *White Supremacy and Racism*.

32. Stephen Jay Gould, *The Mismeasure of Man*, rev. ed. (New York: W. W. Norton, 1996).

33. Feagin, *Racist America*; Joe R. Feagin and Melvin P. Sikes, *Living with Racism: The Black Middle-Class Experience* (Boston: Beacon Press, 1994).

34. Neubeck and Cazenave, *Welfare Racism*; Kenneth J. Neubeck and Noel A. Cazenave, "Welfare Racism and Its Consequences: The Demise of AFD.C. and the Return of the States' Rights Era," in Frances Fox Piven, Joan Acker, Margaret Hallock, and Sandra Morgen, eds., *Work, Welfare and Politics: Confronting Poverty in the Wake of Welfare Reform* (Eugene, Ore.: University of Oregon Press, 2002), pp. 35–53.

35. Winifred Bell, *Aid to Dependent Children* (New York: Columbia University Press, 1965).

36. Ibid.

37. Piven and Cloward, *Regulating the Poor*.

38. Ibid.; Bell, *Aid to Dependent Children*.

39. Piven and Cloward, *Regulating the Poor*.

40. Mink, *Welfare's End*.

41. Abramovitz, *Regulating the Lives of Women*.

42. Neubeck and Cazenave, *Welfare Racism*.

43. Holly Sklar, *Chaos or Community? Seeking Solutions, Not Scapegoats, for Bad Economics* (Boston: South End Press, 1995).

44. Albelda and Tilly, *Glass Ceilings and Bottomless Pits*.

45. Thomas B. Edsall and Mary D. Edsall, *Chain Reaction: The Impact of Race, Rights, and Taxes on American Politics* (New York: W. W. Norton, 1992).

46. Neubeck and Cazenave, *Welfare Racism*.

47. Martin Gilens, *Why Americans Hate Welfare: Race, Media, and the Politics of Antipoverty Policy* (Chicago: University of Chicago Press, 1999).

48. Randy Albelda and Ann Withorn, eds., *Lost Ground: Welfare Reform, Poverty, and Beyond* (Boston: South End Press, 2002); Neubeck and Cazenave, "Welfare Racism and Its Consequences."

49. Neubeck and Cazenave, *Welfare Racism*.

50. Ibid.

51. Peter Brimelow, *Alien Nation: Common Sense about America's Immigration Disaster* (New York: Random House, 1995).

52. Albelda and Withorn, *Lost Ground*; Neubeck and Cazenave, *Welfare Racism*; Sanford F. Schram, Joe Soss, and Richard C. Fording, eds., *Race and the Politics of Welfare Reform* (Ann Arbor: University of Michigan Press, 2003).

53. Neubeck and Cazenave, "Welfare Racism and Its Consequences."

54. Joe Soss, et al., "Setting the Terms of Relief: Explaining State Policy Choices in the Devolution Revolution," *American Journal of Political Science* 45 (2001): 378–403.

55. Jeff Chapman and Jared Bernstein, "Falling through the Safety Net: Low Income Mothers in the Jobless Recovery," *EPI (Economic Policy Institute) Brief* #191 (April 11, 2003), http://www.epinet.org/content.cfm/issuebriefs_ib191.

56. National Partnership for Women and Families (NPWF), *Detours on the Road to Employment* (Washington, D.C.: NPWF, 1999).

57. Kenneth Finegold and Sarah Staveteig, "Race, Ethnicity, and Welfare Reform," in Weil and Finegold, *Welfare Reform*, pp. 203–23.

58. Irene Browne, ed., *Latinas and African American Women at Work: Race, Gender, and Economic Inequality* (New York: Russell Sage Foundation, 1999).

59. Weil and Finegold, *Welfare Reform.*

60. Finegold and Staveteig, "Race, Ethnicity, and Welfare Reform."

61. Pamela J. Loprest, *Who Returns to Welfare?* (Washington, D.C.: The Urban Institute, 2002).

62. Susan Gooden, "The Hidden Third Party: Welfare Recipients' Experiences with Employers," *Journal of Public Management and Social Policy* 5 (1999): 69–83.

63. Susan Gooden, "All Things Not Being Equal: Difference in Caseworker Support toward Black and White Welfare Clients," *Harvard Journal of African American Public Policy* 4 (1998): 23–33.

64. Rebecca Gordon, *Cruel and Usual: How Welfare Reform Punishes Poor People* (Oakland, Calif.: Applied Research Center, 2001): 4–5.

65. Joseph Llobrera, "Food Stamp Caseloads Are Rising," Center on Budget and Policy Priorities (November 12, 2003). http://www.cbpp.org/1-15-02fa.htm.

66. Susmita Pati, Diana Romero, and Wendy Chavkin, *The Impact of Welfare Reform on Health Insurance and Utilization of Food Assistance Programs on Underserved Populations in New York City* (Washington, D.C.: AcademyHealth, 2002).

67. Kenneth J. Neubeck, "Attacking Welfare Racism/Honoring Poor People's Human Rights," in Albelda and Withorn, eds., *Lost Ground*, pp. 113–27.

68. Goldstein, "United States," p. 430.

Chapter 6. The Movement to End Poverty in the United States

1. Martin Luther King, Jr., speech at staff retreat [of the Southern Christian Leadership Conference (SCLC)] by author, transcript, May 1967, at the Penn Center, Frogmore, S.C., p. 2.

2. In November and December of 1967, Dr. King broadcast five Massey Lectures for the Canadian Broadcasting Corporation (CBC). Taken together, they document the evolution in his thinking from a civil rights to a human rights framework. See Martin Luther King, Jr., *The Trumpet of Conscience* (New York: Harper and Row, 1967), p. 60.

3. Martin Luther King, Jr., press conference [announcing the Poor People's Campaign] by author, transcript, December 4, 1967, Atlanta, Ga., papers/unpub/671204–003_Announcing_Poor_Peoples_campaign.htm (accessed December 9, 2002).

4. See Willie Baptist and Mary Bricker-Jenkins, "A View from the Bottom: Poor People and Their Allies Respond to Welfare Reform," *The Annals of the*

American Academy of Political Science 577 (2001): 144–56, for a discussion of the attack on the structure of rights of all U.S. residents signaled by "welfare reform" initiatives of the 1990s, which were purportedly directed primarily—or only—at people receiving Aid to Families with Dependent Children (AFDC). In other words, we argue that AFDC recipients constitute "canaries in the mine."

5. King, speech at staff retreat, p. 10.

6. See, e.g., Jim Davis, "Rethinking Globalisation," *Race and Class* 40, no. 2/3 (1998/99): 37–48; and Jerry Harris, "Globalisation and the technical transformation of capitalism," *Race and Class* 40, no. 2/3 (1998/99): 21–35, for a discussion of the global nature of the transformation. Reisch and Gorin apply the discussion to the practice of social work; see Michael Reisch and Stephen Gorin, "Nature of Work and Future of the Social Work Profession," *Social Work* 46, no. 1 (2001): 9–19. Paula Allman, *Critical Education against Global Capitalism: Karl Marx and Revolutionary Critical Education* (Westport, Conn.: Bergin and Garvey, 2001), provides a useful summary on the debate among Marxists on the precise and potential role of technology in transforming capitalism. Douglas S. Robertson, *The New Renaissance: Computers and the Next Level of Civilization* (New York: Oxford University Press, 1998), applies mathematical modeling to illustrate the catalytic effect of the computer in advancing civilization to a new level in the same manner as language, writing, and printing have done in human history.

7. Much of the data and discussion of overproduction and overcapacity takes the form of the relationships among technology, jobs, outsourcing, and gross domestic product (GDP). A *Chicago Tribune* series by William Neikirk vividly portrayed the links among these elements and some of the people caught in their broiling crosscurrents; see William Neikirk, "The Economics of Glut," *Chicago Tribune*, December 15–18, 2002, http://www.chicagotribune.com/ news/chi-0212150471dec15,1,1110151.story (accessed December 21, 2002). Also in the popular press, the market-oriented *Business Week* ran a special series in March 2003 dispelling myths about outsourcing and revealing the technological basis of production and overproduction. See Bruce Nussbaum et al., "Where Are the Jobs?" *Business Week Online*, March 22, 2004, http://www.businessweek .com/magazine/toc/04_12/B38750412jobs.htm (accessed April 22, 2004). U.S. congressman Barney Frank recently delivered a speech in Congress that provided a well-documented structural analysis of unemployment, pointing out that increased productivity stimulated by technology, and not outsourcing, drove unemployment; see Barney Frank, "Unemployment: A Serious Economic and Social Problem Facing the Country," Special Order Speech of Congressman Barney Frank, March 16, 2004, http://www.house.gov/frank/errataspeech2004 .html (accessed March 17, 2004). Essentially the same analysis is provided by scholars (see, e.g., Kevin L. Kliesen, "The Economy Gets Back on Track but Once Again Leaves Many Workers Behind," *The Regional Economist*, January 2004, http://www.stls.frb.org/publications/re/2004/a/pages/econ_track.html [accessed February 25, 2004] and in commentaries by former government officials representing both parties; see Todd Buchholz, "Only Machines Need Apply," *New York Times*, March 19, 2004, final ed.; and Robert B. Reich, "Why Factory Jobs Are Disappearing All Over," *Public Radio's Marketplace Commentaries*, November 5, 2003, http://www.robertreich.org/reich/20031105.asp (accessed February 28, 2004).

8. See, e.g., Andrew L. Cherry, Jr., *Examining Global Social Welfare Issues: Using MicroCase®* (Belmont, Calif.: Thomson Brooks/Cole, 2005); Chuck Collins, "The Wealth Gap Widens," *Dollars & Sense*, September–October 1999, http://

www.dollarsandsense.org/archives/1999/0999collins.html (accessed May 3, 2004); Adria Scharf, "Wealth Inequality by the Numbers," *Dollars & Sense*, January–February 2004, http://www.findarticles.com/cf_dls/m2548/251/11 2721237/print.jhtml (accessed May 3, 2004); Frank Stricker, "Why American Poverty Rates Stopped Falling in the '70s, and Why a Better Story Was Not Told about It," *Journal of Poverty* 4, no. 4 (2000): 1–21; U.S. Census Bureau, U.S. Department of Commerce, Economics and Statistics Administration, *The Changing Shape of the Nation's Income Distribution: Consumer Income* (Washington, D.C.: U.S. Census Bureau, 2000). Using various measures of income gives rise to debates on the extent of changes and their precise trajectories, but no one argues that the income and wealth gaps have not increased dramatically over time.

9. Indicators are plentiful, and many are succinctly presented in a report by the Economic Policy Institute (EPI), linking economic shifts to family life; see EPI, 2003, "The State of Working America, 2002–03," http://www.epinet.org (accessed January 5, 2003). The report states, "Over the last 30 years, workers in middle-income married-couple families with children have added an average of 20 weeks at work, the equivalent of five more months" (p. 10). For other profiles of the "new class" evolving from the collapsing "middle class," see Martha N. Ozawa and Rebecca Y. Kim, "The Increasing Income Inequality among Children," *Journal of Poverty* 4, no. 3 (2000): 1–19; David K. Shipler, *The Working Poor: Invisible in America* (New York: Alfred A. Knopf, 2004); Julie Stoiber, "First Timers, Families Swell Homeless Ranks," *Philadelphia Inquirer*, October 20, 2003; and Julian Borger, "Long Queue at Drive-In Soup Kitchen," *The Guardian*, November 3, 2003, p. 1.

10. Summarizing a good deal of literature on the topic, Michael Yates, "Poverty and Inequality in the Global Economy," *Monthly Review* 55, no. 9 (February 2004), http://www.monthlyreview.org/0204yates.htm (accessed February 11, 2004), argues that the "social health" of nations is related less to income disparities than to the wealth gap, which is dramatically increasing in the United States and returning in the last decade to 1920s proportions.

11. They have also protected the wealthy nations from the shame of visible starvation and homelessness, but with the augmentation of the notion of "personal responsibility" for one's plight, the burden of shame has effectively been transferred to the individual. In addition, the burden of responsibility for supporting the efforts of individuals to meet their needs has been shifted to nongovernmental organizations (NGOs), state/provincial structures, and such "mediating structures" as churches and charity organizations. This policy and practice of "devolution" not only masks the extent and nature of need but cynically manipulates collective kindness into rescuing national governments that are systematically abrogating their responsibility to safeguard the "common good." To us, this practice reveals the class allegiance of our governments and the (innovative) mechanisms developed to protect class interests during the transition to a globalized, electronics-based economy.

12. Neil Gilbert, *Transformation of the Welfare State* (New York: Oxford University Press, 2002).

13. King, *Trumpet of Conscience*, p. 60.

14. King, speech at staff retreat, p. 10.

15. Our assessment differs from that of Keck and Sikkink, *Activists beyond Borders*. Their analysis, which questions the feasibility of a contemporary U.S. movement based on economic human rights, is based primarily on analysis of poor

people's movements at times and/or in nations whose economic bases and social conditions differ considerably from those prevailing in contemporary U.S. history. We contend, in fact, that the conditions in the United States are becoming more like those in "developing" nations, increasingly generating the circumstances they deem necessary for organizing a U.S. movement. Moreover, our organizing work is intended to document their sine qua non: direct harm and demonstrable causal links (as in people dying from lack of health care) and attacks on core values (as expressed, e.g., in the Declaration of Independence, Roosevelt's "Four Freedoms," and the very notion of "rights" that has often aroused mass action).

16. Adopted by the PPEHRC Steering Committee at its retreat, December 18–21, 2003, at The Highlander Center, New Market, Tenn. The PPEHRC mission statement was fashioned from the KWRU mission statement and is nearly identical.

17. See Chapter 5 by Kenneth Neubeck in this volume.

18. We anticipate a collective need and desire to redefine "jobs" and "work" more inclusively, reflecting the social "use value" of activities such as caregiving in the home, production of art and culture, and so on.

19. See, e.g., Robertson, *The New Renaissance.* For a market-oriented perspective, see U.S. Department of Commerce, Economics and Statistics Administration, "Digital Economy," December 2003, http://www.esa.doc.gov/Digital Economy2003.cfm (accessed May 5, 2004), especially chap. 7. See also Allman, *Critical Education,* on education and consciousness.

20. There are other elements, of course, including communication and information systems, culture and symbols, resources, formal structure, policies, protocols, and the like; these are outside the scope of this discussion.

21. King, *Trumpet of Conscience,* p. 60.

22. Of particular importance is the role of education in movement building; it is so integral to our work that a full exploration would require an entire separate chapter. We hope and expect that the integration of education into our work is clear in this discussion.

23. Willie Baptist, Mary Bricker-Jenkins and M. Dillon, "Taking the Struggle on the Road: The New Freedom Bus—Freedom from Unemployment, Hunger, and Homelessness," *Journal of Progressive Human Services* 10, no. 2 (1999): 7–29; and *Outriders,* prod. and dir. Pamela Yates and Peter Kinoy, 54 min., Skylight Pictures, 1999, videocassette.

24. In fact, the tactical question of pursuing a legislative victory challenged our alliance. Rep. Curry, who could hold hearings on his own authority as a legislator "to evaluate the need for legislation," warned of the risks of passing the resolution, including the possibility of the special committee producing a negative report. NASW-PA, however, desired a legislative victory to maintain the support of the membership for such an unusual initiative (and commitment of resources) and to conform to the national NASW's policy of pursuing bipartisan legislative support. The exigencies of movement building and those of reformism are often uneasy when yoked together.

25. Clearly, we use other tactics as well, including from civil disobedience, mass demonstrations, participatory research, "truth commissions," media campaigns, arts and cultural events, and numerous forms of education in every conceivable setting. In all of these, we focus heavily on leadership development.

26. Marge Piercy, excerpt from "Contribution to Our Museum," in *Living in the Open* (New York: Knopf, 1976): 74–75.

Chapter 7. So Close and Yet So Different

1. Roy J. Romanow, *Building on Values: The Future of Health Care in Canada* (hereafter *Romanow Report*), Commission on the Future of Health Care in Canada, Final Report 2002, xxxiv, 357. http://www.hc-sc.gc.ca/english/care/romanow/hac0086.html.

2. The complicated Clinton plan for health care reform (Health Security Act, l03rd Cong., 1st Sess. [Washington, D.C.: U.S. Government Printing Office]) is described in Ronald Dworkin, "Will Clinton's Plan Be Fair" *The New York Review of Books,* January 13, 1994, p. 20:

> Clinton's act is long and elaborate—1,342 pages and 240,000 words. . . . It aims to achieve universal coverage by requiring every resident of the United States to participate in some form of health plan. To reduce overall costs it would require people not to negotiate directly with a plan as individuals, but to join a large purchasing cooperative (called a regional health-care "alliance") which would use its size and bargaining power to secure the lowest possible rates for health-care coverage. Each alliance would enter into contracts with a variety of plans and would offer its members a choice among them.

3. Romanow, *Romanow Report.* Information about the Canadian health system is available in the United States from Physicians for a National Health Program, 29 E. Madison Suite 602, Chicago, IL 60602, http://www.pnhp.org. A dated but still highly useful and comprehensive source is a series of three articles by John K. Iglehart: "Canada's Health Care System," *The New England Journal of Medicine* (*NEJM*) 315, no. 3 (July 17, 1986): 202–08; *NEJM* 315, no. 12 (Sept. 18, 1986): 778–84; and *NEJM* 315, no. 25 (December 18, 1986): 1623–28.

4. *The Economist,* February 8, 2003, p. 57.

5. *Prairie Messenger* (Saskatchewan), December 10, 2003, pp. 1, 3.

6. C. Stuart Houston, "A Medical Historian Looks at the Romanow Report," *Saskatchewan Law Review* 66 (2003): 542.

7. "A Colloquy on the Romanow Report, Preface, Summary," *Saskatchewan Law Review* 66 (2003): 537.

8. *New York Times,* October 16, 2003, p. A25.

9. Uwe E. Reinhardt, "Why Are There So Many Uninsured Americans?" (paper presented at a symposium by the U.S. Chamber of Commerce, reproduced and circulated by Physicians for a National Health Plan (PNHP), Chicago, 2000.

10. Ibid., p. 4.

11. Ibid., p.13.

12. Fairness and Accuracy in Reporting, "NBC Slams Universal Health Care," November 12, 2002, http://www.fair.org/activism/nbc-oregon.html.

13. . Ellen Pinney, "The Oregon Health Plan, Boon or Bust?" *Alternatives* 97, no. 4 (winter 1997), http://www.alternativesmagazine.com/04/pinney1.html (accessed February 18, 2004).

14. *JAMA* (August 13, 2003), pp. 708–805; Kristen Gerendcher, CBS, *Market Watch,* August 12, 2003.

15. Ibid.

16. Ibid.

17. Royal Commission on Health Services 1 and 11 (Ottawa: Queens' Printer, 1964–65).

18. Romanow, *Romanow Report.*

19. Ibid., Chapter on "Health Care, Citizenship and Federalism," p. 45.

20. See Edwin A. Tollefson, "The Medicare Dispute," in Norman Ward and Duff Spafford, eds., *Politics in Saskatchewan* (Don Mills, ON: Longmans Canada Limited, 1968), pp. 238–79; C. David Naylor, *Private Practice, Public Payment* (Kingston and Montreal: McGill-Queen's University Press, 1986); D. F. Shackleton, *Tommy Douglas: A Biography* (Toronto: McClelland and Stewart, 1975); Janet Walker Gouldner, *The Doctors' Strike: Change and Resistance to Change in Saskatchewan* (n.p., n.d.); Cynthia Krueger, *Prairie Protest: The Medicare Conflict in Saskatchewan* (n.p., n.d.); Seymour M. Lipset, *Agrarian Socialism,* rev. and ex. ed. (Berkeley: University of California Press, 1971).

21. Steve A. Lyons, "The Birth of the Canadian Health Care System: An Interview with Canadian Urologist "Staff" Barootes," PNHP Newsletter, July 1996, pp. 21–24.

22. On the Issues Web site, "John Kerry on Health Care," http://www.issues 2000.org/2004/John_Kerry_Health_Care.htm (accessed July 21, 2004).

23. *Consultation on the Right to Health Care, Session 1, Summary and Assessment,* Science and Human Rights Program of the AAAS, September 18, 1992.

24. Thomas J. Bole III and William B. Bondeson, eds., *Rights to Health Care,* vol. 38, Philosophy and Medicine Series (Boston: Kluwer Academic Publishers, 1991).

25. Baruch A. Brody, "Why the Right to Health Care Is Not a Useful Concept for Policy Debates," in Bole and Bondeson, eds., *Rights to Health Care,* pp. 112, 123.

26. Bole and Bondeson, eds., *Rights to Health Care,* vii.

27. See Ian Shapiro, *The Evolution of Rights in Liberal Theory* (New York: Cambridge University Press, 1986); and Ronald Dworkin, *Taking Rights Seriously* (Cambridge, Mass.: Harvard University Press, 1978).

28. President's Commission for the Study of Ethical Problems in Medicine and Biomedical and Behavioral Research, *Securing Access to Health Care,* vol. 1 (Washington, D.C.: U.S. Government Printing Office, 1983), p. 4.

29. The chapter of the *Romanow Report* on "Primary Health Care" also focuses on issues beyond the provision of health services and considers broader issues of health status.

30. Romanow, *Romanow Report,* chapter on "A New Approach to Aboriginal Health," pp. 211–31.

31. . Ibid., p. 218.

32. The second principle of the preamble reads: "The enjoyment of the highest attainable standard of health is one of the fundamental rights of every human being without distinction of race, religion, political belief, economic or social condition."

Chapter 8. International Labor Rights and North American Labor Law

1. Nelson Lichtenstein, *State of the Union* (Princeton, N.J.: Princeton University Press, 2002), Art. 22.

2. Ibid., p. 270.

3. The Wagner Act, as Peter Irons notes, was based on the interstate commerce clause. "It was simply a 'bet' on the part of the drafters, as one of them put it, that the Supreme Court would ultimately give an expansive reading to the clause." Thus, the drafters borrowed from language in the Supreme Court's

favorable commerce clause decisions, stressing in the act's preamble that denial of the rights to organize and collectively bargain led to "industrial strike or unrest," which interfered with the flow of commerce. Peter Irons, *The New Deal Lawyers* (Princeton, N.J.: Princeton University Press, 1982), pp. 229–30.

4. See generally James Atleson, *Values and Assumptions in American Labor Law* (Amherst: University of Massachusetts Press, 1983), pp. 35–43; Karl Klare, "Judicial Radicalization of the Wagner Act and the Origins of Modern Legal Consciousness, 1937–1941," *Minnesota Law Review* 62 (1978): 267–71.

5. *Emporium Capwell Co. v. Western Edition Community Organization*, 420 U.S. 50 (1975). In *J.I.Case Co. v. NLRB*, 321 U.S. 332 (1944), the Court held that collective bargaining could not be limited by private employment contracts that the employer had signed with some workers. Although the contracts were of uncertain value or meaning, the employer argued that it should not have to bargain with a newly certified union over those topics covered by the individual contracts. The Court rejected this argument, not on the ground that the workers had individual (or collective) rights to engage in collective bargaining but because the board asserted a "public right" to overcome the private "contract rights." See *J.I.Case Co. v. NLRB*, 321 U.S. 332 (1944); *National Licorice v. NLRB*, 309 U.S. 350 (1940). The concept of "public rights" also means that the National Labor Relations Board, not unions or workers, enforces with discretion the statute whether to prosecute or settle.

6. Virginia Leary, "The Paradox of Workers' Rights as Human Rights," in Lance Compa and Stephen Diamond, eds., *Human Rights, Labor Rights, and International Trade* (Philadelphia: University of Pennsylvania Press, 1996), p. 22. The leading North American advocates for treating labor rights as human rights are Roy Adams of McMaster University in Ontario, Canada, and Lance Compa and James Gross at the Industrial Labor Relations School, Cornell University.

7. Professor James Pope has argued that the Thirteenth Amendment, in conjunction with the First Amendment forms the basis for asserting labor's rights. The purpose of the Thirteenth Amendment, as the Supreme Court noted in 1911, is not simply to eliminate slavery but also "to make labor free by prohibiting that control by which the personal service of one man is disposed of or coerced for another's benefit." *Baily v. Alabama*, 219 U.S. 219, 241 (1911). See James Pope, "Labors' Constitution of Freedom," *Yale Law Journal* 106 (1997): 941; and Pope, "The Thirteenth Amendment versus the Commerce Clause," *Columbia Law Review* 102 (2002): 1.

8. The United States has ratified the International Covenant on Civil and Political Rights, albeit with several reservations, but it has ratified only fourteen ILO Conventions.

9. See generally James Gross, "A Human Rights Perspective on United States Labor Relations Law: A Violation of the Right of Freedom of Association," *Employee Rights and Employment Policy Journal* 3 (1999): 65. For excellent analysis of the relationship of labor rights to human rights, see James Gross, ed., *Workers' Rights as Human Rights* (Ithaca, N.Y.: Cornell University Press, 2003). See also, Lance Compa, *Unfair Advantage: Workers' Freedom of Association in the United States under International Human Rights Standards* (New York: Human Rights Watch, 2000), pp. 40–50.

10. Universal Declaration of Human Rights, Art. 20(1); Art. 23(4).

11. International Covenant on Civil and Political Rights, Art. 22.

12. See Appendix 1, Article 8.

13. "Norms on the Responsibilities of Transnational Corporations and Other

Business Enterprises with Regard to Human Rights," UN Doc. E/CN.4/Sub.2/2003/12/Rev.2 (2003).

14. Compa, *Unfair Advantage*, p. 44.

15. Lee Swepston, "Closing the Gap between International Law and U.S. Law," in James Gross, ed., *Workers' Rights as Human Rights*, p. 56.

16. ILO Convention 98, Arts. 1, 3, 4.

17. Fundamental principles of labor rights and human rights were set out in the original ILO constitution of 1919 and in the Declaration of Philadelphia (1944), which was appended to the constitution. The preamble, for instance, refers to "recognition of the principle of freedom of association," and the Declaration of Philadelphia reaffirms that "freedom of expression and association are essential to sustained progress." See Hillary Kellerson, "The ILO Declaration of 1998 on Fundamental Principles and Rights: A Challenge for the Future," *International Labour Review* 137 (1998): 224–25.

18. Compa, *Unfair Advantage*, p. 46. The United States has recognized international labor standards in other contexts. For instance, the Generalized System of Preferences is a statutory system that permits the United States to grant or deny trade preferences to countries that respect labor rights, and it refers to ILO conventions, especially 87. Lance Compa, "Workers' Freedom of Association under International Human Rights Law," in Compa, *Unfair Advantage*, pp. 40–50; Brian Langille, "The ILO and the New Economy: Recent Developments," *The International Journal of Comparative Labour Law and Industrial Relations* 15, no. 3 (1999): 229; Lance Compa, "Going Multilateral," *Connecticut Journal of International Law* 10 (spring 1995): 216; Clyde Summers, "The Battle in Seattle: Free Trade Labor Rights and Societal Values," *University of Pennsylvania Journal of International Economic Law* 22, no. 1 (2001): 61.

19. Compa, *Unfair Advantage*, pp. 48–49. A series of valuable articles are in *International Labour Review* 137, no. 2 (1998); Harold Dunning, "The Origins of Convention 87 on Freedom of Association and the Right to Organize," *International Labour Review* 137, no. 2 (1998): 149.

20. Article 33 of the ILO's constitution grants broad authority to respond to countries that are not in compliance with the obligations of membership: "[T]he Governing Body may recommend that the Conference take such action as it may deem wise and expedient to secure compliance therewith." Article 33 was first invoked in 2000 against Burma. Following a complaint against Burma under Article 26, a commission of inquiry ultimately called on Burma to bring its laws and practices into compliance. After no response was received from Burma, the conference approved a resolution that condemned Burma's refusal to comply with the commission of inquiry's recommendations, prohibited technical assistance except as necessary to implement the recommendations, and banned Burma from most meetings. In March 2000, the governing body requested member states to take appropriate measures with the government of Myanmar (Burma) in relation to Burma's use of forced labor. The situation has not changed, at least formally, nor is it clear that the call for member action has had any effect. As Elliott and Freeman note, the ILO's "slow and tortuous response to Burmese intransigence underscores the unwillingness of the ILO membership to punish miscreants, even when the country in question is a small, poor, isolated one whose violations are egregious and well documented." Kimberly Elliott and Richard Freeman, *Can Labor Standards Improve under Globalization?* (Washington, D.C.: Institute for International Economics, 2003), p. 106.

21. See, e.g., Nichols Valticos, "International Labour Standards and Human

Rights: Approaching the Year 2000," *International Labour Review* 137 (1998): 137. For discussion of the positive effects of ILO standards, see Geraldo Von Potobsky, "Freedom of Association: The Impact of Convention No. 87 and ILO Action," *International Labour Review* 137 (1998): 196. As Potobsky concludes, however, "it is important to understand that international public pressure is the ILO's most powerful weapon, for the ILO does not have power to sanction and its constitution does not allow it to exclude a state and punishment for the violation of international labor standards or principles. Nevertheless, the persistence and perseverance of the supervisory bodies are an extremely powerful weapon in the ILO's armory." Von Potobsky, "Freedom of Association," p. 221.

22. See, e.g., the recent decision by the Canadian Supreme Court holding invalid Ontario's exclusion of agricultural workers from Ontario labor statutes. The Court relied, in part, on ILO Convention 87. *Dunmore v. Ontario (Attorney General)*, 2001 SCC 94. The *Dunmore* decision has led to an outpouring of scholarly analysis. See, e.g., a special issue of the *Canadian Labour and Employment Law Journal* 10, no. 1 (2003). It is far from clear how influential international labor law was in the Court's decision-making process.

23. See, e.g., Lance Compa, "Pursuing International Labour Rights in U.S. Courts," *Industrial Relations (U.K.)* 57 (2002), p. 48, and Compa, "Going Multilateral," 1995.

24. Case no. 1543 (1990).

25. Case no. 1557 (1990).

26. See Brian Burkett, John Craig, and S. Gallagher, "Canada and the ILO: Freedom of Association since 1982," *Canadian Labour and Employment Law Journal* 10, no. 2 (2003): 231.

27. The Supreme Court has stated that "it was early recognized that an employer had a duty to bargain whenever the union representative presented 'convincing evidence of majority support,'" for instance, by the possession of authorization cards, a strike, or a strike vote. Yet, in the same case as this statement was made, the Court upheld an NLRB rule that basically permitted the employer to reject objective evidence of majority support and force an election. *NLRB v. Gissel Packing Co, Inc.*, 395 U.S. 575 (1969).

28. See Kate Bronfenbrenner, "We'll Close! Plant Closings, Plant-Closing Threats, Union Organizing and NAFTA," *Multinational Monitor* 18, no. 3 (March 1997): 8–14; "Raw Power: Plant-Closing Threats and the Threat to Union Organizing," *Multinational Monitor* 21 (December 2000): 24–30; "The Role of Union Strategies in NLRB Certification Elections," *Industrial and Labor Relations Review* 50, no. 2 (1997): 195.

29. See Paul Weiler, "Promises to Keep: Securing Workers' Rights to Self-Organization under the NLRA," *Harvard Law Review* 96 (1983): 1778.

30. Ibid., pp. 1779–80.

31. James Atleson, "Law and Union Power: Thoughts on the United States and Canada," *Buffalo Law Review* 42 (1994): 478.

32. Ibid., p. 480; William Cooke, *Union Organizing and Public Policy: Failure to Secure Union Contracts* (Kalamazoo, Mich.: W. E. Upjohn Institute for Employment Research, 1985), p. 98.

33. Cited at Paul Weiler, *Governing the Workplace* (Cambridge, Mass.: Harvard University Press, 1990), p. 114.

34. In 2002, the General Accounting Office found that 25 million private sector workers and 7 million public sector workers do not have the right to form unions. AFL-CIO, "Time for Reform," http://www.afl-cio.org.

35. Patricia Hughes, "*Dunmore v. Ontario (Attorney General)*: Waiting for the Other Shoe," *Canadian Labour and Employment Law Journal* 10, no. 1 (2003): 27.

36. *NLRB v. Mackay Radio and Telegraph*, 304 U.S. 333 (1938). For one of many criticisms of this doctrine, see Atleson, *Values and Assumptions*, pp. 1–34.

37. See James Atleson, "An Injury to One . . . : Transnational Labor Solidarity and the Role of Domestic Law," in Gross, ed., *Workers' Rights as Human Rights*, p. 160.

38. Collective agreements in the United States generally bar strikes during the term of the contract, although some unions have negotiated limited exceptions to the contractual prohibition. Even if there is no contractual no-strike clause, strikes may still be barred by judicial interpretation of arbitration provisions. In an important U.S. Supreme Court decision, strikes are barred if they involve matters that could be resolved by the grievance process even in the absence of a no-strike clause. *Local 174, Teamsters v. Lucas Flour*, 369 U.S. 95 (1962).

39. There may also be specific legislation prohibiting or hampering the ability of national workers' organizations to affiliate with international confederations. See *World Labour Report: Industrial Relations, Democracy and Social Stability* (Geneva: ILO, 1997–98), pp. 37–38.

40. James Atleson, "Reflections on Labor, Power, and Society," *Maryland Law Review* 44 (1985): 841.

41. K. W. Wedderburn, "Industrial Relations," in H. R. Hahlo, J. Graham Smith, and Richard W. Wright, eds., *Nationalism and the Multinational Enterprise* (New York: Oceana Publications, 1973), p. 244.

42. See, e.g., C. Fisk, D. Mitchell, and C. Erickson, "Union Representation of Immigrant Janitors in Southern California: Economic and Legal Challenges," in Ruth Milkman, ed., *Organizing Immigrants* (Ithaca, N.Y.: Cornell University Press, 2000), p. 199.

43. Quoted in Anthony Forsyth, "Trade Union Rights for the New Millennium" (London: International Centre for Trade Union Rights, 1988), p. 9. Atleson, "An Injury to One," pp. 178–79. A more detailed analysis of domestic barriers to international solidarity efforts is James Atleson, "The Voyage of the Neptune Jade: The Perils and Promises of Transnational Labor Solidarity," *Buffalo Law Review* 52, no. 1 (spring 2004).

44. See Atleson, "An Injury to One," p. 160.

45. Ibid., pp. 177–78.

46. See James Atleson, "Confronting Judicial Values: Rewriting the Law of Work in a Common Law System," *Buffalo Law Review* 45 (1997): 455–56. For a discussion of the values inherent in modern as well as historical labor decision-making in the United States, see Atleson, *Values and Assumptions*.

47. See James Atleson, "Law and Union Power," p. 500.

48. See Leary, "Paradox of Workers' Rights as Human Rights," p. 43.

Chapter 9. Deconstructing Barriers

1. J. Bickenbach, *Disability and Social Policy* (Toronto: University of Toronto Press, 1993), p. 14.

2. World Health Organization (WHO), "WHO Publishes New Guidelines to Measure Health" (News Release 1/48, November 15, 2001), http://www.who.int/inf-pr-2001/en/pr2001-48.html.

3. T. Shakespeare, "What is a Disabled Person?" in M. Jones and L. A. Basser

Marks, eds., *Disability, Divers-Ability and Legal Change* (The Hague: Martinus Nij-hoff Publishers, 1999), p. 25.

4. M. H. Rioux and M. J. Prince, "The Canadian Political Landscape of Dis-ability: Policy Perspectives, Social Status, Interest Groups and the Rights Move-ment," in A. Puttee, ed., *Federalism, Democracy and Disability Policy in Canada* (Montreal and Kingston: McGill-Queen's University Press, 2003), p. 11.

5. M. D. Lepofsky, "The Latimer Case: Murder Is Still Murder When the Victim Is a Child with a Disability," *Queen's Law Journal* 27 (2001): 324.

6. Bickenbach, *Disability*, p. 12; see also ibid., pp. 61–92.

7. Rioux and Prince, "Landscape of Disability," p. 12.

8. Ibid., p. 13.

9. Bickenbach, *Disability*, p. 13; see also ibid., pp. 93–134.

10. Ibid., 13, also pp. 135–81.

11. See M. Oliver, *The Politics of Disablement: A Sociological Approach* (New York: St. Martins Press, 1990).

12. M. Jones and L. A. Basser Marks, eds., "Law and the Social Construction of Disability" in Jones and Basser Marks, *Disability, Divers-Ability and Legal Change*, p. 3.

13. Shakespeare, "What Is a Disabled Person?" p. 31.

14. The WHO's guidelines for the International Classification of Function-ing, Disability and Health explicitly rejects this classification; see WHO, "New Guidelines to Measure Health."

15. See J. Bickenbach, "Minority Rights or Universal Participation: The Poli-tics of Disablement," in Jones and Basser Marks, *Disability, Divers-Ability and Legal Change*, p. 101.

16. Shakespeare, "What Is a Disabled Person?" p. 31.

17. I. Zola, "Toward the Necessary Universalizing of a Disability Policy," *The Milbank Quarterly* 67 (1989): 421, as cited in Bickenbach, "Minority Rights," p. 111.

18. Universal Declaration of Human Rights.

19. Bickenbach, "Minority Rights," p. 112.

20. The ADA prohibits discrimination in employment, government, public accommodations, commercial facilities, transportation, and telecommunica-tions.

21. See M. D. Lepofsky, "The Long, Arduous Road to a Barrier-Free Ontario for People With Disabilities: The History of the *Ontarians with Disabilities Act*—The First Chapter," *National Journal of Constitutional Law* 15 (2004): 125

22. See also S. Tjorman, "Canada's Federal Regime and Persons with Disabili-ties," in D. Cameron and F. Valentine, eds., *Disability and Federalism: Comparing Different Approaches to Full Participation* (Montreal and Kingston: McGill-Queen's University Press, 2001), p. 151; M. J. Prince, "Canadian Federalism and Disabil-ity Policy Making," *Canadian Journal of Political Science* 34 (2001): 791.

23. Tjorman, "Canada's Federal Regime," p. 157.

24. Ibid., pp. 151–52.

25. See Canada Health and Welfare, *Obstacles: Disabled Persons in Canada* (Ottawa: Minister of Supply and Services, 1981); Federal Task Force on Disability Issues, *Equal Citizenship for Canadians with Disabilities: The Will to Act* (Ottawa: Min-ister of Supply and Services, 1996); Federal/Provincial/Territorial Ministers Responsible for Social Services, *In Unison: A Canadian Approach to Disability Issues* (Ottawa: Minister of Supply and Services, 1998), and *In Unison 2000: Persons with Disabilities in Canada* (Ottawa: Minister of Supply and Services, 2001). See also

Government of Canada, *Advancing the Inclusion of Persons with Disabilities* (Ottawa: Minister of Supply and Services, 2002).

26. Section 15(1) of the Charter states, "Every individual is equal before and under the law and has the right to equal protection and equal benefit of the law without discrimination and, in particular, without discrimination based on race, national or ethnic origin, color, religion, sex, age or physical or mental disability."

27. Section 9 of the South African Constitution also protects people with disabilities from direct and indirect discrimination by the state.

28. See also W. Boyce et al., *A Seat at the Table: Persons with Disabilities and Policy Making* (Montreal and Kingston: McGill-Queen's University Press, 2001), especially chap. 4, "The Canadian Charter of Rights and Freedoms: The Political Battle Over Four Words." See also M. D. Lepofsky, "A Report Card on the *Charter*'s Guarantee of Equality to Persons with Disabilities after 10 Years—What Progress? What Prospects?" *National Journal of Constitutional Law* 7 (1996): 263.

29. M. D. Lepofsky and J. Bickenbach, "Equality Rights and the Physically Handicapped," in A. F. Bayefsky and M. Eberts, eds., *Equality Rights and the Canadian Charter of Rights and Freedoms* (Toronto: Carswell, 1985), pp. 323, 338.

30. Ibid., p. 275.

31. Y. Peters, "The Constitution and the Disabled," *Health Law Review* 2 (1993): 1.

32. UNGA Resolution 347 (XXX), December 9, 1975.

33. Peters, "Constitution and the Disabled," par. 25.

34. See S. Armstrong, "Disability Advocacy in the Charter Era," *Journal of Law and Equality* 2 (2003): 33.

35. Government of Canada, *Advancing the Inclusion*, p. 31.

36. Ibid., p. 36.

37. Ontario Human Rights Commission, *The Opportunity to Succeed: Achieving Barrier-Free Education for Students with Disabilities* (Toronto: Ontario Human Rights Commission, 2003), referring to *Eldridge v. British Columbia (Attorney General)*, (1997) 3 Supreme Court Reports 624.

38. 38. Notably, the federal government provides funding for the education of First Nations students who live on reserves and of Inuit students, and it works with the provinces to improve post-secondary financial assistance programs.

39. Boyce et al., *A Seat at the Table*, p. 12.

40. Ibid.

41. H. Noah, *Reviews of National Policies for Education* (Paris: OECD, 1976), pp. 54–56, quoted in Boyce et al., *A Seat at the Table*, p. 12.

42. (1997) 1 Supreme Court Reports 241 (hereafter *Eaton*).

43. Federal Task Force, *Equal Citizenship for Canadians with disabilities*, chap. 5.

44. Government of Canada, *Advancing the Inclusion*, p. 35.

45. Ibid., p. 39.

46. 46. According to *Advancing the Inclusion*, approximately 10 percent of the OF budget is allocated for Aboriginal Canadians with disabilities.

47. M. J. Prince, "Designing Disability Policy in Canada," in Puttee, ed., *Federalism, Democracy and Disability Policy in Canada*, p. 34. Only federally regulated employers are governed by the act.

48. We refer to the program as the Canada/Quebec Pension Plan because, while the federal government operates the CPP for the rest of Canada, the government of Quebec operates an analogous plan for that province.

49. Government of Canada, *Advancing the Inclusion*, p. 36.

50. Tjorman, "Canada's Federal Regime," p. 171.
51. Rioux and Prince, "Landscape of Disability," pp. 22–23.
52. See, e.g., *Masse v. Ontario (Ministry of Community and Social Services)* (hereafter *Masse*) (1996), 134 Dominion Law Reports (4th) 20; *Gosselin v. Quebec (Procureur General)*, (hereafter *Gosselin*) (2002) Supreme Court Reports 429; *Falkiner v. Ontario (Ministry of Community and Social Services, Income Maintenance Branch)* (hereafter *Falkiner*) (2002) Ontario Judgments 1771.
53. See *Masse*.
54. See *Falkiner*.
55. See *Gosselin*.
56. Tjorman, "Canada's Federal Regime," p. 171.
57. CCSD, *Children and Youth with Special Needs* (November 2001), http://www.ccsd.ca/pubs/2001/specialneeds/specialneeds.pdf.
58. Roehr Institute, *Count Us In: A Demographic Overview of Childhood and Disability in Canada* (Toronto: Roehr Institute, 2000).
59. Ontario Human Rights Commission, *Education and Disability: Human Rights Issues in Ontario's Education System* (Toronto: Ontario Human Rights Commission, 2003), p. 16.
60. Ibid., p. 17.
61. Ibid., p. 16.
62. Ibid.
63. CCSD, *Disability Information Sheet Number 2* (2001), http://www.ccsd.ca/drip/research/dis2.pdf.
64. CCSD, *Disability Information Sheet Number 3* (2001), pp. 7–8, http://www.ccsd.ca/drip/research/dis3.pdf.
65. CCSD, *Disability Information Sheet Number 9* (2003), pp. 7–8, http://www.ccsd.ca/drip/research/dis9/dis9.pdf.
66. CCSD, *Disability Information Sheet Number 10* (2003), p. 2, http://www.ccsd.ca/drip/research/dis10/dis10.pdf.
67. Ibid., pp. 2–3.
68. CCSD, *Disability Information Sheet Number 8* (2002), pp. 2–3, http://www.ccsd.ca/drip/research/dis8/dis8.pdf.
69. G. Fawcett, *Living with Disability in Canada: An Economic Portrait* (Ottawa: Human Resources Development Canada, 1996).
70. Income Security Advocacy Centre, *Denial by Design: The Ontario Disability Support Program* (Toronto: Income Security Advocacy Centre, 2003).
71. Ibid., p. 7.
72. Ibid., pp. 13–15.
73. Ibid., p. 8.
74. Ibid., pp. 33–34.
75. Ibid., pp. 34–35.
76. CCSD, *Disability Information Sheet Number 10*, pp. 5–6.
77. Bickenbach, Disability, p. 227.

Chapter 10. The Economic Rights of Migrant and Immigrant Workers in Canada and the United States

I would like to thank Jessica Higginbottom for her research assistance for this chapter and Dan Milisavljevic for his careful editorial assistance. The participants at the workshop held at the State University of New York, Buffalo, in October 2003, also provided a number of helpful comments on this chapter.

1. Stephen Castles and Mark Miller, *The Age of Migration: International Population Movements in the Modern World* (London: Macmillan Press, 1993), pp. 51–52.

2. In its 2000 *Guide to Naturalization,* the U.S. Immigration and Naturalization Service tells applicants for citizenship, "We are very pleased you want to become a U.S. citizen. The United States is a nation of immigrants. Throughout our history, immigrants have come here seeking a better way of life and have strengthened our nation in the process." *Guide to Naturalization* (Washington, D.C.: Immigration and Naturalization Service, 2000).

3. Douglas Massey, "Why Does Immigration Occur?" in Charles Hirschman, Philip Kasinitz, and Josh DeWind, eds., *The Handbook of International Migration* (New York: Russell Sage Foundation, 1999), pp. 48–49.

4. Immigration also raises a number of broader issues about human rights that cannot be discussed in this context. For instance, there are important debates about the extent to which immigrants have, and should have, the right to engage in cultural practices that are common (and acceptable to at least some segments of the population) in their homelands.

5. "Diversity immigration" is the one major U.S. category that does not have a parallel within the Canadian immigration program. This provision makes visas available to persons from countries with low rates of immigration to the United States and is operated as a lottery.

6. George Borjas, *Heaven's Door: Immigration Policy and the American Economy* (Princeton, N.J.: Princeton University Press, 1999); Neil Bissoondath, *Selling Illusions: The Cult of Multiculturalism in Canada* (Toronto: Penguin Books, 1994), p. 132.

7. Citizenship and Immigration Canada, *Becoming a Canadian Citizen,* 2003, http://cicnet.ci.gc.ca/english/citizen/becoming-howto.html.

8. Stephen Castles and Godula Kosack, *Immigrant Workers and Class Structure in Western Europe* (London: Oxford University Press, 1973), p. 474.

9. Barry Edmonston, Jeffrey Passel, and Frank Bean, "Perceptions and Estimates of Undocumented Migration to the United States," in Frank Bean, Barry Edmonston, and Jeffrey Passel, eds., *Undocumented Migration to the United States: IRCA and the Experience of the 1980s* (Santa Monica, Calif.: Rand Corporation, 1990), p. 11.

10. Castles and Miller, *Age of Migration,* p. 91.

11. Frank Bean, Barry Edmonston, and Jeffrey Passel, Introduction, in Bean, Edmonston, and Passel, eds., *Undocumented Migration,* p. 3.

12. See "The Americas," *The Migration News* 11, no. 1 (2004): 1–23.

13. Department of Homeland Security, "Immigrants Admitted by Type and Selected Class of Admission, Fiscal Years 1986–2001" (Washington, D.C.: Bureau of Citizenship and Immigration, 2003), http://uscis.gov/graphics/shared/aboutus/statistics/IMM01yrbk/IMM2001list.htm (accessed July 20, 2004).

14. Ibid.

15. Peter Li, *Destination Canada: Immigration Debates and Issues* (Toronto: Oxford University Press, 2003), p. 48.

16. Marina Jiminez, "200,000 Illegal Immigrants Toiling in Canada's Underground Economy," *Toronto Globe and Mail,* November 15, 2003, p. A4.

17. Borjas, *Heaven's Door,* p. 203.

18. Immigration and Naturalization Service, "Estimates, Fiscal Year 2000," http://www.bcis.gov/graphics/shared/aboutus/statistics/Est2000.pdf.

19. Leo Chavez, "Immigration Reform and Nativism: The Nationalist Re-

sponse to the Transnationalist Challenge," in Juan Perea, ed., *Immigrants Out! The New Nativism and the Anti-Immigrant Impulse in the United States* (New York: New York University Press, 1997), p. 73. Analysts in Canada have also argued that much of the anti-immigrant discourse of recent years is racially based, but couched in racially neutral language. According to Peter Li, "[T]he term *immigrants* frequently becomes a code, in the sense that it contains a subtext, to refer to non-white-immigrants, their cultural diversity, and indeed, the urban problems they are believed to have created." See Li, *Destination Canada*, p. 46. See also Sean Hier and Joshua Greenberg, "News Discourse and the Problematization of Chinese Migration to Canada," in Frances Henry and Carol Tator, eds., *Discourses of Domination: Racial Bias in the Canadian English Language Press* (Toronto: University of Toronto Press, 2002), pp. 142–43.

20. Li, *Destination Canada*, p. 43.

21. James Gimpel and James Edwards, *The Congressional Politics of Immigration Reform* (Boston: Allyn and Bacon, 1999), p. 68.

22. Borjas, *Heaven's Door,* pp. 192–93.

23. Nandita Sharma, "On Being *Not* Canadian: The Social Organization of 'Migrant Workers' in Canada," *Canadian Review of Sociology and Anthropology* 38, no. 4 (2001): 415–39.

24. Citizenship and Immigration Canada, "Information Sharing Arrangement among Citizenship and Immigration Canada, U.S. Immigration and Naturalization Service and the U.S. Department of State," 2003, http://www .cic.gc.ca/english/policy/smu/smu-bkgrnd.html.

25. Deborah Waller Meyers, "Does Smarter Lead to Safer? An Assessment of the U.S. Border Accords with Canada and Mexico," *International Migration* 41, no. 4 (2003): 5–44.

26. Vic Satzewich and Lloyd Wong, "Immigration, Ethnicity and Race: The Transformation of Transnationalism, Localism, and Identities," in Wallace Clement and Leah Vosko, eds., *Changing Canada: Political Economy as Transformation* (Montreal and Kingston: McGill-Queen's University Press, 2003), p. 367; see also Citizenship and Immigration Canada, "Information Sharing," and Meyers, "Does Smarter Lead to Safer?"

27. *An Act Respecting Immigration to Canada and the Granting of Refugee Protection to Persons Who Are Displaced, Persecuted or in Danger, Statutes of Canada,* chap. 27, sections 49–50, 2001.

28. Yasmeen Abu-Laban and Christina Gabriel, *Selling Diversity: Immigration, Multiculturalism, Employment Equity, and Globalization* (Peterborough: Broadview Press, 2002), p. 81.

29. Citizenship and Immigration Canada, "Length of Time You Must Support a Sponsored Relative or Family Member," http://www.cis.gc.ca/english/ sponsor/support.html (2003).

30. Austin Fragomen, "The Illegal Immigration Reform and Immigrant Responsibility Act of 1996: An Overview," *International Migration Review* 31, no. 2 (1997): 441.

31. Abu-Laban and Gabriel, *Selling Diversity,* p. 52.

32. Ibid.

33. Fragomen, "Illegal Immigration Reform," p. 441.

34. Ibid., p. 447.

35. Ibid., pp. 448–50.

36. Arthur Helton, "The New Convention from the Perspective of a Country of Employment: The U.S. Case," *International Migration Review* 25, no. 4 (1991): 852.

37. Chavez, "Immigration Reform and Nativism."

38. Kristin Hill Maher, "Who Has Access to Rights? Citizenship and Exclusions in an Age of Migration," in Alison Brysk, ed., *Globalization and Human Rights* (Los Angeles: University of California Press, 2002), p. 21; see also George Sanchez, "Face the Nation: Race, Immigration and the Rise of Nativism in Late-Twentieth-Century America," in Hirschman, Kasinitz and DeWind, eds., *The Handbook of International Migration.*

39. Maher, "Who Has Access to Rights?" p. 29.

40. Fragomen, "Illegal Immigration Reform," p. 447.

41. Commission for Labor Cooperation, *Protection of Migrant Agricultural Workers in Canada, Mexico and the United States* (Washington, D.C.: Secretariat of the Commission for Labor Cooperation, 2002), p. 37.

42. Ibid.

43. Ibid., p. 38.

44. Vic Satzewich, *Racism and the Incorporation of Foreign Labour: Farm Labour Migration to Canada since 1945* (London: Routledge, 1991).

45. Sharma,"On Being *Not* Canadian."

46. See Commission for Labor Cooperation, *Protection,* pp. 11–13, for details.

47. Ibid., p. 10.

48. Ibid., pp. 44–49.

49. See Appendix 1.

50. Gurcharn Basran and Li Zong, "Devaluation of Foreign Credentials as Perceived by Non-white Professional Immigrants," *Canadian Ethnic Studies* 30, no. 1 (1998): 6–23; see also Li, *Destination Canada,* pp. 112–15.

51. Vic Satzewich, Wsevolod Isajiw, and Eugene Duvalko, "Recent Immigrants from Ukraine in Toronto: Social Networks and the Economic Adjustment Process" (paper presented at the Ukraine and Its Diaspora Conference, Harvard University, March 26–28, 2003).

52. The term "visible minority" is used in Canada as a euphemism for "non-white" racialized groups. Within Canadian federal government legislation, the following groups are considered visible minorities: Chinese, blacks, South Asians, Arabs, West Asians, Filipino, Latin American, Japanese, and Korean.

53. Li, *Destination Canada,* p. 109.

54. American research on immigrant earnings is also plentiful and is complicated by the notable earnings and income disparities within the native-born population between blacks and whites. As in Canada, immigrants to the United States are diverse in terms of their countries of origins, their class backgrounds, and their time of arrival. As a result, some of the gross categories that are used to construct dependent variables that measure a combination of "race," ethnicity and skin color may be questionable. For instance, Waters and Eschbach (see note 55, following) note that the category of "Asian male" includes Cambodians and Laotians, who arrived in the United States with relatively low levels of education, and Asian Indian and Filipino men, who have relatively high levels of education.

55. Mary Waters and Karl Eschbach, "Immigration and Ethnic and Racial Inequality in the United States," *Annual Review of Sociology* 21 (1995): 433.

56. See, e.g., Borjas, *Heaven's Door,* p. 51; Waters and Eschbach, "Immigration"; and Jeffrey Reitz and Raymond Breton, *The Illusion of Difference: Realities of Ethnicity in Canada and the United States* (Toronto: C. D. Howe Institute, 1994).

57. Li, *Destination Canada,* p. 112.

58. Reitz and Breton, *Illusion of Difference,* p. 122.

59. Gimpel and Edwards, *Congressional Politics*, p. 85. See also Rey Koslowski, "Economic Globalization, Human Smuggling, and Global Governance," in David Kyle and Rey Koslowski, eds., *Global Human Smuggling: Comparative Perspectives* (Baltimore: Johns Hopkins University Press, 2001), p. 357.

60. Annette Bernhardt, "Wal-Mart Makes Workers Pay," *Atlanta Journal-Constitution*, October 29, 2003.

61. Steve Miller, "Wal-Mart Lawsuit Seen as Trend for U.S. employers," *Washington Times*, November 24, 2003.

62. Commission for Labor Cooperation, *Protection*, pp. 41–42.

63. See "*Hoffman Plastic Compounds, Inc. v. NLRB*: Supreme Court Bars Undocumented Worker from Receiving Back Pay Remedy for Unlawful Firing," *Immigrants' Rights Update* 16, no. 2 (2002): 1.

64. Gimpel and Edwards, *Congressional Politics*, p. 292.

65. Mark Miller, "Toward Understanding State Capacity to Prevent Unwanted Migration: Employer Sanctions Enforcement in France, 1975–1990," *West European Politics* 17, no. 2 (1994): 140–67; and Mark Miller, "The Sanctioning of Unauthorized Migration and Alien Employment," in David Kyle and Rey Koslowski, eds., *Global Human Smuggling: Comparative Perspectives* (Baltimore: Johns Hopkins University Press, 2001).

66. Cynthia Bansak and Steven Raphael, "Immigration Reform and the Earnings of Latino Workers: Do Employer Sanctions Cause Discrimination?" *Industrial and Labor Relations Review* 54, no. 2 (2001): 275–95.

67. Ibid., p. 279.

68. *Act Respecting Immigration, Statutes of Canada*, c. 27, pt. 124.

69. Miller, "Unauthorized Migration and Alien Employment," p. 325.

70. "The Americas," p. 6.

71. Steven Greenhouse, "Wal-Mart Raids by U.S. Aimed at Illegal Immigrants," *New York Times*, October 24, 2003.

72. Koslowski, "Economic Globalization," p. 352.

73. Government Accounting Office (GAO), *Immigration Reform: Employer Sanctions and the Question of Discrimination, Report to Congress* (Washington, D.C.: United States General Accounting Office, 1990), p. 6.

74. Ibid., pp. 6–7; see also Bansak and Raphael, "Immigration Reform," p. 277; Leah Haus, "Openings in the Wall: Transnational Migrants, Labor Unions, and U.S. Immigration Policy," *International Organization* 49, no. 2 (1995): 285–313.

75. Christian Joppke, "The Legal-Domestic Sources of Immigrant Rights: The United States, Germany and the European Union," *Comparative Political Studies* 34, no. 4 (2001): 339–66.

76. Ibid., p. 340.

77. Ibid., pp. 340–41.

78. *International Convention on the Protection of the Rights of All Migrant Workers and Their Families*, G.A. res. 45/158, annex, 45 UN GAOR Supp. (No. 49A) at 262, Un.Coc. A/45/49 (1990), available at http://www1.umn.edu/humanrts/instree/n8icprmw.htm.

79. Office of the United Nations High Commissioner for Human Rights, "Status of Ratifications of the Principal International Human Rights Treaties, as of November, 2003" (New York: United Nations, 2003).

80. David Weissbrodt, "Comprehensive Examination of Thematic Issues Relating to the Elimination of Racial Discrimination: The Rights of Non-Citizens" (working paper prepared for the Sub-Commission on Prevention of Dis-

crimination and Protection of Minorities, Commission on Human Rights, Economic and Council of the United Nations, 1999), pp. 2–4.

81. Helton, "New Convention," p. 853.

82. Commission for Labor Cooperation, *Protection*, p. 1.

83. Secretariat of the Commission for Labor Cooperation, *Report on the Migrant Worker Guide Focus Group* (Washington, D.C.: Secretariat of the Commission for Labor Cooperation, 2001), p. 1.

84. David Weissbrodt, "General Comment on the Rights of Non-Citizens" (prepared for the United Nations Sub-Commission on the Promotion and Protection of Human Rights, Advanced Edited Version, E/CN.4/Sub.2/2003/23, May 26, 2003), p. 4.

Chapter 11. The Netherlands

I wish to thank Ineke Boerefijn, Fons Coomans, and Tiemo Oostenbrink for their comments.

1. Less than twice the size of the state of New Jersey, with a population of 16.1 million inhabitants (July 2003, est.).

2. See Peter Baehr, Monique Castermans-Holleman, and Fred Grünfeld, *Human Rights in the Foreign Policy of the Netherlands* (Antwerp: Intersentia, 2002). An article by the same authors with the same title appeared in *Human Rights Quarterly* 24, no. 4 (November 2002): 992–1010.

3. Based on life expectancy at birth; adult literacy rate; combined primary, secondary and tertiary enrolment rate; and GDP per capita. UN Development Program, *Human Development Report 2003* (New York: Oxford University Press, 2003), pp. 237 ff.

4. CIA World Factbook, http://www.oD.C.i.gov/cia/publications/factbook/print/nl.html (accessed December 20, 2003).

5. Fried van Hoof, "De Praktische Betekenis van Economische, Sociale en Culturele Rechten in Nederland?" (The practical significance of economic, social and cultural rights in the Netherlands?), in M. K. C. Arambulo, A. P. M. Coomans, and B. C. A. Toebes, eds., *De Betekenis van Economische, Sociale en Culturele Rechten in de Nederlandse Rechtsorde: Vrijblijvend of Verplichtend?* (Leiden: Stichting NJCM-Boekerij, 1998), p. 10; translated from the original Dutch.

6. For recent observations about the way in which the ESC Committee deals with the implementation of the Covenant, see Fons Coomans, "The Role of the UN Committee on Economic, Social and Cultural Rights in Strengthening Implementation and Supervision of the International Covenant on Economic Social and Cultural Rights," *Verfassung und Recht Übersee* (VRÜ) 35 (2002): 182–200.

7. The very latest consideration of a report by the Netherlands by the Committee on the Rights of the Child on January 19, 2004, and its Concluding Observations (CRC/C/15/Add. 227) dated January 30, 2004, are *not* covered by this chapter.

8. In the Dutch legal tradition, there is no hierarchy among the fundamental rights. This creates an obvious problem whenever there is a conflict among rights. This issue was at the background of the public controversy, when politician Pim Fortuyn (who was assassinated on May 6, 2002) declared in an interview that the "odd" Article 1 of the Netherlands Constitution, which prohibits discrimination on the grounds of religion, political views, race, gender, or on what-

ever other grounds, should be abolished in favor of freedom of expression. *De Volkskrant* (Amsterdam), February 9, 2002. This view had especially to do with his abhorrence of Islam, which he considered "a backward culture": "Sir, if I could acquire sufficient juridical support, I would say: no Moslem should enter [this country]." Ibid., translated from the original Dutch.

9. Ministry of Foreign Affairs of the Kingdom of the Netherlands, *Human Rights and Foreign Policy* (memorandum presented to the Lower House of the States General of the Kingdom of the Netherlands, May 3, 1979, by the minister for foreign affairs and the minister for development co-operation, official English version), p. 137. It sets a limit, however, where refugees are concerned. Persons who have left their country for economic reasons—in other words, because they could not avail themselves of their economic and social rights—are termed "economic migrants," who cannot claim refugee status under the terms of the UN Refugee Convention of 1951.

10. Ministry of Foreign Affairs, *2001 Memorandum on Human Rights Policy*, official English version, p. 5.

11. Van Hoof, "De Praktische Betekenis," p. 8; translated from the original Dutch.

12. Ibid., p. 11.

13. Ibid., p. 14.

14. Advisory Council on International Affairs, *Commentary on the 2001 Memorandum on Human Rights Policy*, report no. 23 (2001), official English version (2001), p. 9.

15. See also the foreign minister's response (July 24, 1995) to the Advisory Committee on Human Rights and Foreign Policy's advisory report on economic, social, and cultural rights. See also F. Coomans and F. van Hoof, eds., *The Right to Complain about Economic, Social and Cultural Rights* (Utrecht: SIM Special no. 18, 1995).

16. At the time of this writing (winter 2004) the said optional protocol seems not to have progressed much beyond the thinking stage. The Economic and Social Council endorsed in its decision 2002/254 of July 25, 2002, a move of the Commission for Human Rights to establish an open-ended working group with a view to consider options regarding the elaboration of such an optional protocol. In its 2003 session, the commission asked the working group to meet for a period of ten working days prior to its sixtieth session (2004). Commission for Human Rights, res. 2003/18, pars. 12 and 13. See also Coomans, "Role of the UN Committee," pp. 195–99, and *Report of the International Seminar: The Proposal for an Optional Protocol to the International Covenant on Economic, Social and Cultural Rights: Issues and Open Questions* (organized by the German Institute for Human Rights, Berlin, January 30 and 31, 2003).

17. Dutch section of the International Commission of Jurists (Nederlands Juristencomité voor de Mensenrechten [hereafter: NJCM]), *Commentary on the Second Periodic Report of the Netherlands Submitted in Accordance with Article 16 of the International Covenant on Economic, Social and Cultural Rights*, December 8, 1997, p. 4.

18. Van Hoof, "De Praktische Betekenis," p. 10; translated from the original Dutch.

19. P. B. Cliteur, *Rechtsfilosofie: Een Thematische Benadering* (Legal philosophy: A thematic approach), Nijmegen: Ars Aequi Libri, 2002, pp. 187–202. For a similar view, see Elies Steyger, "Over Staatstaken, Sociale Grondrechten en Mensenrechten" (About tasks of the state, basic social rights, and human rights), in

A. P. M. Coomans, A. W. Heringa, and I. Westendorp, eds., *Economische, Sociale en Culturele Rechten* (Leiden: Stichting NJCM-Boekerij, 1994), pp. 23–29.

20. NJCM has, however, criticized the Netherlands report to the ESC Committee for lacking information on the progress made in achieving the observance of the rights: "In general, the report is of a rather descriptive nature and does not contain an analysis or opinion of the government on the state of affairs concerning the implementation of economic, social and cultural rights, nor on the developments since the last report. . . . The Dutch report makes very few references to the problems and obstacles encountered in the process of (progressively) realizing the rights laid down in the Covenant." NJCM, *Commentary on the Second Periodic Report of the Netherlands Submitted in Accordance with Article 16 of the International Covenant on Economic, Social and Cultural Rights*, December 8, 1997, p. 3.

21. Economic and Social Council, *Concluding Observations of the Committee on Economic, Social and Cultural Rights: Netherlands, 16/06/98*, E/C.12/Add. 25, p. 2.

22. NJCM, *Commentary on the Second Periodic Report of the Netherlands* (emphasis added).

23. "All persons are equal before the law and are entitled without any discrimination to the equal protection of the law. In this respect, the law shall prohibit any discrimination and guarantee to all persons equal and effective protection against discrimination on any ground such as race, color, sex, language, religion, political or other opinion, national or social origin, property, birth or other status."

24. *S. W. M. Broeks v. The Netherlands*, comm. no. 172/1984, and *Zwaan-de Vries v. The Netherlands*, comm. no. 182/1984, decision April 9, 1987, A/42/40. Cf. Aalt Willem Heringa, "Article 26 CCPR and Social Security: Recent Dutch Cases Invalidating Discriminatory Social Security Laws," *SIM Newsletter, Netherlands Quarterly of Human Rights* 6 (1988), pp. 19–26; Aleidus Woltjer, *Wetgever, Rechter en het Primaat van de Gelijkheid: Over Primaten in het Recht* (Legislature, judiciary and the primacy of equality: About primacy in law) (The Hague: Boom, 2002); with a summary in English, pp. 101–8.

25. See note by Tom Zwart, *NJCM Bulletin* 12 (1987): 384–91. See also Manfred Nowak, *U.N. Covenant on Civil and Political Rights: CCPR Commentary* (Kehl: N. P. Engel, 1993), p. 470. However, in *Vos v. The Netherlands*, the committee found that gender-specific distinctions in other social security laws were based on reasonable and objective criteria. At the time, the General Disablement Benefits Act made a distinction according to sex, in that a disabled woman whose (former) husband died, did not retain the right to a disability allowance but was entitled to a widow's pension. In contrast, a disabled man whose (former) wife died retained the right to a disability allowance. Two members of the committee, however, disagreed, claiming that, in that case, Article 26 of the Covenant had also been violated (see Nowak, *CCPR Commentary*, p. 471).

26. See the petition initiated by NJCM and signed by ten leading Dutch human rights scholars, submitted to the Dutch minister of foreign affairs, in connection with the International Covenant on Civil and Political Rights. *SIM Newsletter, Netherlands Quarterly of Human Rights* 6 (1988): 128–31. When asked by members of the Human Rights Committee, the Netherlands delegation had this to say: "The Government certainly had no intention of denouncing the Covenant. It had been suggested in some quarters that it might do so and might then become a party again and enter a reservation to Article 26, but that option was no longer under consideration. There had also been some suggestion that it

might denounce the Optional Protocol in order to avoid difficult decisions or views of the Committee, but this Government was not accustomed to handling problems in that manner and it would be highly unlikely to denounce a protocol in whose creation it had played a prominent part." CCPR/C/SR.861, p. 12, par. 57, as quoted in Ineke Boerefijn, Herman von Hebel, and Aleidus Woltjer, "Nederlandse Rapportage bij het Mensenrechtencomité" (Netherlands reporting to the Human Rights Committee), *NJCM Bulletin* 14 (1989): 104.

27. Economic and Social Council, *Concluding Observations*, par. 12.

28. The Netherlands government had previously reported to the ESC Committee that in child care facilities it lagged behind the rest of Europe; in the late 1980s, organized child care facilities were available in only 200 of the 700 municipalities. Economic and Social Council, *Implementation of the International Covenant on Economic, Social and Cultural Rights, Second Periodic Report: Netherlands 05/08/96*, E/1990/6/Add. 11, par. 30.

29. Office of the High Commissioner for Human Rights, *Concluding Observations of the Committee on the Elimination of Discrimination against Women: Netherlands, 31/07/2001*, A/56/38, pars. 203 and 204.

30. Ibid, par. 229. This optional protocol offers the possibility to submit communications on behalf of individuals or groups of individuals claiming to be victims of a violation of any of the rights set forth in CEDAW. Such communications will be considered by the Committee on the Elimination of Discrimination against Women. It thus contains an important additional instrument for the protection of rights of women.

31. Economic and Social Council, *Implementation of the International Covenant on Economic, Social and Cultural Rights*, par. 124. No information was provided about paternity leave, as, for instance, practiced in Sweden.

32. NJCM, *Commentary on the Second Periodic Report of the Netherlands*, p. 12, and NJCM, *Commentary on the Second and Third Periodic Report of the Netherlands on the Implementation of the Convention on the Elimination of All Forms of Discrimination against Women*, December 28, 2000, p. 13.

33. Economic and Social Council, *Summary Record of the 14th Meeting of the Committee on Economic, Social and Cultural Rights*, May 6, 1998, EC.12/1998/SR.14, p. 4.

34. Mr. Potman (the Netherlands) in ibid.

35. See Kinderrechtencollectief, *Opgroeien in de Lage Landen: Kinderrechten in Nederland: Tweede Rapport van het Kinderrechtencollectief over de Implementatie van het VN-Verdrag inzake de Rechten van het Kind in Nederland* (Growing up in the low countries: Children's rights in the Netherlands: Second report of the Children's Rights Collective on the implementation of the UN Convention on the Rights of the Child in the Netherlands) (Amsterdam: Defence for Children International Nederland, 2002), p. 21.

36. NJCM, *Commentary on the Second Periodic Report of the Netherlands*, p. 22.

37. Ibid., p. 23.

38. Economic and Social Council, Committee on Economic, Social and Cultural Rights, *Summary Record of the 15th Meeting: Netherlands, 11/05/98*, E/C.12/1998/SR.15, par. 13.

39. Ibid., par. 18.

40. Ibid., pars. 27–29.

41. Economic and Social Council, *Concluding Observations*, pars. 19 and 27. High school students from the age of 16 as well as university students must pay tuition fees.

42. Ibid., par. 7. The representative of the Netherlands had limited himself to acknowledging that his country had entered the reservation to Article 26 "because it felt that the article might be interpreted as giving children an individual right to social security." Committee on the Rights of the Child, *Summary Record of the 579th Meeting: Netherlands, 08/10/99,* CRC/C/SR. 579, par. 7.

43. Article 26(1): "States Parties shall recognize the right of every child to benefit from social security, including social insurance, and shall take the necessary measures to achieve the full realization of this right in accordance with their national law."

44. At the time of this writing (winter 2004), however, the reservations were still on the books.

45. "States Parties shall undertake all appropriate legislative, administrative, and other measures for the implementation of the rights recognized in the present Convention. With regard to economic, social and cultural rights, States Parties shall undertake such measures to the maximum extent of their available resources and, where needed, within the framework of international cooperation."

46. Committee on the Rights of the Child, *Concluding Observations of the Committee on the Rights of the Child: Netherlands, 26/10/99,* CRC/C.15/Add. 114, par. 13.

47. I.e., over fifty years of age. Economic and Social Council, *Implementation of the International Covenant on Economic, Social and Cultural Rights, Second Periodic Report,* par. 27.

48. Economic and Social Council, *Committee on Economic, Social and Cultural Rights, Summary Record of the 17th Meeting, 12/05/98,* E/C.12/1998/SR. 17, par. 33.

49. NJCM, *Commentary on the Second Periodic Report of the Netherlands,* p. 5. It also expressed its concern about the lack of protection against disability discrimination and about the scattered initiatives to promote the employment opportunities of *young* disabled persons. See further Aart Hendriks, *Gelijke Toegang tot de Arbeid voor Gehandicapten: Een Grondrechtelijke en Rechtsvergelijkende Analyse* (Equal access to employment for people with disabilities: An analysis from a human rights and comparative law perspective) (Deventer: Kluwer, 2000).

50. Economic and Social Council, *Concluding Observations,* pars. 14, 16, 24, and 25. A new law on the discrimination of handicapped persons was scheduled to enter into force in late 2004.

51. NJCM, *Commentary on the Second and Third Periodic Report of the Netherlands,* pp. 26–27.

52. Office of the High Commissioner on Human Rights, *Concluding Observations of the Committee on the Elimination of Discrimination Against Women,* par. 215.

53. Data from the Central Bureau of Statistics (CBS), the Netherlands.

54. Data from the Immigration and Naturalization Service of the Ministry of Justice. Estimates for 2003 are even lower and are expected to be about fourteen thousand.

55. Economic and Social Council, *Implementation of the International Covenant on Economic, Social and Cultural Rights, Second Periodic Report,* par. 53.

56. NJCM, *Commentary on the Second Periodic Report of the Netherlands,* p. 4, n. 3.

57. Committee on the Elimination of Racial Discrimination, *Summary Record of the Public Part of the 1414th meeting: Finland, Netherlands, 16/08/2000,* CERD/C/SR. 1414, par. 20.

58. *Concluding Observations of the Committee on the Elimination of Racial Discrimination, Netherland* [*sic*], CERD/C/304/Add. 104, par. 14.

59. Economic and Social Council, *Implementation of the International Covenant on Economic, Social and Cultural Rights, Second Periodic Report,* par. 48.

60. NJCM, *Commentary on the Second Periodic Report of the Netherlands,* p. 6.

61. Ibid., p. 11.

62. Economic and Social Council, *Implementation of the International Covenant on Economic, Social and Cultural Rights, Second Periodic Report,* par. 247 (e).

63. NJCM, *Commentary on the Second Periodic Report of the Netherlands,* pp. 17, 26. NJCM, *Commentary on the Second and Third Periodic Report of the Netherlands,* p. 17.

64. Article 12, ICESCR: "The States Parties to the present Covenant recognize the right of everyone to the enjoyment of the highest attainable standard of physical and mental health." See Appendix 1. Article 12(2) of the Women's Convention: "to ensure to women appropriate services in connection with pregnancy, confinement and the post-natal period, granting free services where necessary."

65. NJCM, *Commentary on the Second Periodic Report of the Netherlands,* p. 21.

66. Office of the High Commissioner for Human Rights, *Concluding Observations of the Committee on the Elimination of Discrimination Against Women,* pars. 203–206.

67. *Concluding Observations of the Committee on the Rights of the Child,* par. 23.

68. Ibid., par. 28.

69. Ibid., par. 29.

70. *Concluding Observations of the Committee on the Elimination of Racial Discrimination, Netherlands,* pars. 11 and 12.

71. Ibid., par. 15.

72. Steven Bouckaert and Sarah D'Hondt, "The Growing Impact of Human Rights Standards on the Socioeconomic Status of Undocumented Migrants in Belgium: A Few Illustrations," in Peter van der Auweraert, Tom de Pelsmaeker, Jeremy Sarkin, and Johan Vande Lanotte, eds., *Social, Economic and Cultural Rights: An Appraisal of Current European and International Developments* (Antwerp: Maklu, 2002), pp. 289–311. The authors distinguish three categories of undocumented migrants: (1) rejected migrants are those who tried unsuccessfully to obtain a legal status through one of the existing migration procedures; (2) clandestine migrants are foreigners who have never tried to obtain a legal residence status; and (3) tolerated undocumented migrants are those who cannot be deported from the territory for one reason or another, mostly humanitarian. See ibid., p. 292.

73. Ibid., p. 298.

74. The Western European states occupy the following positions on the UNDP's Human Development Index, which ranks 173 states: (1) Norway, (2) Iceland, (3) Sweden, (5) The Netherlands, (6) Belgium, (10) Switzerland, (11) Denmark, (12) Ireland, (13) United Kingdom, (14) Finland, (15) Luxembourg, (16) Austria, (17) France, (18) Germany, (19) Spain, (21) Italy, (23) Portugal, and (24) Greece. The United States is (7) and Canada is (8). UNDP, *Human Development Report 2003,* pp. 237 ff.

75. And, in the case of children's rights, to the Children's Rights Collective.

76. "From the clash of opinions emerges the truth."

77. Almost ten years ago, the Dutch expert on ESC rights, Fons Coomans, had the following to say about the subject: "So far, the Committee [on ESC rights] has been rather reluctant in judging a certain situation as a violation of an ICESCR rule, or in naming a state in violation of the treaty. . . . [I]t is not simple to determine the action of a state as the violation of a right." A. P. M. Coomans,

"Schendingen van Economische, Sociale en Culturele Rechten" (Violations of economic, social and cultural rights), in A. P. M. Coomans, A. W. Heringa, and I. Westendorp, eds., *De Toenemende Betekenis van Economische, Sociale en Culturele Mensenrechten* (Leiden: Stichting NJCM-Boekerij, 1994), p. 65; translated from the original Dutch. See, however, *Maastricht Guidelines on Violation of Economic, Social and Cultural Rights* of 1997, http://www.rechten.unimaas.nl/humanrights (accessed August 27, 2003).

78. See appendix 1, Article 2, par. 1.

79. ESC Committee, General Comment 3, *The Nature of State Party Obligations,* 5th sess., 1990.

80. See Aart Hendriks and Vivien Lenos, "Mensenrechten in het Sociaal Recht" (Human rights in social law), *NJCM Bulletin* 27 (2002): 230: "In the Netherlands there exist, in 2001, still great differences in remuneration. These differences are in many cases connected to protected grounds of discrimination, in particular sex and race" (translated from the original Dutch).

81. The situation would seem to be somewhat different in politics. Five of the present sixteen ministerial positions are held by women, while 55 of the 150 members of the directly elected Second Chamber and 24 of the 75 members of the indirectly elected First Chamber are women.

82. Though, as was pointed out earlier in the chapter, the notion of paternity leave is not yet well developed in the Netherlands.

83. A recent study shows that in Amsterdam the separation between "black" and "white" schools is almost complete. See "Scheiding naar Ras en Klasse is Volledig" (Separation according to race and class is complete), *NRC Handelsblad* [Rotterdam], August 26, 2003.

84. According to Dr. Ruben Gowricham, professor of multicultural cohesion and transnational problems at Tilburg University, *NRC Handelsblad* [Rotterdam], August 9–10, 2003.

Contributors

Editors

RHODA E. HOWARD-HASSMANN is Canada Research Chair in International Human Rights at Wilfrid Laurier University in Ontario, Canada, and professor emerita at McMaster University. She holds a Ph.D. in sociology from McGill University (1976) and is a Fellow of the Royal Society of Canada (1993). Dr. Howard-Hassmann is the author of *Colonialism and Underdevelopment in Ghana* (1978), *Human Rights in Commonwealth Africa* (1986), *Human Rights and the Search for Community* (1995), and *Compassionate Canadians: Civic Leaders Discuss Human Rights* (2003); she is also co-editor (with Jack Donnelly) of *International Handbook of Human Rights* (1987). She has published numerous articles and book chapters on human rights and development in Africa; women's rights; Canadian foreign and refugee policy; and theoretical, methodological, and sociological issues in international and Canadian human rights. Her current research is on the question of what the West owes Africa.

CLAUDE E. WELCH, JR., is SUNY Distinguished Service Professor and professor of political science at the University at Buffalo, The State University of New York. He also directs the Program in International and Comparative Legal Studies. His books include *NGOs and Human Rights: Promise and Performance* (2001, edited), *Protecting Human Rights in Africa* (1995), *Asian Perspectives on Human Rights* (1990, co-edited) and *Human Rights and Development in Africa* (1984, co-edited). He has published eight other books, more than thirty-five chapters and over forty articles in *Human Rights Quarterly* and other professional journals. He is currently working on a book, *Protecting Human Rights Globally*. Professor Welch serves on the advisory committee of the Africa Division of Human Rights Watch and the board of the Institute for Human Rights and Development in Africa. He has also been a consultant to the MacArthur Foundation and the U.S. Institute of Peace, among others.

Authors

SARAH ARMSTRONG, MINDY NOBLE, AND PAULINE ROSENBAUM each received a degree from McMaster University in Hamilton, Ontario, Canada. While at McMaster University, the three were students in the Theme School on International Justice and Human Rights under the directorship of Dr. Rhoda Howard-Hassmann. Their interest in disability issues was sparked by a course on human rights and disability, taught by Professor Mary Tremblay of McMaster's Occupational Therapy Programme. After they graduated from McMaster, Ms. Armstrong, Ms. Noble, and Ms. Rosenbaum attended the Faculty of Law at the University of Toronto. While at law school, they collaborated on academic and community-oriented projects involving disability, poverty, women's and children's issues, international human rights, and public interest law. They were awarded the Gordon C. Cressy Student Leadership Award for their work. Ms. Armstrong, Ms. Noble, and Ms. Rosenbaum received LL.B. degrees in 2002 from the University of Toronto. They were admitted to the Bar of Ontario in 2003.

JAMES B. ATLESON, SUNY Distinguished Teaching Professor in the Law School, University at Buffalo, The State University of New York, joined its staff in 1964. He has also taught at the Texas, Minnesota, Georgetown, and the University of Pennsylvania law schools. With his J.D. from Ohio State and LL.M. from Stanford, Professor Atleson has written two major books: *Labor and the Wartime State: The Continuing Impact of Labor Relations during World War II* (1998), *Values and Assumptions in American Labor Law* (1983, 2nd printing 1984), and coauthored *Labor Law and Collective Bargaining in Private Employment* (1978). He has also authored many other articles and essays. He has been a labor arbitrator since the early 1970s and belongs to the National Academy of Arbitrators, the American Arbitration Association, and FMCS Panel of Arbitrators as well as other panels.

PETER R. BAEHR is honorary professor of human rights at Utrecht University (Netherlands). He taught at the University of Amsterdam (international relations) from 1961 to 1976 and at Leiden University (human rights) from 1986 to 1996. Professor Baehr directed SIM, the Netherlands Institute of Human Rights, in 1990–98, concurrent with his professorial position in Utrecht. His recent books in English include *Human Rights in the Foreign Policy of the Netherlands* (2004, coauthored, new and revised edition), *Human Rights: Universality in Practice* (2001, paperback edition), *Innovation and Inspiration: Fifty Years of the Universal Declaration of Human Rights* (1999, co-edited), and *The United Nations at the End of the*

Nineties (1999, coauthored, new and revised edition). Among his major recent professional activities are editor, *Netherlands Quarterly of Human Rights* (1990–present) and member of the Commission on Human Rights of the Advisory Council on International Problems (1997–present).

WILLIE BAPTIST is the education director of the Kensington Welfare Rights Union and a member of the War Council. He is also co-coordinator of the University of the Poor, the educational arm of the Poor People's Economic Human Rights Campaign. He is formerly homeless. With his family, he was on welfare for ten years, participating in workfare as a condition for survival.

MARY BRICKER-JENKINS is professor of social work at Temple University. She is also assistant director of the Kensington Welfare Rights Union's (KWRU) Education Committee, co-chair of the Social Work Strategy Subcommittee, and an honorary member of KWRU's War Council (governing body). She is co-chair of the School of Social Work and Social Transformation of the University of the Poor.

BARBARA WAKE CARROLL is a professor in the Political Science department at McMaster University, Hamilton, Canada. She was formerly a manager/policy analyst for the governments of Alberta, Manitoba, and New Brunswick, and the government of Canada, mainly Canada Mortgage and Housing. She has been a visiting faculty member at the University of Waikato, New Zealand, and the University of Bordeaux, France. She is the author or coauthor of four books and some fifty articles and monographs on organization theory, public management, and policymaking. Within public policy, her main areas of interest are housing policy and development in sub-Saharan Africa. She has been involved with the non-profit housing sector in Canada as a facilitator, analyst, and board member for thirty-five years.

DAVID P. FORSYTHE is University Professor and Charles J. Mach Distinguished Professor of Political Science at the University of Nebraska-Lincoln. He has held postdoctoral fellowships at Princeton and Yale and visiting professorships in Denmark, Ireland, the Netherlands, and Switzerland. His publications include *Human Rights in International Relations* (2000, translated into Arabic, Chinese, and Bulgarian), *Human Rights and Comparative Foreign Policy* (2000, edited), *The United States and Human Rights* (2000, edited), and *The United Nations and Changing World Politics* (2000; with two other authors, 4th ed. forthcoming).

ERIC A. HEINZE is currently a doctoral candidate at the University of Nebraska-Lincoln (UNL), in the Department of Political Science and Program on Human Rights and Human Diversity. He has taught courses in U.S. politics, comparative politics, foreign policy, and international law and served as the assistant to the director of the Human Rights Program at UNL during academic year 2003–4. His dissertation deals with moral and legal aspects of humanitarian intervention. His articles have appeared in *Politics, Human Rights and Human Welfare, Polity, Journal of Conflict Studies,* and *The International Journal of Human Rights.*

VIRGINIA A. LEARY is SUNY Distinguished Service Professor Emerita at the University at Buffalo, The State University of New York, and holds the Fromm Chair in International and Comparative Law (Hastings Law School). She received her undergraduate degree from the University of Utah, her J.D. (Order of the Coif) from the University of Chicago, and her Ph.D. from the Institute of International Studies (Geneva). Prior to coming to Buffalo in 1975, she worked at the International Labor Organization. Professor Leary also served as Ariel Sallows Chair of Human Rights (University of Saskatchewan) in 1986–87 and as Hoskins and Harcourt Distinguished Professor in Human Rights (University of Toronto) in 1994.

KENNETH J. NEUBECK is professor emeritus of sociology at the University of Connecticut, where he served as director of the university's undergraduate minor in human rights. He is co-author (with Noel A. Cazenave) of *Welfare Racism: Playing the Race Card against America's Poor* (2001), along with other publications on economic inequality, racism, poverty, and welfare reform. In addition, Professor Neubeck is the author of major textbooks published with McGraw-Hill, including *Sociology: Diversity, Conflict, and Change* (2005, written with Davita Silfen Glasberg) and *Social Problems: A Critical Approach* (1997, coauthored with Mary Alice Neubeck). He is currently preparing a monograph focusing on the gap between U.S. welfare policy and respect for economic human rights. Professor Neubeck has long been an activist on civil rights and anti-poverty issues and most recently has worked with advocacy groups on such issues as racial equity in welfare reform.

BRIAN OREND is director of international studies and associate professor of philosophy at the University of Waterloo in Canada. He has published three books and dozens of articles. His latest book, *Human Rights: Concept and Context* (2002), has been used as a required textbook in courses at more than twenty-five universities worldwide, including Stanford and Johns Hopkins. This book also won designation as an "outstanding academic title" from *Choice* magazine in 2002. His other writings deal with the ethics of war and peace and include *War and International Justice: A Kantian Perspective* (2000), *Michael Walzer on War and Justice* (2000), and the entry "War" in the *Stanford Encyclopedia of Philosophy*. Professor Orend received his Ph.D. in 1998 from Columbia University in New York City.

VIC SATZEWICH is professor of sociology, McMaster University, Hamilton, Ontario, and is past president of the Canadian Sociology and Anthropology Association (2002–3). He has published in *The Canadian Review of Sociology and Anthropology, Economy and Society, Ethnic and Racial Studies, The International Journal of Comparative Race and Ethnic Relations, International Sociology, The Journal of Historical Sociology*, and *Social History/ Histoire sociale*. His books include *Racism and the Incorporation of Foreign Labour: Farm Labour Migration to Canada since 1945* (1991) (with Terry Wotherspoon), *First Nations: Race Class and Gender Relations* (1993), and *The Ukrainian Diaspora* (2002). He is also editor of *Racism and Social Inequality in Canada: Concepts, Controversies and Strategies of Resistance* (1998) and *Deconstructing a Nation: Immigration, Multiculturalism and Racism in '90s Canada* (1992).

DAVID WEISSBRODT has taught at the University of Minnesota Law School since 1975 and is the Fredrikson and Byron Professor of Law. He teaches international human rights law and other subjects. Weissbrodt has authored a dozen books in addition to 150 articles about human rights, immigration law, and torts. Weissbrodt helped establish several human rights organizations, including the Center for Victims of Torture and the University of Minnesota Human Rights Library (http:// www.umn.edu/humanrts). As a member of the UN Sub-Commission on the Promotion and Protection of Human Rights (1996–2003), Weissbrodt assisted in preparing UN human rights norms for companies, served as UN special rapporteur on the rights of non-citizens, and was in 2001 elected chairperson of the sub-commission. Professor Weissbrodt was the first U.S. citizen ever to chair the sub-commission and the first U.S. citizen since Eleanor Roosevelt to head a UN human rights body.

Index

Acknowledgments

This volume took shape over several years, through numerous telephone calls, innumerable e-mails, and face-to-face discussions. Ultimately, financial support turned our intellectual speculations into this book. The Canadian Embassy to the United States supported us through its Canadian Studies Conference Grant Program. The Baldy Center for Law and Social Policy, directed by Lynn Mather, and the Canadian-American Studies Committee, directed by Lorraine Oak, both at the University at Buffalo, The State University of New York, also generously provided funds. We are most grateful to all these organizations for their faith in this project.

Many people helped us to produce *Economic Rights in Canada and the United States*. We acknowledge, in particular, the crucial role of the Baldy Center staff, notably its assistant director, Laura Mangan. She brought several important qualities to the conference in October 2003, at which authors presented drafts of their chapters. Her long-standing commitment to human rights, administrative efficiency, energy, and inextinguishable goodwill brought both a human face and intellectual depth to our deliberations. Ellen Kausner and Ann Gaulin, other members of the Baldy staff, spent many hours with the myriad of details an international gathering of that sort demanded.

We also relied on several graduate students, who brought a variety of strengths to our efforts. They included, at the University of Buffalo, Alison Berkowitz, Aditi Grover, and Blake Webber. Lisa Daniel, Gabe Gilman, and Nil Satana also assisted at the October 2003 workshop. On the Canadian side, Anthony P. Lombardo compiled and edited our book proposal and acted as rapporteur at the October 2003 workshop. Both he and Dan Milisavljevic provided invaluable research assistance to Rhoda Howard-Hassmann. Dan Milisavljevic also took over full responsibility in the summer of 2004 for editing and preparing the final manuscript. Rhoda Howard-Hassmann is especially grateful to these two brilliant young Canadians for their efficiency, their patience, and their sense of humor. Indexing was ably handled by Jane Morris.

Finally, as editors, we would like to thank our contributors for their willingness to join in this project, accept our instructions, meet our deadlines, and make time in their schedules to attend our workshop at the University at Buffalo. All our contributors are extremely busy scholars and practitioners, with many other claims on their attention. Yet they all agreed with us that the human rights community should pay more attention to economic rights in Western developed countries and were therefore willing to make time for this project. This book is a genuine collective effort.

Rhoda E. Howard-Hassmann and Claude E. Welch, Jr.